Six Key Approaches to Counselling and Therapy

Richard Nelson-Jones

SAGE Publications
Los Angeles • London • New Delhi • Singapore

SAGE Publications Ltd.
1 Oliver's Yard
55 City Road
London EC1Y 1SP

SAGE Publications Inc
2455 Teller Road
Thousand Oaks, California 91320

SAGE Publications India Pvt Ltd.
B1/I 1 Mohan Cooperative Industrial Area
Mathura Road, New Delhi 110 044
India

SAGE Publications Asia-Pacific Pte Ltd
33 Pekin Street #02-01
Far East Square
Singapore 048763

British Library Cataloguing in Publication data
A catalogue record for this book is available from the British Library

ISBN: 978-0-8264-4969-6 (pbk)

Typeset by Paston PrePress Ltd., Beccles, Suffolk
Printed and bound in Great Britain by
Athenaeum Press Ltd., Gateshead, Tyne & Wear

Contents

Preface

Welcome to *Six Key Approaches to Counselling and Therapy*. I intend this book as an authoritative and accessible textbook for those embarking on the study of different therapeutic approaches in a wide range of educational, professional and voluntary sector settings.

CONTENTS

In this book, whose focus is on individual therapy, I present two approaches selected from each of the three main schools influencing contemporary therapy practice: the psychodynamic school, Freud's psychoanalysis and Jung's analytical therapy; the humanistic school, person-centred therapy and gestalt therapy; and the cognitive-behavioural school, rational emotive behaviour therapy and cognitive therapy. In addition, I discuss the structure and function of theories, review issues in evaluating therapeutic approaches, provide a glossary, and include appendices on training information and journal information.

I selected the six approaches presented here because of their prominence within each school, reflecting both the richness of the approach's concepts and the number of its adherents. The chapters on these approaches are drawn from the thirteen counselling and therapy approaches presented in my longer and more comprehensive textbook *The Theory and Practice of Counselling and Therapy* (3rd edition), also being published by Continuum. Important reasons for publishing this shorter book include both enhancing consumer choice and addressing the teaching and learning needs of those wanting a more easily manageable amount of content than in the longer book.

FEATURES

I draw your attention to the following features of the book, which I hope will make it attractive for you:

Authoritative

This book, which is written from primary sources, provides up-to-date and accurate presentations of each counselling and therapy approach. For instance, when preparing the book, I contacted living theorists for their most recent material. In addition, I gave either the theorists themselves or prominent adherents of the approach the opportunity to preview chapters and to suggest alterations.

Thorough and clear presentation

Each of the six approaches is in a standard chapter format that helps to ensure that the approach is thoroughly and clearly presented. Though you may not understand the meaning of some of the following headings now, once you start working with the book you should experience no difficulty in so doing.

Introduction
  Originator's biography

Theory
  Basic concepts
  Acquisition
  Maintenance

Therapy
  Therapeutic goals
  Process of therapy
  The therapeutic relationship
  Therapeutic interventions
  Case material
  Further developments

Annotated bibliography

References

Focus on fundamentals

The chapters emphasize presenting the theory and practice of the originator of each approach. Some contributions by other adherents of the approach are mentioned in the 'Further developments' section of each chapter. However, the chapters present the basic or classical version of each approach. Getting down to basics is important, since introducing developments from the original approach too soon can be confusing. In all of the chapters I review the originator's case material and in most chapters I give directions about accessing audiovisual resources. If available and where budgets permit, I encourage lecturers to use audio-cassettes and videotapes of the originators engaging in therapy as an accompaniment to using this book.

Personal focus

Originating counselling and therapy approaches is a personal journey. A distinctive feature of this book is the degree to which the lives of the originators are seen as important in understanding the development of their therapeutic approaches. Learning about counselling and therapy approaches is also a personal journey. Each chapter ends not only with review questions, but with personal questions as well that encourage you to relate the material to your own life.

Aids to comprehension and revision

Boxes are used throughout the book to highlight concepts and provide examples of specific interventions. Towards the end of each chapter, I provide a summary and review questions designed to help you learn and revise material for assignments and course requirements.

Help with further reading

I encourage you to use the chapters in this book as stepping stones to reading primary sources. Each chapter ends with an annotated bibliography and with a listing of references.

Simple English

I have tried to use simple, accessible English, while remaining sensitive to the distinctive therapeutic languages used by the different theorists.

ACKNOWLEDGEMENTS

I acknowledge with gratitude the distinctive contributions of all the originators of counselling and therapy approaches presented in this book. While accepting full responsibility for any shortcomings, I am extremely grateful to the following people for contributing to the preparation of and for previewing chapters: Dr Judith Beck, Ann Casement, Professor Petruska Clarkson, Dr Albert Ellis and Professor Brian Thorne. In addition, a special word of appreciation for Professor Danny Wedding, co-editor of the best-selling American textbook *Current Psychotherapies*, who gave me pre-publication access to all the relevant chapters in the sixth edition of that book. I also thank Philip Sturrock, Janet Joyce and Karen Haynes at Continuum, who were involved in the decision to commission this book. Last but not least, I thank the production staff at Continuum for their work in copy-editing and bringing this book to life.

Since each of the six approaches is presented as a self-contained unit, you can choose which parts to study in the order that best suits your purposes. I hope that you enjoy reading and interacting with this book and share my enthusiasm for studying and learning more about counselling and therapy approaches.

I welcome feedback on this book. If you have any comments you would like to share with me you can either send them or e-mail them to me at the following address:

Richard Nelson-Jones
Cognitive-Humanistic Institute
Suite 715, Supakit Condominium
90/1 Moo 8, Soi Suthep 4
Suthep Road
Chiang Mai
Thailand 50200
e-mail: rnjchi@loxinfo.co.th

Introducing Counselling and Therapy Approaches

It may be that each person who develops his own system of psychotherapy writes, in the final analysis, his own case history.

Viktor Frankl

I invite you on an intellectual, practical and personal journey through six of the most interesting and important approaches to contemporary counselling and therapy. Though you may not have thought of it this way, you already started your journey as a personality theorist long ago as you developed ideas about what makes people 'tick' and 'what makes the world go around'. Already, many of you will have had differing degrees of exposure to the ideas covered here and may have incorporated some of them into your personal view of how people think, feel and behave. In this book, I aim to assist you to move further along the path towards developing your theory of human development and gaining practical knowledge about how to conduct counselling and therapy.

A useful distinction exists between *schools* of counselling and therapy and *theoretical approaches* to counselling and therapy. A theoretical approach presents a single position regarding the theory and practice of counselling and therapy. A school of counselling and therapy is a grouping of different theoretical approaches which are similar to one another in terms of certain important characteristics that distinguish them from theoretical approaches in other counselling and therapy schools.

Probably the three main schools that influence contemporary individual counselling and psychotherapy practice are the psychodynamic school, the humanistic school, and the cognitive-behavioural school. Sometimes the humanistic school incorporates existential therapeutic approaches and then gets the broader title of being the humanistic-existential school. Be careful not to exaggerate the differences between counselling and therapy schools, since there are similarities as well as differences between them. Box 1.1 briefly describes

---

Box 1.1   Three counselling and therapy schools

The psychodynamic school

The term *psychodynamic* refers to the transfer of **psychic or mental energy** between the different structures and levels of consciousness within people's minds. Psychodynamic approaches emphasize the importance of **unconscious influences** on how people function. Therapy aims to increase clients' abilities to exercise **greater conscious control** over their lives. Analysis or interpretation of dream can form a central part of therapy.

The humanistic school

The humanistic school is based on humanism, a system of values and beliefs that emphasizes the better qualities of humankind and people's abilities to develop their **human potential**. Humanistic therapists emphasize enhancing clients' abilities to **experience their feelings** and think and act in harmony with their underlying tendencies to **actualize themselves** as unique individuals.

The cognitive-behavioural school

Traditional behaviour therapy focuses mainly on changing observable behaviours by means of providing different or rewarding consequences. The cognitive-behavioural school broadens behaviour therapy to incorporate the contribution of **how people think** to creating, sustaining and changing their problems. In cognitive-behavioural approaches, therapists **assess** clients and then intervene to help them to **change specific ways of thinking and behaving** that sustain their problems.

some distinguishing features of the psychodynamic, humanistic and cognitive-behavioural schools.

Box 1.2 introduces the theoretical approaches, grouped according to counselling and therapy school, selected for inclusion in this book. So that readers can obtain a sense of the history of the development of ideas within counselling and therapy, I have included the dates of the originators of each approach. With the exception of Rogers' person-centred therapy coming before Perls' gestalt therapy, the ordering of the chapters on the counselling and therapy approaches presented in this book corresponds to the birth dates of their originators. Those of you requiring further brief introductions to the different approaches are referred to the summaries

---

Box 1.2 Six counselling and therapy approaches

Psychodynamic school

Classical psychoanalysis *Originator: Sigmund Freud (1856–1939)*
Pays great attention to unconscious factors related to infantile sexuality in the development of neurosis. Psychoanalysis, which may last for many years, emphasizes working through the transference, in which clients perceive their therapists as reincarnations of important figures from their childhoods, and the interpretation of dreams.

Analytical therapy *Originator: Carl Jung (1875–1961)*
Divides the unconscious into the personal unconscious and the collective unconscious, the latter being a storehouse of universal archetypes and primordial images. Therapy includes analysis of the transference, active imagination and dream analysis. Jung was particularly interested in working with clients in the second half of life.

Humanistic school

Person-centred therapy *Originator: Carl Rogers (1902–87)*
Lays great stress on the primacy of subjective experience and how clients can become out of touch with their actualizing tendency through introjecting others' evaluations and

treating them as if their own. Therapy emphasizes a relationship characterized by accurate empathy, respect and non-possessive warmth.

Gestalt therapy   *Originator: Fritz Perls (1893–1970)*
Individuals become neurotic by losing touch with their senses and interfering with their capacity to make strong contact with their environments. Therapy emphasizes increasing clients' awareness and vitality through awareness techniques, experiments, sympathy and frustration, and dream work.

Cognitive-behavioural school

Rational emotive behaviour therapy   *Originator: Albert Ellis (1913–)*
Emphasizes clients re-indoctrinating themselves with irrational beliefs that lead to unwanted feelings and self-defeating actions. Therapy involves disputing clients' irrational beliefs and replacing them with more rational beliefs. Elegant or profound therapy entails changing clients' philosophies of life.

Cognitive therapy   *Originator: Aaron Beck (1921–)*
Clients become distressed because they are faulty processors of information with a tendency to jump to unwarranted conclusions. Therapy consists of educating clients in how to test the reality of their thinking by interventions such as Socratic questioning and conducting real-life experiments.

provided at the end of each chapter. The descriptions given in Box 1.2 reflect the position of the originators of the different positions, rather than developments within a theoretical approach stimulated by others.

So far, I have presented the different schools and theoretical approaches as though they are separate. In reality, many counsellors and therapists regard themselves as working in either eclectic or integrative ways. A detailed discussion of eclecticism and integration is beyond the scope of this introductory book. Suffice it for now to say that eclecticism is the practice of drawing from different counselling and therapy schools in formulating client problems and implementing treatment interventions. Integration refers to attempting to blend together theoretical concepts and/or practical interventions drawn from different counselling and therapy approaches into coherent and integrated wholes.

COUNSELLING AND PSYCHOTHERAPY

The word 'therapy' is derived from the Greek word 'therapeia' meaning healing. Literally, psychotherapy means healing the mind or the soul. Nowadays, most commonly the meaning of psychotherapy is broadened to become that of psychological therapy involving healing the mind by psychological methods which are applied by suitably trained and qualified practitioners. However, as illustrated in this book, there are different approaches to psychotherapy and, consequently, it is more accurate to speak of the psychotherapies than of a uniform method of psychotherapy. Moreover, there are different goals for psychotherapy including dealing with severe mental disorder, addressing specific anxieties and phobias, and helping people find meaning and purpose in their lives. Each of the different therapeutic approaches may be more suitable for attaining some goals than others.

Does counselling differ from psychotherapy? The British Association for Counselling's *Code of Ethics and Practice for Counsellors* states that 'Counselling may be concerned with developmental issues, addressing and resolving specific problems, making decisions, coping with crisis, developing personal insight and knowledge, working through feelings of inner conflict or improving relationships with others' (BAC, 1998, p.1). Attempts to differentiate between counselling and psychotherapy are never wholly successful. Both counselling and psychotherapy represent diverse rather than uniform knowledge and activities and both use the same theoretical models.

Nevertheless, some people try to distinguish counselling from psychotherapy. For instance, psychotherapists may be more thoroughly trained; psychotherapy may focus more deeply on uncovering unconscious influences and be longer term; and psychotherapy may be more a medical term that characterizes the work of psychiatrists and clinical psychiatrists, whereas counselling relates more to activities in non-medical settings: for example, college counselling centres. All these distinctions can be refuted: for example, there are psychodynamic counsellors; both counselling and therapy can be either brief, medium-term or long-term; and much counselling is performed both by medically and non-medically qualified people inside and outside of medical settings.

Though some perceive different shadings of meaning between counselling and psychotherapy, when it comes to the offering of professional as contrasted with voluntary services, similarities outweigh differences. The terms are frequently used interchangeably and most theorists view their work as applicable to both counselling and psychotherapy, Carl Rogers and Albert Ellis being prime examples. In this book, I use the terms 'counselling' and 'therapy' interchangeably.

DEFINING TERMS

Throughout this book, for the sake of consistency, for the most part I use the terms 'therapy', 'therapist' and 'client'. *Therapy* refers both to the theoretical approach and to the process of helping clients. It is notable that the originators of most therapeutic approaches included the word therapy in their approach's title: for instance, person-centred therapy, gestalt therapy, rational emotive behaviour therapy and cognitive therapy. *Therapist* refers to the providers of therapy services to clients, be they psychoanalysts, psychiatrists, clinical psychologists, counselling psychologists, counsellors, social workers or other suitably trained and qualified persons. *Client* refers to the recipient of therapeutic services whether inside or outside of medical settings.

WHAT IS A COUNSELLING AND THERAPY THEORY?

A theory is a system of suppositions or ideas explaining something. Hall and Lindzey write: 'A theory is an unsubstantiated hypothesis or speculation concerning reality which is not yet definitely known to be so. When the theory is confirmed it becomes a fact' (Hall and Lindzey, 1970, p. 10). These authors make the division between theory and fact too rigid. Rather, a theory is a formulation of the underlying principles of certain observed phenomena which have been verified to some extent. A criterion of the power of a theory is the extent to which it generates predictions which are confirmed when relevant empirical data are collected. The more a theory receives confirmation or verification, the more accurate it is. Facts strengthen rather than replace theories.

Functions of counselling and therapy theories

What do counselling and therapy theories do? Why are they useful? Therapists cannot avoid being counselling and therapy theorists. All make assumptions about how clients become and stay the way they are and about change. Three of the main functions of counselling and therapy theories are providing conceptual frameworks, providing languages, and generating research.

Theories as conceptual frameworks

Therapists are decision-makers. They continually make choices about how to think about clients' behaviour, how to treat them, and how to respond on a moment-by-moment basis during therapy sessions. Theories provide therapists with concepts that allow them to think systematically about human development and the therapeutic process.

Counselling and therapy theories may be viewed as possessing four main dimensions if they are to be stated adequately: (1) a statement of the *basic concepts* or assumptions underlying the theory; (2) an explanation of the *acquisition* of helpful and unhelpful behaviour; (3) an explanation of the *maintenance* of helpful and unhelpful behaviour; (4) an explanation of how to help clients *change* their behaviour and *consolidate* their gains when therapy ends. Box 1.3 shows

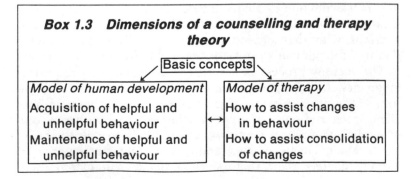

Box 1.3 Dimensions of a counselling and therapy theory

Basic concepts

Model of human development
Acquisition of helpful and unhelpful behaviour
Maintenance of helpful and unhelpful behaviour

Model of therapy
How to assist changes in behaviour
How to assist consolidation of changes

how counselling and therapy theories can be viewed as containing a model of human development and a model of therapy.

When reading about the different counselling and therapy theories, you may observe that many if not most have significant gaps in their conceptual frameworks. They are partial rather than complete or comprehensive theories. Arguably, some of the missing concepts in the theories are implicit rather than explicit. In addition, theorists select for more thorough treatment those dimensions of a theory that they consider important. For instance, Ellis' rational emotive behaviour theory has a wider variety of explanatory concepts concerning how behaviour is maintained than how it is initially acquired.

Theories as languages

Swiss psychiatrist Carl Jung used to stress that, since all clients are different individuals, therapists require a different language for each client (Jung, 1961). Another function of theories is similar to that provided by languages. Languages are vocabularies and linguistic symbols that allow communication about phenomena. Like the major spoken languages of English, French, Spanish and Mandarin Chinese, the different theorists develop languages for the phenomena they wish to describe: for instance, cognitive, psychoanalytic or person-centred languages. Language can both unite and divide. It can encourage communication between people who speak the same language, but discourage communication if not. Each theoretical position has concepts described in unique language. However, the uniqueness of the language may mask common elements among theories: for example, the meaning of conditions of worth in person-centred therapy overlaps with that of super-ego in Freud's psychoanalytic therapy, though you would not know this from the language!

The therapy process is a series of conversations requiring languages. In any therapeutic relationship there are at least four kinds of conversations going on: namely, therapist and client inner and outer speech. All therapists who operate out of explicit theoretical frameworks are likely to talk to themselves about clients in the language of that framework. In varying degrees their therapeutic practice will match their language. Therapists do not always act according to how they think. Furthermore, in varying degrees therapists share their theoretical language with clients. For example, unlike in rational emotive behaviour therapy, the language in which person-centred theory is expressed tends not to be shared with clients. Instead, person-centred therapists try to reflect and match clients' outer speech.

Clients are also theorists, though usually without the sophistication of their therapists. Approaches like rational emotive behaviour therapy and cognitive therapy actively try to influence the language in which clients talk to themselves so that it becomes helpful rather than harmful. These approaches educate clients to converse with themselves. In a sense the therapist's language is being exported to and imported by clients so that they can better assist themselves once therapy ends.

Theories as sets of research hypotheses

The social psychologist Kurt Lewin is reported to have said that 'Nothing is more practical than a good theory'. Para-phrasing him, perhaps 'Nothing is more scientific than a good theory'. Theories can both be based on research and stimulate research. For example, cognitive-behavioural therapy is based on research into how people think and how both people and animals behave. Furthermore, cognitive-behavioural approaches, such as rational emotive behaviour therapy and cognitive therapy, have stimulated research into their pro-cesses and outcomes.

Theories also provide therapists with frameworks within which to make predictive hypotheses during their practice of therapy. Whether acknowledging it or not, all therapists are practitioner-researchers. Therapists make hypotheses every time they decide how to work with specific clients and how to respond to single or a series of client utterances.

Clients are also practitioner-researchers who make predic-tions about how best to lead their lives. If valid theories of counselling and therapy are transmitted to clients, they may increase the accuracy with which clients can predict the consequences of their behaviours and, hence, gain more control over their lives.

Limitations of counselling and therapy theories

All counselling and therapy theories should carry the psycho-logical equivalent of health warnings. They can be used for ill as well as for good. The following are some potential disadvantages of theories.

Restriction of focus

A criticism of many theories is that they present partial truths as whole truths. Rogers may be viewed as an example of this tendency to over-generalize. He posits a unitary diagnosis of all clients' problems, namely that they are out of touch with their actualizing tendencies, and sees the helping relationship as necessary and sufficient in all instances (Rogers, 1957). Ellis focuses on irrational beliefs at risk of paying insufficient attention to other aspects of thinking, for instance perceiving accurately or using coping self-talk. Freud emphasizes unco-vering unconscious material through the analysis of dreams, but says little about developing specific effective behaviours to deal with everyday problems. The trend to eclecticism among many therapists, who draw upon aspects from different theories, attests to this negative aspect of the major theories.

Therapist rigidity

A function of theory is that it meets insecure therapists' need for certainty. Instead of acting as effective practitioner-researchers who test their theoretical hypotheses, such thera-pists allow theory to interfere with the accuracy with which they assess and treat clients. However, a beneficial side-effect of theoretical faith may be that it provides therapists with confidence that then gets transmitted to clients. Unfortunately, such confidence can be misplaced.

Tendencies to theoretical rigidity are heightened by the institutionalizing of theoretical approaches, with prescribed training routes. On the positive side, the institutionalizing of theoretical approaches can foster useful research and train-ing. On the negative side, organizations and associations representing theoretical approaches can turn into self-congratulatory status systems that reinforce rigidity. Preferment goes to those who toe the line rather than those who are too interested in theoretical breadth.

The different languages of theoretical approaches can disguise similarities between them. Theoretical rigidity is fostered when language differences lead therapists only to talk with those speaking the same language rather than to a broader sharing of knowledge and experience.

Depowering clients

Some theories may lead to pathologizing clients by focusing more on what is wrong rather than on what is right. In addition, theories can make clients' problems out to be more severe than they are. For instance, psychoanalysts can view learned ineffective behaviour as symptomatic of deeper underlying conflicts. Further, if clients give negative feedback to analysts they can be labelled as resisting and acting out their negative transferences rather than having their feedback taken seriously.

The language of theories can create a power imbalance between therapists and clients. Therapists who think in a special theoretical language which they do not share can put themselves in superior–inferior relationships with clients. Furthermore, the language of some theories does little to empower clients once they end therapy. Ideally, the language of therapy is that of self-helping. Clients who are unable to articulate what to think and do when faced with problems after therapy are less likely to maintain gains than clients who can instruct themselves appropriately.

Supporting the status quo

Counselling and therapy theories can contain many assumptions about how people should behave and about the causes of their behaviour. For example, possibly all theories in this book insufficiently take into account cultural differences. Instead, theorists present their ideas as more culture-universal and less culture-specific than they really are. In addition, theories of counselling and therapy, by focusing on individuals, couples and families, can either ignore or underestimate how much socio-environmental conditions like poverty, poor housing and racial discrimination may contribute to explaining ineffective behaviour. Though feminist and gender-aware theorizing is attempting to redress the balance, most theories insufficiently take into account the influence of sex-role conditioning. In addition, theories tend to assume heterosexuality and insufficiently take into account the needs of gay, lesbian and bisexual clients.

CREATING YOUR OWN THEORETICAL APPROACH

There is no psychology; there is only biography and autobiography.

Thomas Szasz

Every reader of this book is engaging in the process of creating their own theoretical approach. Theory creation is both a subjective process of making sense of material as well as an external process of reading, learning, researching and practising therapeutic skills. How can you make yourself a better theorist and hence a more effective therapist? The following are some suggestions.

Work with this book

Though based on the writings of the original theorists, this book is a secondary source. Nevertheless, it should provide you with a faithful overview of some of the main counselling and therapy theories. To understand any theory you need to master its basic concepts. It is insufficient just to read about them. You will need actively to work on understanding and memorizing them. At the end of each theory chapter I provide review questions that test your knowledge of basic concepts.

Get personal

Jung observed: 'My life is a story of the realisation of the unconscious' (Jung, 1961, p. 17). What about your life story and what are you trying to realize through your interest in counselling and therapy? Applying the different theories to your own life is one way to make learning more personal, involving and interesting. What do the theories say that seems applicable to you and why? Another way to understand the theories is to think about how applicable they are to past, present or future clients. What in different theories might prove useful in your practical work and why? In addition, you can compare and contrast different theories in an attempt to critically evaluate their strengths and weaknesses for you as a person and as a therapist. At the end of each chapter I provide personal questions so that you may apply your learnings and insights to yourself.

Still a further way to learn about the theories is to try to develop a theoretical approach of your own. For over twenty years I asked counselling and counselling psychology students taking my theory classes to write a paper presenting their current theoretical approach.

Read primary sources

Primary sources are books and articles written by the theorists themselves. Ultimately, there is no substitute for reading primary sources. You will gain a much broader and deeper impression of the different theories if you read widely the works of their originators. You can also learn about how the originators applied their counselling and therapy theories by reading case studies of their work. I include a section on case material towards the end of each chapter on the different therapies. In addition, after describing the work of each theorist, I provide a brief annotated bibliography plus other primary source references.

Read secondary sources

You can read secondary sources other than this book. Some secondary sources are counselling and therapy textbooks and you should always look out for the most recent editions. My *The Theory and Practice of Counselling and Therapy* (Nelson-Jones, in press) includes descriptions of seven more theoretical positions in addition to the six presented in this book. This larger book also contains chapters on cultural and gender perspectives. *Current Psychotherapies* is a widely respected edited book containing a mixture of primary and secondary sources (Corsini and Wedding, 2000). All major therapy approaches beget many secondary source books: for instance, Mearns and Thorne's *Person-Centred Counselling in Action* (1999).

A warning about reading secondary sources. Choose care-fully, because some secondary source writers do not really understand the theoretical positions they present. The follow-ing are three more traps into which secondary source textbook writers can fall. The first is to mix the writings of the original theorist together with recent developments in theory, so the student has difficulty in knowing which is which. A second trap is to merge the writings of different theorists into the same chapter: for example, to have a chapter combining either psychodynamic theories or humanistic theories. A problem with this approach is that no theory gets presented thor-oughly. If you doubt this point, look at the next two chapters on Freudian psychoanalysis and Jung's analytical therapy and see how wellnigh impossible it would be to combine them so that readers obtain a good introduction to both Freudian and Jungian theory and practice. A third trap is for secondary source writers only to present case examples of their own work. A risk here is that this secondary source case material does not truly reflect how the originator practised or practises therapy.

Watch and listen to audiovisual material

You can obtain a further insight into the different theorists by watching films and videotapes and listening to audio-cassettes of them discussing their theories and working with clients. For instance, audiovisual material is available for theorists like Rogers, Perls, Ellis and Beck.

Attend training courses and workshops

You may expand your knowledge and skills in the different theories by attending training courses and workshops run by competent adherents of the different approaches. Introductory theories of counselling and therapy courses are likely to be limited in presenting different approaches both by time con-straints and lecturer preferences. You may get a much more thorough introduction to any single approach if you attend workshops and courses run by specialists. However, when considering training courses and workshops, be careful about spreading yourself too thinly.

Undergo supervision

A good way to learn about the theory and practice of a counselling approach is to be supervised by a practitioner skilled in it. For instance, you can learn the theory and practice of one therapeutic approach more thoroughly by being supervised by someone knowledgeable and competent in that approach. You can then broaden how you work by obtaining supervision from practitioners of one or more different approaches.

Undergo personal therapy

If a counselling and therapy approach particularly appeals to you, one way to learn about its theory and practice is to become a client of a skilled practitioner in the approach. For some approaches, for example, psychoanalysis and analytical therapy, a training analysis is an integral part of learning the approach.

Evaluate theoretical approaches

In creating your own theoretical approach you will undoubtedly undergo a process of evaluating the existing theoretical approaches. Many considerations go into evaluating theoretical approaches: for instance, how well you understand the theoretical approaches you are trying to evaluate, how thoroughly each approach is researched, and how their goals differ. I leave a more detailed discussion about evaluating counselling and therapy approaches to this book's final chapter.

SUMMARY

- *A theoretical approach presents a single position regarding the theory and practice of counselling and therapy.*
- *A school of counselling and therapy is a grouping of different theoretical approaches which are similar to one another in terms of certain important characteristics that distinguish them from approaches in other counselling and therapy schools.*
- *Probably the three main schools that influence contemporary*

individual counselling and psychotherapy practice are the psychodynamic school, the humanistic school and the cognitive-behavioural school.

- *Therapy is derived from the Greek word for healing. Though there may be variations of emphasis between counselling and therapy, there are more similarities than differences.*
- *A theory is the formulation of the underlying principles of certain observed phenomena which have been verified to some extent. Three of the main functions of counselling and therapy theories are providing conceptual frameworks, providing languages and generating research.*
- *Counselling and therapy theories can be for good or ill. Potential limitations of therapy theories include restriction of focus, therapist rigidity, depowering clients and supporting the status quo.*
- *In addition to working with this book, you can create your own theoretical approach by applying the theories to yourself; reading primary sources, secondary sources and case studies; watching and listening to audiovisual material; attending training courses and workshops; and undergoing supervision and personal therapy by skilled practitioners.*

REVIEW AND PERSONAL QUESTIONS

Review questions

1. What are the distinguishing characteristics of the following schools of counselling and therapy:

   - psychodynamic?
   - humanistic?
   - cognitive-behavioural?

2. To what extent do you consider the terms 'counselling' and 'therapy' describe different activities and why?
3. What is a theory?
4. What are the functions of counselling and therapy theories?
5. What are some potential limitations or disadvantages of counselling and therapy theories?

Personal questions

1. Do you consider yourself a prospective counsellor and/or a prospective therapist and why?
2. Describe your present preferences regarding counselling and therapy theoretical approaches.
3. How can you best learn about counselling and therapy theoretical approaches?
4. How can you best develop a theoretical approach to guide your counselling and therapy practice?

ANNOTATED BIBLIOGRAPHY

Corsini, R. J. and Wedding, D. (eds) (2000) *Current Psychotherapies* (6th edn). Itasca, IL: Peacock.

This book is a mixture of primary and secondary sources. Chapters on cognitive, existential, multimodal, person-centred and rational emotive therapies are written by their originators, sometimes with co-authors. Secondary source chapters review psychoanalytic, Adlerian, gestalt, behaviour and family therapy. There is also a strong chapter on Asian psychotherapies.

Nelson-Jones, R. (in press) *The Theory and Practice of Counselling and Therapy* (3rd edn). London: Continuum.

In addition to covering the six approaches contained in the present volume, this book has further chapters on reality therapy, existential therapy, logotherapy, behaviour therapy – theory, behaviour therapy – practice, multimodal therapy, cognitive-humanistic therapy, cultural issues and gender issues.

REFERENCES

British Association for Counselling (1998) *Code of Ethics and Practice for Counsellors*. Rugby: Author.
Corsini, R. J. and Wedding, D. (eds) (2000) *Current Psychotherapies* (6th edn). Itasca, IL: Peacock.
Hall, C. S. and Lindzey, G. (1970) *Theories of Personality*. New York: John Wiley.
Jung, C. G. (1961) *Memories, Dreams and Reflections*. London: Fontana Press.
Mearns, D. and Thorne, B. (1999) *Person-Centred Counselling in Action* (2nd edn). London: Sage.

Nelson-Jones, R. (in press) *The Theory and Practice of Counselling and Therapy* (3rd edn). London: Continuum.

Rogers, C. R. (1957) 'The necessary and sufficient conditions of therapeutic personality change'. *Journal of Consulting Psychology*, **21**, 95–104.

Freud's Psychoanalysis

*We believe that civilisation has been built up, under
the pressure of the struggle for existence, by sacri-
fices in the gratification of primitive instincts.*

Sigmund Freud

INTRODUCTION

A woman who is very anxious to bear children always reads
'storks' instead of 'stocks'. The notion of Freudian slips, or
people inadvertently betraying their underlying thoughts, has
become part of Western culture. Furthermore, humour about
Freudian psychoanalysis is common, with Woody Allen being
a prime example. For instance, when asked 'How long have
you been in psychoanalysis?', he replied 'Twenty-one years?'
When further asked 'How is it going?', he answered 'Slowly.'
In the film *Annie Hall*, the character played by Woody Allen
observes: 'I was depressed ... I was suicidal; as a matter of fact
I would have killed myself but I was in analysis with a strict
Freudian and if you kill yourself they make you pay for the
sessions you miss.'

Sigmund Freud, the originator of psychoanalysis, is easily
the best-known of the theorists whose work is described in
this book. Freud, an Austrian, lived the first forty-four years of
his life in the second half of the nineteenth century. This was a
period of intellectual ferment with a crucial issue being the
challenges posed by Darwin's ideas on the evolution of the
species. Around this time, psychology was gradually starting
to separate itself from philosophy. Freud, like William James
in the United States, was interested in both areas. Along with
the intellectual challenges, the old ways of life were also being
challenged by the industrial revolution and technological
inventions like the discovery of electricity and the motor car.

Freud also lived in a time of conflict, a major theme of his work. One area of conflict was that between the strait-laced 'Victorian' public morality of late nineteenth-century Austria and human sexuality. To a large extent public acknowledgement of sexuality was frowned upon, which fostered widespread ignorance of healthy sexual functioning. Another area of conflict was that caused by human aggression. The nineteenth century had started with the Napoleonic wars, in the second half of the century the Franco-Prussian war took place, and, in the second decade of the twentieth century, matters were to get worse with the horrors of the First World War. Though Freud died within a month of the start of the Second World War he was very conscious of the factors leading up to it, not least because all his professional life, as a Jew, he had been acutely aware of the anti-Semitism in his homeland and he was to die in exile, a refugee from Nazism.

SIGMUND FREUD (1856–1939)

Sigmund Freud was born at Freiberg, a small town in what is now the Czech Republic. He was the eldest son of his father's second wife, who subsequently bore five daughters and two other sons. Jones (1963) writes of Freud's mother's pride in and love for her first-born and also mentions that between the ages of 2 and $2\frac{1}{2}$ Freud's libido had been aroused towards his mother on seeing her naked. Freud writes: 'My parents were Jews, and I have remained a Jew myself' (Freud, 1935, p. 12). His father, Jakob, was a wool merchant who moved his family to Vienna when Freud was 4 years old. Freud's early years in Vienna were hard and, throughout his upbringing, his family appears to have been short of money.

When he was 9 Freud went to high school (Sperl Gymnasium), where he was at the top of his class for seven years, enjoyed special privileges, and was required to pass few examinations. Freud was a hard worker who enjoyed reading and studying. On leaving school with distinction at age 17 he faced the choice of a career, which for a Viennese Jew had to be in industry, business, law or medicine. He recalls not feeling any particular predilection for medicine, since his interests were directed more towards human concerns than natural objects. Freud writes: 'and it was hearing Goethe's beautiful essay on Nature read aloud by Professor Carl Bruhl just before I left school that decided me to become a medical student' (Freud, 1935, p. 14).

In 1873 Freud enrolled at the University of Vienna to study medicine, though while he was there his academic interests were more wide-ranging. In 1876 he began the first of his researches, a study of the gonadic structure of eels. Soon afterwards he entered Ernst Brücke's physiological laboratory, where he worked, with short interruptions, from 1876 to 1882. During this period Freud focused chiefly on work connected with the histology of nerve cells. He found 'rest and satisfaction' in Brücke's laboratory as well as scientists 'whom I could respect and take as my models' (Freud, 1935, p. 15). He thought especially highly of Brücke himself. Freud recalls being decidedly negligent in pursuing his medical studies. Nevertheless, in 1881 he passed his final examinations to become a doctor of medicine with the grade of 'excellent'.

In 1882 Freud left Brücke's laboratory, where the year before he had been appointed a demonstrator. For financial reasons, probably influenced by falling in love, Freud decided to earn his living as a physician. He entered the General Hospital of Vienna, where he gained experience in various departments and became an active researcher in the Institute of Cerebral Anatomy. During this period, 'with an eye to material considerations, I began to study nervous diseases' (Freud, 1935, p. 18). Because of inadequate opportunities for learning this subject, Freud was forced to be his own teacher. He published a number of clinical observations on organic diseases of the nervous system and, in 1885, was appointed lecturer in neuropathology. Around this period Freud both took cocaine and conducted research into its use. Jones (1963) observes: 'For many years he suffered from periodic depressions and fatigue or apathy, neurotic symptoms which later took the form of anxiety attacks before being dispelled by his own analysis' (pp. 54–5). Cocaine apparently calmed the agitation and eased the depression. Jones also mentions that all his life Freud was subject to severe bouts of migraine which were refractory to any treatment.

On the award of a travelling fellowship Freud went to Paris where, from October 1885 to February 1886, he studied at the Sâlpetrière (hospital for nervous diseases) under Charcot. He was very impressed by Charcot's investigations into hysteria, confirming the genuineness of hysterical phenomena, including hysterical paralyses and contractures by hypnotic suggestion. In 1886 Freud returned to Vienna to marry Martha Bernays and set up a private practice as a specialist in nervous diseases. His 'therapeutic arsenal contained only two weapons, electrotherapy and hypnotism' (Freud, 1935, p. 26). He soon dropped electrotherapy and increasingly realized the limitations of hypnotic suggestion. During the period 1886 to 1891 he did little scientific work, though in 1891 he jointly published the first of his studies on the cerebral paralyses of children.

In the early 1880s Freud had developed a close friendship with Joseph Breuer, a prominent Viennese physician, who told him how, between 1880 and 1882, he had successfully treated a young girl with hysterical symptoms. His method was to hypnotize her deeply and then encourage her to express in words her memories of earlier emotional situations which were oppressing her. In the late 1880s Freud began repeating Breuer's technique with his own patients, being aware 'of the possibility that there could be powerful mental processes which nevertheless remained hidden from the consciousness of man' (Freud, 1935, p. 29). In 1893 Freud and Breuer wrote a preliminary paper on the cathartic method and, in 1895, published their book *Studies on Hysteria*.

During the 1890s the transition from catharsis to psycho-analysis proper took place. Jones (1963) writes: 'there is ample evidence that for ten years or so – roughly comprising the nineties – he suffered from a very considerable psychoneurosis ... yet it was just in the years when the neurosis was at its height, 1897–1900, that Freud did his most original work' (p. 194). Although he showed no conversion symptoms, he had extreme alterations of mood between elation and self-confidence, and depression and inhibition. In the latter moods Freud could neither write nor concentrate, apart from his professional work. In addition, he had occasional attacks of dread of dying and also became very anxious about travelling by rail.

During the period 1887 to 1900 Freud had an intense friendship with Wilhelm Fleiss, a nose and throat specialist two years his junior. Fleiss saw sexual problems as central to his own work, encouraged Freud and gave him permission to develop his theories. Jones notes Freud's dependency on Fleiss' good opinion and calls him Freud's 'sole public' during this period. Jones rated Fleiss as intellectually far inferior to Freud.

Against this background, Freud started developing his ideas on the sexual bases of neuroses, abandoned hypnotism yet retained his practice of requiring the patient to lie on a sofa while he sat behind. During 1897 to 1899 he wrote his major work, *The Interpretation of Dreams*. In the summer of 1897 Freud undertook a psychoanalysis of his own unconscious, and this self-analysis generated material for the book. Freud discovered his childhood passion for his mother and jealousy of his father, which he considered a pervasive human characteristic; he termed it the Oedipus complex. It took eight years to sell the first edition of 600 copies of *The Interpretation of Dreams*. Jones (1963) observes of Freud's self-analysis: 'The end of all that labor and suffering was the last and final phase in the evolution of Freud's personality. There emerged the serene and benign Freud, henceforth free to pursue his work in imperturbable composure' (p. 205). Fromm's (1959) biography is less kind, suggesting that Freud continued to exhibit some insecurity and egotism in areas of both his professional and personal life. In 1905 Freud published what is perhaps his other major work, *Three Contributions to the Theory of Sex*, which traces the development of sexuality from its earliest childhood beginnings.

In his autobiographical study Freud observed that, after the preliminary cathartic period, the history of psychoanalysis falls into two phases. From 1895–96 until 1906 or 1907 he worked in isolation, but thereafter the contributions of his pupils and collaborators increasingly grew in importance. The historical development of Freud's ideas will be left at this stage. Suffice it to say that for the remainder of his life he published numerous books and articles not only on psychoanalysis as a method of treating the disturbed, but also on the relevance of his theories to everyday life. In 1910, at a congress held in Nuremberg, the analysts formed themselves into an International Psychoanalytical Association divided into a number of local societies, but under a common president. By 1935 the number of the Association's supporters had considerably increased. The growth of psychoanalysis, however, was not smooth, and it aroused considerable antipathy.

Freud was in the habit of smoking an average of twenty cigars a day and, in 1923, learned that he had cancer of the jaw. He lived the last sixteen years of his life in pain which was often extreme, and a total of thirty-three operations were performed on his jaw. In 1938 Nazism caused Freud to leave Austria with his family and settle in his admired England, which he had first visited when he was 19. He died in London a year later.

Freud had observed that he was by temperament a conquistador or adventurer, with the accompanying traits of curiosity, boldness and tenacity. A modern term for Freud might be an 'ideas person'.

THEORY

Where id was, there shall ego be.

Sigmund Freud

BASIC CONCEPTS

Although many of Freud's basic concepts are to be found in *The Interpretation of Dreams*, he was developing and refining his ideas continuously. Thus the same concept may appear in different sources, only some of which will be mentioned here. In general, this chapter represents Freud's later presentation of his work.

The pleasure principle

Originally presented as the unpleasure principle, the pleasure principle follows from the constancy hypothesis that 'the mental apparatus endeavours to keep the quantity of excitation in it as low as possible or at least to keep it constant' (Freud, 1961, p. 3). Thus everything which increases the quantity of excitation will be felt as unpleasurable and anything which diminishes it will be experienced as pleasurable. Freud qualified the idea of the dominance of the pleasure principle by observing that, although in the mind there exists a strong tendency towards the pleasure principle, there are also other forces opposing it, with the final outcome not always fulfilling the tendency towards pleasure.

The instincts

Instincts represent somatic or biological demands upon the mind. While acknowledging the possibility of distinguishing many instincts, Freud assumed that these could be grouped into two basic instincts: *Eros* and the *destructive instinct*. The erotic instincts 'seek to combine more and more living substance into even greater unities', while the death instincts 'oppose this effort and lead what is living back to an inorganic state' (Freud, 1973, p. 140). Eros includes the instincts of self-preservation, the preservation of the species, ego-love and object-love, and its energy is called *libido*. Throughout life the basic instincts may either work together (for instance, the sexual act is also an act of aggression) or oppose each other.

Freud saw instincts as historically acquired and conservative, and stated: 'It seems, then, that an instinct is an urge inherent in life to restore an earlier state of things' (Freud, 1961, p. 30). Given the assumption that living things appeared later than inanimate ones and arose out of them, the death instinct may be viewed as a compulsion to repeat this earlier inorganic state. Consequently, the aim of all life is death. Eros, however, does not follow the same formula. Freud considered that sexual instincts were the single exception among the instincts in not seeking to restore an earlier state of things.

Freud viewed the inclination to aggression as an original instinctual disposition in human beings. He quoted Plautus: '*Homo homini lupus*', a translation of which is 'Man is a wolf to man'. The aggressive instinct is the derivative and main representative of the death instinct. The evolution of civilization represents the struggle between the life and death instincts in the human species. The fateful question that Freud posed at the end of *Civilization and its Discontents* was whether Eros would assert itself, 'But who can foresee with what success and what results?' (Freud, 1962c, p. 92).

The unconscious and consciousness

Heavily influenced by his study of dreams, Freud made a distinction between the unconscious and consciousness. From the very beginning, he stated that there were two kinds of unconscious. Hence, Freud asserted that there were three levels of consciousness.

- *The unconscious* (Ucs), or unconscious proper, is material that is inadmissible to consciousness through repression. In other words, with the unconscious the censorship on material coming into awareness is very strong indeed. The object of psychoanalysis is to help make some of this material accessible to awareness, though strong resistances may be aroused during the process, not least because of the forbidden sexual connotations of much of what is being repressed.
- *The preconscious* (Pcs) consists of everything that can easily exchange the unconscious state for the conscious one. Thus the preconscious is latent and capable of becoming conscious, while the unconscious is repressed and unlikely to become conscious without great difficulty. Material may remain in the preconscious, though usually it finds its way into consciousness without any need for psychoanalytic intervention. The preconscious may be viewed as a screen between the unconscious and consciousness, with, as in the case of dreams, modifications being made in unconscious material through censorship.
- *Consciousness* (Cs or Pcpt Cs) has the function of a sense organ for the perception of psychical qualities. Unlike the two kinds of unconscious, consciousness has no memory and a state of consciousness is usually very transitory. Material becomes conscious, or flows into the consciousness sense-organ, from two directions: the external world and inner excitations. Furthermore, the function of speech enables internal events such as sequences of ideas and intellectual processes to become conscious.

Structure of the mental apparatus

Freud structured the mental apparatus into three systems or agencies: the id, the ego and the super-ego. Psychological well-being depends on whether these three systems are interrelating effectively. Box 2.1 shows Freud's own sketch of the structural relations of the mental apparatus, though he acknowledges that the space occupied by the unconscious id ought to have been much greater (Freud, 1973, p. 111).

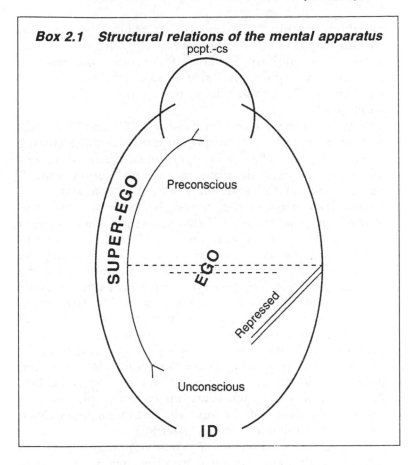

Box 2.1 Structural relations of the mental apparatus
pcpt.-cs

SUPER-EGO

Preconscious

EGO

Repressed

Unconscious

ID

- *The id* or 'it' is the oldest of these systems and contains everything that is inherited and fixed in the constitution. The instincts, which originate in the somatic organization, find their mental expression in the id. The id, filled with energy from the instincts, strives to bring about the satisfaction of instinctual needs on the basis of the pleasure principle. Thus the activity of the id is directed towards securing the free discharge of quantities of excitation. The psychical processes of the id are known as primary processes because they are present in the mental apparatus from the first. Furthermore, no alteration in the id's mental processes is produced by the passage of time. Freud viewed the id as 'a chaos, a cauldron full of seething emotions', which 'knows no judgements of values: no good and evil, no morality' (Freud, 1973, pp. 106–7). The id consists of wishful impulses. It is not governed by logic, and this applies especially to the law of contradiction, since it contains contrary impulses side by side. In short, the id is the individual's primary subjective reality at the unconscious level.

- *The ego* or 'I' is first and foremost a bodily ego ultimately derived from bodily sensations, in particular those coming from its surface. The ego is a portion of the id which has undergone a special development or modification through the influence of the external world. The ego acts as an intermediary between the id and the external world and ideally represents reason and common sense, whereas the id contains instinctual passions and would destroy itself without the intervention of the ego. The ego strives to bring the reality principle to bear upon the id in substitution for the pleasure principle. The processes of the ego, which include perception, problem-solving and repression, are later developments or secondary processes, in contrast to the original or primary processes of the id. Nevertheless, the ego seeks pleasure and the avoidance of unpleasure, differing from the id only in the means of attaining common ends. A foreseen increase in unpleasure is met by a signal of anxiety. As Box 2.1 shows, the perceptual-conscious system (pcpt.-cs) is the top or outer layer of the ego, which also includes much preconscious and unconscious material.

  The ego is in control of voluntary movement, but interposes thought between experiencing a need and acting on it. The ego deals with external events through perception, memory, avoiding excessive stimuli, adapting to moderate stimuli, and engaging in activities designed to modify the external world to its advantage. Regarding internal events in relation to the id, the ego attempts to control instinctual demands by deciding the timing and manner of their gratification or by suppressing their excitations. Freud makes the analogy of the id being the horse, while the ego is the rider. He observes that often, however, the ego is weak in relation to the id and so is in the habit of transforming the id's will into action as if it were its own.

- *The super-ego* is a residue formed within the ego in which parental influence is prolonged. Parental influence may be broadly defined as including cultural, racial and family influences. As the person grows up, the nature of the 'parental' influence may vary, partly because parents may behave differently. In addition, teachers, admired figures in public life and many others may contribute to the development of an individual's super-ego, which normally departs more and more from original parental influences.

The function of the super-ego, which engages in self-observation, is to contain the demands of the id through moral influence on the ego. Originally, the child engages in instinctual renunciation through fear of loss of love or through fear of aggression from an *external* or parental authority. Subsequently, a secondary situation develops in which the external restraint is internalized and thus instinctual renunciation comes about through fear of an *internal* authority, or super-ego.

A characteristic of the super-ego is the ego-ideal, based on the admiration which the child felt for the perfection it saw in its parents and which it strives to emulate. In fact the terms 'super-ego' and 'ego-ideal' are virtually synonymous. The ego-ideal consists of both precepts – 'You ought to be like this' – and prohibitions – 'You ought not to be like that'. These precepts and prohibitions are based in part on the identifications and repressions resulting from the resolution of the Oedipus complex. They represent the individual's conscience, transgressions of which are likely to result in a sense of inferiority and guilt and also possibly in a need for punishment. Freud observed: 'The super-ego is the representative for us of every moral restriction, the advocate of a striving towards perfection – it is, in short, as much as we have been able to grasp psychologically of what is described as the higher side of human life' (Freud, 1973, p. 98).

In addition to the demands of the instincts and of the external world, the ego has to take into account the demands of the super-ego. Individuals vary in the severity of their super-egos, which may be benign or punitively harsh and restricting. Conflicts can arise between ego and super-ego, with large portions of both agencies remaining unconscious.

Anxiety

Freud defined anxiety as a specific state of unpleasure accompanied by motor discharge along definite pathways. He saw anxiety as the universal reaction to the situation of danger and the ego as the sole seat of anxiety. In later life, a source of anxiety which is involuntary occurs whenever a dangerous situation arises. Another source is anxiety generated by the ego when danger is merely threatened and the ego feels weak in relation to it. Hence there are three kinds of anxiety, one for each of the ego's three 'taskmasters':

- *realistic* anxiety regarding the dangers of the external world
- *moral* anxiety regarding conflict with the super-ego
- *neurotic* anxiety regarding conflict with the strength of the id's instinctual impulses.

Thus anxiety is either a reaction to actual danger or a signal involving the perception of impending danger.

Psychical energy, cathexis and anti-cathexis

Psychoanalysis is often referred to as having a dynamic view of psychology. What this means is that the concept of psychical or mental energy and its distribution among the id, ego and super-ego is central to psychoanalysis. The id is the source of this somatically based psychical energy, being filled with energy reaching it from the instincts. Sexual excitation is an example of instinctual psychical energy. As the ego and the super-ego are formed they also become charged with energy.

The words 'cathexis' and to 'cathect' describe the idea of psychical energy being drawn to mental agencies and processes, somewhat analogous to an electric charge. Cathexes are the charges of instinctual energy seeking discharge, whereas anti-cathexes are charges of energy which block and inhibit such discharge. The id has only primary-process instinctual cathexes seeking discharge. However, the ego and the super-ego have both urging cathexes and restraining anti-cathexes. Throughout life the ego is the avenue by which libidinal cathexes are transferred to objects and into which they may also be withdrawn again. Two characteristics of libidinal cathexes are mobility – the ease with which they pass from one object to another — and, in contrast, fixation, or being bound to particular objects.

Bisexuality

Freud observed that it was a long-known anatomical fact that in every normally formed male or female there are traces of the apparatus of the other sex, though in atrophied form. Anatomically there may have been an original predisposition to bisexuality, which in the course of the development of the human species has largely been altered to monosexuality.

Psychologically, Freud considered that the sexual impulse is probably entirely independent of its object and therefore is not originated by chemical attraction. Another way of stating this is that there is only one libido and it cannot be assigned a sex. Therefore the direction of both heterosexual and homosexual object selection requires further explanation. By studying covert sexual excitations, psychoanalytic research discovered that all men were capable of homosexual object selection and actually accomplish this in the unconscious. Furthermore, homosexual libidinous feelings 'play no small role as factors in normal psychic life' and an even greater role as 'causative factors of disease' (Freud, 1962a, p. 10).

Freud considered that the same free attachment to male and female objects as observed in childhood and primitive and prehistoric states forms the basis on which both normal and homosexual or inverted sexual development takes place. A degree of homosexuality is congenital in everyone, with the final determination of sexual behaviour being the result of the intensity of constitutional predisposition as well as of life experiences and restrictions in one or the other direction. Both the woman and the man develop out of a child with a bisexual disposition.

ACQUISITION

Infantile sexuality and amnesia

Freud distinguished between the sexual impulse, the sexual object and the sexual aim. The sexual impulse is the sexual aspect of libido, the sexual object is the person in whom sexual attraction is lodged, and the sexual aim refers to the action, such as touch or intercourse, towards which the sexual impulse strives. Freud further made a sharp distinction between 'sexual' and 'genital', considering that sexual life consists of gaining pleasure from erotogenic zones of the body and that this is not necessarily in the service of reproduction. In addition, sexual life includes affectionate and friendly impulses often called 'love'. In a sense, all adult sexual behaviour whose goal is not reproduction, a heterosexual object and intercourse may be considered perverse. Adult sexual behaviour does not suddenly emerge at puberty but has developed out of prior sexual dispositions and experiences.

Sexual life starts soon after birth. Infantile sexuality, in the absence of genital maturation and of ego and super-ego development, lacks a central co-ordinating focus. Instead the component sexual instincts seek their own pleasure. Infantile sexuality is fundamentally auto-erotic in that the infant finds its pleasure in the object of its own body. Freud considered that the infantile sexual disposition contained great tendencies to perversion and that normal sexual behaviour develops partly in response to organic changes and partly as a result of psychic inhibitions and repressions.

The years of childhood are when the individual is most impressionable. Nevertheless, people are largely unaware of the beginnings of their sexual life and tend to view their childhood as if it were a prehistoric time. However, infantile and childhood sexual experiences leave deep traces in the individual's psychical life, acting as significant determinants for future development. Freud used the term 'infantile amnesia' to refer to the phenomenon by which a veil is drawn over early sexual experiences.

Sexual development

The onset of sexual life is diphasic. The first or pre-genital stage of sexual development is a steady process that reaches a climax towards the end of a child's fifth year. There follows a lull or period of latency. The second or genital stage starts with the re-emergence of the sexual impulse at menarche or puberty. The pre-genital and genital stages of sexual organization are distinguished by whether or not the genital zones have assumed a dominating role.

The pre-genital stage (birth to about age 6)

The pre-genital stage itself consists of three separate phases of sexual organization through which individuals normally pass smoothly, though fixations or arrested development may occur at each phase. Both sexes seem to pass through the early stages of sexual development in the same manner.

- *Oral phase (first eighteen months)*   The first organ to be an erotogenic zone is the mouth, and hence sexual development starts with the *oral* phase. The infant's act of sucking goes beyond that needed for the taking of nourishment to what may be viewed as the seeking of sexual organ pleasure independent of nourishment. The oral phase can be further subdivided. The first sub-stage is where there is a focus only on oral incorporation, whereas the second sub-stage is 'oral-sadistic', with the emergence of biting activity. These two sub-stages of the oral phase are the first manifestation of the phenomenon of ambivalence.
- *Anal phase (18 months to 3 years of age)*   The second organ to become an erotogenic zone is the anus, and normal sexual development proceeds from the oral to the *sadistic-anal* phase. The active aspect of this phase is the impulse for mastery (sadism), with the strengthening of the musculature of the body and control of sphincter functions. The erotogenic mucous membrane of the anus also manifests itself as an organ with a passive sexual aim. Character traits associated with this phase are orderliness, parsimony and obstinacy, which together define the so-called 'anal character'.
- *Phallic phase (from about age 3 to 5 or 6)*   The third organ to become an erotogenic zone is the genital apparatus. The period of sexual development in which the male sexual organ (the phallus) and the female clitoris become important is known as the *phallic* phase, which starts in about the child's third year. Here pleasure is obtained from masturbation. During the phallic phase the sexuality of early childhood reaches its greatest intensity, and it is during this phase that male and female sexual development become differentiated. The *Oedipus* phase is part of the phallic phase for both sexes (see Box 2.2).

Box 2.2   The Oedipus complex

For boys

At an early age the little boy develops an object-cathexis for his mother and identifies with his father. During the phallic phase the body's libidinal object-cathexis of his mother intensifies and he wishes to be rid of his father and take his father's place with his mother. The threat of castration causes the boy to abandon and repress his incestuous wishes. The resolution of the boy's Oedipus complex involves renouncing his object-cathexis of his mother, which may lead to an identification with his mother or, more normally, to an intensification of his identification with his father, consolidating the masculinity in his character. The Oedipus situation is often more complex because of the child's bisexual disposition. Thus, instead of affection for his mother and ambivalence towards his father, he may have a mixture of affection for and ambivalence towards each parent. Freud observes that 'in both sexes the relative strength of the masculine and feminine sexual dispositions is what determines whether the outcome of the Oedipus situation shall be an identification with the father or with the mother' (Freud, 1962b, p. 23). Perhaps it is more accurate to consider the outcome as a predominant rather than an exclusive identification with one or the other parent. Freud further asserts that, especially with neurotics, a bisexual Oedipus complex should be assumed.

For girls

As with the boy, the girl's mother is the first object of her love. During the phallic phase the clitoris is her predominant erotogenic zone. Freud considered that during the girl's development to femininity she should change both her predominant erotogenic zone (to the vagina) and also the sex of her love object. The powerful attachment of the girl to her mother is ended when the girl, discovering the inferiority of her clitoris and the fact that she does not have a penis, holds her mother responsible. Penis envy or the wish for a penis is a very important feminine trait. The wish for a penis-baby from the father replaces the wish for a penis, and it is at this stage that the girl has entered her Oedipus situation, desiring her father and wishing to be rid of her mother. Again the situation may be complicated by her bisexual disposition. Girls remain in their Oedipus situation for an indeterminate length of time and resolve it late and often incompletely. Whereas the boy is encouraged to surmount the Oedipus complex through fear of castration, the girl has no such motivation. As time goes by the female Oedipus complex weakens, partly as a result of inevitable disappointment in her father.

The latency period (about age 6 to 12)

The period from around the beginning of the child's sixth year – probably later for girls – to menarche and puberty constitutes the sexual latency period. Latency may be total or partial and, during this period, sexual inhibitions develop. One of the mechanisms by which sexual energy is diverted is called sublimation or the displacement of libido to new aims and cultural pursuits. Furthermore, as the individual develops, libidinous impulses may call forth contrary anti-cathexes or reactions (reaction formations) such as disgust, shame and morality.

The genital stage (age about 12 and onward)

The *genital* stage, which starts at menarche or puberty, involves the subordination of all sources of sexual feeling to the primacy of the genital zones. Earlier libidinal cathexes may be retained, included in sexual activity or preliminary or auxiliary acts, or in some way repressed or diverted. Puberty brings a greater increase of libido in boys, but in girls there is an increase in repression, especially regarding clitoral sexuality. Also at menarche and puberty, along with the overcoming of incestuous object-choices, comes the breaking away from parental authority. Given a reasonably adequate prior sexual development, the individual is now ready to engage in a heterosexual genital relationship.

Identification

Identification is an important concept for understanding ego and super-ego development. Identification may be viewed in three ways:

- as the original form of emotional tie with an object;
- as a regressive substitute for a libidinal object-tie by means of introjection of the object with the ego, so that the ego assumes the characteristics of the object (for example, a female patient imitating her father's cough);
- as a feeling generated by the perception of a common quality with another person who is not libidinally cathected.

The development of the super-ego may be seen in terms of identification with the parental agency, by which young people, wishing to be like their parents, mould their egos after the fashion of those taken as their models. Identification is part of the normal process of development. However, the ego may be restricted, as well as enhanced, depending on the nature of the identification.

Defence mechanisms

During the child's early years its ego is relatively feeble, yet it has to deal with strong instinctual sexual impulses. At this stage anxiety may be generated by loss of an object or loss of love, which may persist into later life. Later sources of anxiety include fear of castration during the phallic phase, and fear of the super-ego during and after the latency period.

In order to cope with the sources of anxiety the ego utilizes defence mechanisms. Freud doubted that the ego could do without them during normal development. In many instances, however, the ego pays a high price for the use of the mechanisms, since they restrict its functioning, also using in their anti-cathexes psychical energy which might better be expended elsewhere. Defence mechanisms are infantilisms which operate unconsciously and may impede realistic behaviour long after they have outlived their usefulness. Individuals do not make use of all the possible mechanisms of defence, but select some, which then become fixated in their egos. The establishment of defence mechanisms is largely a feature of the child's struggle against its sexuality during the first five years of life. When the ego observes that an emerging instinctual demand may place it in danger, as Box 2.3 describes, there are five main defensive ways in which the ego strives to contain the threatening instinctual cathexis.

Box 2.3   The ego's main mechanisms of defence

Repression

Purposely forgetting something and remaining unaware of having done this. The process of repression is of two kinds:

- material which is in the preconscious and hence admissible to consciousness is pushed back into the unconscious;
- unconscious material may be forbidden by censorship to enter the preconscious and hence has to remain unconscious.

For example, either kind of repression might apply to an individual's latent sexually perverted impulses. Repression is the central underlying defence mechanism of the ego, the basis of all other defences.

Reaction formation

Adapting thoughts, feelings and behaviours that are the opposite to one's true thoughts and feelings. The ego acknowledges impulses that are contrary to the ones by which it is threatened. For instance, sexual impulses may be warded off by excessive shame, disgust and loathing of sexuality.

Projection

The ego deals with the threat of an unacceptable instinctual impulse by externalizing it. Thus individuals, instead of acknowledging the extent of their own libidinal and aggressive impulses, may become very aware of such characteristics in others and actually attribute them incorrectly.

Fixation

Where people become highly anxious about moving on to the next phase of their sexual development, they may lag behind or become fixated in varying degrees to an earlier stage in terms of satisfaction of their instincts. For instance, children may cling dependently to their mothers' love rather than make new object-cathexes.

Regression

Resuming behaviours appropriate to an earlier stage of sexual development. Under threat, an individual returns to an earlier phase at which s/he may previously have been fixated. In fact, regressions may be of two kinds: a return to the incestuous objects first cathected by the libido and a return of the sexual organization as a whole to an earlier phase.

Normal development

To summarize, the Freudian view of the normal development of personality may be seen in terms of three interrelated strands.

- The individual's libidinal development, which starts with a mixture of constitutional and infantile predispositions which mature into genital sexuality in successive but over-lapping phases, interrupted by the latency period.
- The development of both the ego, as it gains in ability to mediate between instinctual demands and the reality of the external world, and the super-ego, based on identifications with parental influences.
- The establishment of favoured defence mechanisms on the part of the ego to ward off the anxiety caused by the strength and persistence of the id's libidinal impulses.

Thus normal development may be viewed as passing through successive stages of sexual maturation without major fixations and regressions, developing an ego which copes reasonably effectively with the external world, developing a super-ego based on identifications which are constructive and not punitively moralistic, and evolving defence mechanisms which drain off some of the energy of the id without serious restriction of ego functioning. Normal development is a dynamic process entailing a continuing distribution and redistribution of psychical energy among id, ego and super-ego, the three systems of the mental apparatus.

Development and activation of neurosis

Freud saw biological, phylogenetic and psychological factors as each contributing to neurosis.

The biological factor

The human animal is born relatively unfinished and thus has to undergo a protracted period of helplessness and dependence. This helplessness creates the initial situation of danger regarding fear of object loss, which in turn creates the human being's need to be loved, which it never renounces.

The phylogenetic factor

This is inferred from the interruption in human sexual development of the latency period, whereas the sexual maturation of related animals proceeds uninterrupted. Freud believed that something momentous must have taken place in the history of the human species to bring about this situation and that its pathogenic importance is that most of the instinctual demands of infantile sexuality are treated as dangers to be guarded against by the ego. Furthermore, there is the danger that the sexual impulses of puberty will follow their infantile prototypes into repression.

The psychological factor

This involves three elements which together make for a pathogenic neurotic conflict.

- *Frustration of sexual impulses* or the damming up of the sexual instinct by the ego. Repressions are especially likely to take place in infancy and early childhood, when the ego is underdeveloped and feeble in relation to the strength of the sexual impulses. Freud observed: 'We recognise the essential precondition of neuroses in this lagging of ego development behind libidinal development' (Freud, 1949, p. 113). The process of repression takes place under the influence of anxiety, in that the ego anticipates that satisfaction of the emerging sexual cathexis will lead to danger. In fact the ego allows an initial reproduction of the feared unpleasure. This feeling of anxiety brings the unpleasure–pleasure mechanism into operation and so causes the ego to repress the dangerous instinctual impulse. By the act of repression, however, the ego has renounced a portion of its organiza-

---

Box 2.4   Examples of normal and neurotic development

Freud (1973) gives as an example of normal and neurotic development the story of the caretaker's and the landlord's daughters. When young, the two girls played games which took on a sexual character, including exciting each other's genitals. These experiences awakened sexual impulses which afterwards found expression in masturbation.

Normal development

The caretaker's daughter, unscarred by her early sexual activity, which she regarded as natural and harmless, took a lover and became a mother.

Neurotic development

While still a child, the landlord's daughter, as a result of education, developed the idea that she had done something wrong. She turned into an intelligent and high-minded girl who renounced her sexuality and whose subsequent neurosis precluded her from marrying. While consciously unaware of her sexual impulses, unconsciously these impulses were still attached to her experiences with the caretaker's daughter. Freud observes that, owing to the higher moral and intellectual development of her ego, she came into conflict with the demands of her sexuality.

tion and the repressed instinctual impulse remains inaccessible to its influence.

- *Transformation of frustrated sexual impulses into neurotic symptoms* Frustrated sexual impulses may not disappear, instead being transformed into neurotic symptoms. Freud saw symptoms such as hysterical or conversion symptoms as the substitute satisfactions for the frustrated sexual instincts. Repression, however, does not always result in symptom formation. For instance, in a successful dissolution of the Oedipus complex the repressed sexual impulses may be destroyed, with their libido being put permanently to other uses.

- *Inadequacy of previously used repressions* While repressions may be effective during early childhood and the latency period, they may turn out to be inadequate with the reawakening and intensification of the sexual instincts at menarche and puberty. When this occurs the individual may experience an intense neurotic conflict with all its suffering. Without assistance in undoing its repressions, the ego will have little or no influence over the transformed instincts of the repressed id. Furthermore, the conflict is often heightened through an alliance of the id and super-ego against the ego.

MAINTENANCE

Freud considered that neuroses are acquired only during early childhood, up to the age of 6, even though the symptoms of the neurotic conflict may not appear until much later. He acknowledged the truth of the common assertion that the child is psychologically father of the man or woman. Neurotic people, despite their suffering, are unable to heal their disordered egos and thus their misery is maintained. The reason for this is that, by definition, the significant repressions made by their weak childhood egos are unconscious. Thus their egos pay the price of their defensive operations by not having conscious access to the material through which the neurotic conflict might be resolved. Neurotic people's egos are weakened by their repressions, and their personality functioning is impaired by psychical energy being utilized in harmful defensive anti-cathexes. Further, as long as the repressions continue, so do the conditions for the formation of neurotic symptoms through the rechannelling of frustrated libidinous impulses.

In a broader sense, maintenance of neurosis results from the unsatisfactory way in which society tries to regulate sexual matters. Freud considered that what is described as morality, or the group super-ego, requires a bigger sacrifice of libidinal impulses than is necessary or desirable. He found it impossible to side with conventional sexual morality and considered that anyone with real self-knowledge would be protected against the dangers of morality, while possibly adopting a lifestyle different from the conventions of their society.

THERAPY

The interpretation of dreams is the royal road to a knowledge of the unconscious activities of the mind.

Sigmund Freud

THERAPEUTIC GOALS

The goals of psychoanalysis are threefold:

- *a less constricted id* – the freeing of impulse;
- *a stronger ego* – the strengthening of reality-based ego functioning, including widening its perceptions so that it appropriates more of the id;
- *a more humane super-ego* – the alteration of the contents of the super-ego so that it represents humane rather than punitive moral standards.

A definition of a neurotic is someone who is incapable of enjoyment and efficiency. To be capable of enjoyment, neurotics require the ability to deploy their libido on to real objects instead of transforming it into symptoms. To live efficiently, the ego needs to have the energy of the libido at its disposal rather than wasting energy in warding off libidinous impulses through repression. Furthermore, people's super-egos need to be such as to allow them libidinal expression and the efficient use of their egos.

Freud considered psychoanalytic treatment effective for a

number of nervous diseases, such as hysteria, anxiety states and obsessional neurosis. Since the alliance between the analyst and the client's ego is a mutual one, the client's ego needs to have retained a minimum degree of coherence or reality orientation. This is not to be expected with psychotics, with whom, therefore, psychoanalysis is contra-indicated.

PROCESS OF THERAPY

Freud saw the practice of psychoanalysis as comprising three main parts:

- inducing clients' weakened egos to participate in the intellectual work of interpretation to fill in the gaps of their mental resources and transfer to their analysts the authority of their super-egos;
- stimulating clients' egos to struggle against each of the id's demands and to defeat the resistances arising in connection with them;
- restoring order to clients' egos 'by detecting material and impulses which have forced their way in from the unconscious' (Freud, 1949, p. 77). Such material is both traced back to its origin and exposed to criticism.

Psychoanalysis is a process of re-educating the ego. Repressions were instituted when clients' egos were weak. However, not only have clients' egos now grown stronger, but they possess allies in analysts. Methods by which analysts help weakened egos to lift their repressions, gain insight and make realistic decisions are discussed below. The pathogenic conflicts of neurotics are different from normal mental conflicts because of the ego's weakness relative to the other mental agencies.

Classical psychoanalytic therapy often involves at least four sessions a week, with each session lasting for a minimum of 45 minutes. A course of psychoanalytic therapy may last for several years (Arlow, 2000). Freud considered that ultimately the success of psychoanalysis depended upon the quantitative relationship between the amount of energy analysts can mobilize in clients to their advantage in comparison with the amount of energy of the forces working against them.

THE THERAPEUTIC RELATIONSHIP

As I write this section, I am looking at pictures of Freud's consulting rooms in Vienna and Hampstead. In each, there is a couch which has no back, but one end is raised so that the client's head may comfortably rest there. Cushions are placed at the back of the couch against the wall. A Middle Eastern rug hangs on the wall just above the couch, which itself has a thick Middle Eastern cover. Freud's tub chair facing into the room is placed against the wall behind the raised part of the couch. The nature and positioning of the furniture in psycho-analysis indicates that this is going to be a relationship far removed from normal social interaction: for example, the client cannot see the therapist who, in turn, cannot directly see the client's face.

Seated behind the couch and thus physically keeping out of the way, the analyst encourages the client to say whatever comes into her or his mind without censorship. A major feature of the therapeutic relationship is the development of transference, which is discussed below.

As well as the positioning of client and therapist, a number of other features of the therapist–client relationship aim to encourage clients to reveal the intimate secrets of their minds. Therapists remain anonymous in terms of their own personal life and views. Furthermore, any form of immature personal gratification from the therapeutic relationship is forbidden; for instance, meeting the therapist's own needs for friendship and affection. In addition, confidentiality is strictly observed.

Analysts keep their relationships with clients formal. At the same time they are both intensely involved with helping clients gain insight, compassionate, yet emotionally detached. Much power resides with analysts who, like Freud, decide which interpretations are valid and when and how their clients are resisting the therapeutic process.

The practical aspects of the therapeutic contract are strictly regulated. For example, clients are expected to adhere to a fixed schedule of appointments and fees. However, even Freud had problems with bad debts, one of which contributed to the following slip of the tongue and possibly reveals the uncon-scious fulfilment of a wish. Freud reported repeatedly address-ing a patient Mrs James, who was refusing to pay for her treatment, as Mrs Smith, who paid her fees promptly (Freud, 1960).

THERAPEUTIC INTERVENTIONS

Free association

A basic pact lies at the heart of analytic relationships. Freud (1949) stated: 'The patient's sick ego promises us the most complete candor ... we, on the other hand, assure him of the strictest discretion and put at his service our experience in interpreting material that has been influenced by the unconscious' (p. 63). The fundamental rule for clients is that of free association. Clients must tell their analysts everything that occurs to them, even if it is disagreeable and even if it seems meaningless. As far as possible, clients are encouraged to put their self-criticism out of action and share all their thoughts, feelings, ideas, memories and their associations. The object of free association is to help lift repressions by making unconscious material conscious.

Transference

From early in his career Freud attached great importance to his relationships with clients. He discovered that clients perceive their analysts as reincarnations of important figures from their childhoods and transfer on to them moderate to intense feelings and emotions appropriate to these earlier models. Freud speaks of transference love and observes that this love is ambivalent, being a mixture of affection with a reverse side of hostility, exclusiveness and jealousy. Transference represents a development of the original neurosis into a transference neurosis in relation to the analyst.

The transference has at least three advantages:

- It may start by being positive, which helps analysts, since their clients work to please them. The weak ego can become stronger and the client may achieve gains out of love for the analyst.
- When clients place analysts in the place of their fathers or mothers, they give them access to the power their super-egos have over their egos. Analysts as new super-egos can use their power for 'a sort of *after-education* of the

neurotic' (Freud, 1949, p. 67). They can remedy earlier
errors in parental education. However, analysts need to
always respect their clients' demand for independence.

- In transference, clients reproduce, rather than just remember, important parts of their life history. They act out in
front of their analysts mental attitudes and defensive reactions connected with their neuroses.

Almost invariably transference becomes negative and hostile,
thus turning into resistance. The onset of negative transference is connected with analysts frustrating their clients by
being unwilling to satisfy their erotic demands towards them.
The revival of pathogenic conflicts gives analysts access to
much repressed material, insight into which helps to
strengthen their clients' egos.

Handling transference is a critical skill of analysts, who
must again and again show clients the prototype of their
feelings in their childhoods. Analysts need to take care that
transferences do not get out of hand. They can forewarn
clients of this possibility and be alert to early signs of this
happening. They can also encourage clients not to act out their
transferences outside of the analytic setting.

Resistance

Free association is not really free, in that clients associate
within the context of the analytic situation. Thus everything
that occurs to them has some reference to that situation and
they are likely to resist reproducing the repressed material. At
its simplest level, resistance involves intentionally not adher-
ing to the fundamental rule. Even if this level of resistance is
overcome, resistance will find less obvious means of expression. The client's ego is fearful of potential unpleasure caused
by exploring material that it has repressed in the unconscious.
The ego protects itself from the repressed id by means of anti-
cathexes. The more threatening the repressed material, the
more tenaciously the ego clings to its anti-cathexes and the
more remote are clients' associations from the unconscious
material that their analysts seek.

Freud described all the forces that oppose the work of
recovery as clients' resistances. He outlined five kinds of
resistance:

- The repression resistance described above.
- The transference resistance mentioned earlier.
- The resistance to forgoing the gain from illness.
- The resistance of the id, which may resist a change in the direction of its satisfaction and need to 'work through' to a new mode of satisfaction.
- The resistance, emanating from the super-ego, of the unconscious sense of guilt or need for punishment which resists any success through analysis. Clients must remain ill for they deserve no better. This is the most powerful kind of resistance and the one analysts most dread.

The struggle to overcome resistances is the main work of psychoanalysis and this part of analytic treatment cannot easily be hurried. Forces helping analysts to overcome resistances are clients' needs for recovery, any intellectual interest they may have in the analytic process and, most importantly, their positive transferences with their analysts.

Interpretation

Interpretations are constructions or explanations. They can focus both on what has happened to clients and been forgotten and on what is now happening to clients without their understanding it. Interpretation is the means by which material that is repressed and unconscious is transformed into preconscious material and consciousness.

Analysts employ interpretation not only to understand the impulses of the id, but also to help clients to gain insight into the defence mechanisms and resistances their egos use both to cope with the repressed material and to thwart the analytic endeavour. Part of the work of interpretation consists of filling in memory gaps. Analysts interpret the impulses that have become subject to repression and the objects to which they have become attached with the aim of helping clients to replace these repressions by acts of judgement appropriate to their present-day rather than to their childhood situations. The analyst works with the client's ego, encouraging it to overcome resistances and to take control of hitherto repressed libidinal energy. Unconscious impulses are exposed to criticism by being traced back to their origin.

The material for interpretation is obtained from a number

of sources. These include the clients' free associations, para-praxes or slips of the tongue, dreams, and their transference relationships with their analysts. Analysts need to clearly distinguish between their own and their clients' knowledge. Appropriate timing of interpretations is very important, since if attempted at the wrong time, they meet with resistance. Therefore clients need to be very near to the moment of insight before analysts make interpretations. Further, the closer interpretations are to the details of what has been forgotten, the easier it is for clients to accept them. The later stages of psychoanalysis involve a working through by repeated interpretations, and this is often the most difficult and frequently an incomplete part of analysis.

Interpretation of dreams

Interpreting dreams represents an important – sometimes the most important – part of the analyst's work. When Freud's clients were told to communicate to him every idea or thought that occurred in relation to a particular topic, among other things they told him their dreams. This taught Freud that 'a dream can be inserted into the psychical chain that has to be traced backwards in the memory from a pathological idea' (Freud, 1976, p. 175). During sleep the ego reduces its repression and thus unconscious material becomes conscious in the shape of dreams. Freud saw dreams as wish-fulfilments, being the disguised fulfilment of repressed wishes. However, even in sleep the ego still retains some censorship over repressed material and the latent dream thoughts are distorted so as to make the manifest dream content less threatening. Dreams, in fact, are compromises between repressed id impulses and the defensive operation of the ego.

The interpretation of a dream involves understanding the latent dream thoughts which are disguised by the process of dream work. Elements of dream work involve condensing the latent dream thoughts into a much smaller dream content, displacing the psychical intensity between elements, and using symbolism. Frequently, symbols in dreams represent sexual material. For instance, all elongated objects, such as sticks, tree trunks, knives, daggers and umbrellas may stand for the penis. The opening of an umbrella may symbolize an erection. Boxes, cases, chests, cupboards and ovens represent the uterus. A dream of going through a suite of rooms is a brothel or harem dream. Not all dream symbols are sexual: for instance, emperors or empresses may represent parents.

Freud prepared clients in two ways for working with their dreams. First, he asked them to increase the attention they paid to their psychical perceptions. To enhance this, it was advantageous that they 'lie in a restful attitude' (Freud, 1976, p. 175). However, he soon abandoned also stressing that they

---

Box 2.5   An example of dream interpretation

The context

Freud had been giving psychoanalytic treatment to Irma, a good friend of his and his family's. The treatment was partially successful in that Irma was relieved of her hysterical anxiety, but without losing all somatic symptoms. One day Freud received a visit from a junior colleague called Otto, who had been staying with Irma and her family at a country resort. Otto answered Freud's enquiry about Irma with: 'She's better, but not quite well.' Freud was annoyed at Otto's words, detecting reproof in them. That evening he wrote out Irma's case history with the idea of giving it to Dr M, a common friend.

The dream

The following night or morning, Freud had a dream, which he noted down as soon as he awoke. The dream involved Irma, Otto, Dr M and a friend called Leopold. Without going into great detail, in the dream Otto was implicated in infecting Irma by giving her an injection with a syringe that was probably unclean.

The interpretation of the dream

The conclusion of Freud's interpretation of his dream was that, in it, he was not responsible for the persistence of Irma's present pains; rather, Otto was. Freud observed of his dream: 'Thus its content was the fulfillment of a wish and its motive was a wish' (Freud, 1976, p. 196).

need shut their eyes. Second, he explicitly insisted that clients abandon all criticism of the thoughts they perceived (a feature of free association). Clients differed in the ease with which they could adopt the required mental attitude and abandon their critical functions.

Box 2.5 provides a brief illustration, taken from *The Interpretation of Dreams*, of Freud interpreting one of his own dreams (Freud, 1976, pp. 180–99). Dream interpretation can be a complex, multi-layered and lengthy process. For example, Freud took about twenty pages to describe the interpretation of the dream illustrated in Box 2.5. In addition, in his famous study of Dora, a case of hysteria, Freud's descriptions of his interpretations of her first and second dreams take up about thirty and twenty pages, respectively (Freud, 1963).

CASE MATERIAL

Accounts of analyses by other therapists lose the flavour of how Freud actually worked. Freud published few case studies, possibly because he feared breaking confidentiality. Those wishing to become familiar with how Freud worked are encouraged to read one or more of the following case studies.

- *Dora* was an 18-year-old, young woman. Freud's analysis revealed her hysterical symptoms as manifestations of repressed sexual impulses that included her homosexual love for an older admirer's wife (Freud, 1963).
- *Hans*, 5 years old, feared a horse would bite him if he went out into the street. Freud helped Hans' doctor father treat him, and his analysis demonstrated that Hans' fear expressed phallic phase dynamics, including the Oedipus complex and castration anxiety (Freud, 1955a).
- *Schreber* was an appeals court judge who wrote an account of his illness, diagnosed as paranoia. Based only on Schreber's written account, Freud's analysis demonstrated how Schreber's paranoid delusions were related to his latent homosexuality (Freud, 1958).
- *Wolf Man*, in his twenties, had contracted gonorrhoea, which in turn triggered castration anxiety. Freud's analysis established the relationship between the castration anxiety

and a frightening childhood dream involving wolves that followed real or imagined observation of parental sexual intercourse (Freud, 1955b).

FURTHER DEVELOPMENTS

Psychoanalytic theory possesses a unique historical interest not only in terms of its being an early major psychological theory, but also because of its influence on other theorists. Other analysts influenced by Freud include Jung, Adler, Horney, Sullivan and Fromm, the last four of whom are sometimes termed the 'neo-Freudians'. In addition, under the leadership of Melanie Klein, a British school of psychoanalysis emerged, emphasizing the importance of primitive fantasies of loss (the depressive position) and persecution (the paranoid position) in the pathogenesis of mental illness. Winnicott and Bowlby were other prominent British analysts whose work was influenced by Freud.

Freud has influenced humanistic and existential psychologists and psychiatrists to varying degrees. For example, points of contact with transactional analysis include the tripartite structure of personality and the importance of early experience. Furthermore, Rogers' concept of levels of awareness resembles Freud's idea of levels of consciousness. In addition, May and Yalom's version of existential dynamics, motivated by underlying death anxiety, also has its origins in psychoanalysis.

Classical psychoanalysis, based on the Freudian model, continues to develop and evolve. One stimulus for change is that problems tend to alter with the times: for instance, hysteria and conversion symptoms are less frequent now, but there is an increase in clients suffering from masochistic character disorders and from narcissistic neuroses (Arlow, 2000). Clients often complain of inner emptiness, lack of goals, and of inability to form lasting love relationships.

In addition, some analysts have developed forms of brief psychoanalytic therapy. Reasons for brief psychoanalysis include hoped-for cost-effectiveness; the fact that governments, health insurers and most private individuals cannot afford long-term therapy; and to meet the pressing need to treat more people.

SUMMARY

- Psychoanalytic theory groups human instincts into two broad categories: the erotic or life instincts and the death or destructive instincts. The energy of the life instincts is termed 'libido'. To a large extent people are motivated by the pleasure principle. Mental life takes place on conscious, preconscious and unconscious levels.
- The mental apparatus consists of three agencies: the id, which is constantly striving for instinctual satisfaction; the super-ego, which represents parental and moral influence; and the ego, which aims to meet the instinctual demands of the id on the basis of the reality principle.
- The ego has three taskmasters – the external world, the id and the super-ego – and each may cause it anxiety. Psychical energy is distributed between the three mental agencies, which may be in harmony or in conflict with each other.
- People are sexual from infancy, though they tend to be subject to amnesia about this. Humans are constitutionally bisexual and infantile sexuality contains great tendencies towards perversion.
- Sexual development takes place in two phases: a pre-genital phase up to the end of the fifth year and a genital phase starting at menarche and puberty. The period in between is the latency period. There are some differences in sexual development between the sexes, including development during the Oedipus situation.
- While the child's ego is relatively weak, it develops defence mechanisms to ward off the strong sexual impulses emanating from the id. Thus much of its early sexual life becomes repressed or is not allowed access to consciousness. Excessive repression may lead to the development of neurosis. Since the ego is weakened by having to maintain the repression, it does not have access to the repressed material, and the repressed impulses become transformed into neurotic symptoms.
- The goals of psychoanalysis include the freeing of impulse, the strengthening of reality-based ego functioning, and humanizing the super-ego's standards.
- While clients reclined, Freud would sit in a tub chair out of sight at the head of the client's couch. He encouraged clients

to free associate or tell the analyst everything, however disagreeable it may be.

- *Transference occurs when clients perceive their analysts as reincarnations of important figures from their childhoods and transfer on to them moderate to intense feelings and emotions appropriate to these earlier people. Analysts require great skill in showing clients the prototypes of their feelings in their childhoods.*
- *Resistances are all the forces that oppose the work of a client's recovery. The struggle to overcome resistances is the main work of psychoanalysis and cannot easily be hurried.*
- *Interpretation is the means by which analysts transform material which is repressed and unconscious into preconscious material and consciousness. Material for interpretations comes from clients' free associations, slips of the tongue, dreams and transference relationships with their analysts.*
- *The interpretation of a dream involves understanding the latent dream thoughts which are disguised by the process of dream work.*
- *Freudian psychoanalysis has been the precursor of many other analytic schools, including the object-relations approach of Melanie Klein, the British psychotherapist. Classical psychoanalysis, based on the Freudian model, continues to develop and evolve.*

REVIEW AND PERSONAL QUESTIONS

Review questions

1. How did Freud view the instincts?
2. Describe each of Freud's three levels of consciousness.
3. How did Freud describe the id, the ego and the super-ego and their functions?
4. Why is psychoanalysis often referred to as presenting a dynamic view of psychology?
5. Describe each stage and phase of a person's sexual development.
6. What is the function of defence mechanisms? Illustrate with specific examples.
7. Describe Freud's views on the development and maintenance of neurosis.

8. In psychoanalysis, what is meant by the term 'transference' and why is it so important?
9. In psychoanalysis, what is meant by the term resistance and why is it so important?
10. Describe as best you can how Freud approached the interpretation of a dream.

Personal questions

1. Can you think of material or events in your life which you might view as evidence for unconscious mental processes? If so, provide examples (e.g. dreams).
2. What are some of the significant influences which contributed to the formation of your super-ego? With what moral guidelines, if any, do you consider that your super-ego restricts you in the realistic pursuit of pleasure?
3. Are you aware that your ego uses defence mechanisms to ward off anxiety? If so, what are they? Do you consider that your use of defence mechanisms is normal or neurotic?
4. What do you consider the relevance of Freud's ideas on the interpretation of dreams to interpreting your own dreams?
5. What is the relevance of Freud's work to understanding your life?
6. How has Freud influenced the way you think about and practise counselling and therapy?

ANNOTATED BIBLIOGRAPHY

Freud, S. (1976; original edn 1900) *The Interpretation of Dreams.* Harmondsworth: Penguin Books.

This book is Freud's major work. In it he reviews the scientific literature about dreams, demonstrates his method of interpreting dreams, and discusses dreams as fulfilments of wishes, distortion in dreams, the material and sources of dreams, dream-work, and the psychology of the dream process. The present translation is based on the reprint of the eighth edition (1930), the last published during Freud's life. This volume is part of The Pelican Freud Library, which is intended to contain all Freud's major writings.

Freud, S. (1962a; original edn 1905) *Three Contributions to the Theory of Sex.* New York: E. P. Dutton.

This book is Freud's major statement on the nature and development of human sexuality. The three contributions are entitled the sexual aberrations, infantile sexuality, and the transformations of puberty. Apart from *The Interpretation of Dreams*, this was the only other book that Freud kept more or less systematically up to date.

Freud, S. (1949; original edn 1940) *An Outline of Psychoanalysis*. New York: W.W. Norton.

Written just before Freud's death, this book provides an excellent concise introduction to psychoanalysis. The book consists of three parts: the mind and its workings, the practical task, and the theoretical yield.

Jones, E. (1963) *The Life and Work of Sigmund Freud*, edited and abridged in one volume by Lionel Trilling and Steven Marcus. New York: Anchor Books. Also available in a Penguin edition.

Written in three volumes by a close associate, this book is the definitive biography of Freud. It records the main facts of Freud's life and relates his personality and life experiences to the development of his ideas. In addition, the book traces the history of the psychoanalytic movement during Freud's lifetime.

Hall, C. S. (1954) *A Primer of Freudian Psychology*. New York: Mentor Books.

This concise book presents Freud's ideas on the organization, dynamics, development of, and stabilized personality. It is a highly recommended secondary source.

REFERENCES

All Freud's writings can be found in the twenty-four volumes of:

Freud, S. (1953–73) *Standard Edition of the Complete Works of Sigmund Freud*. London: Hogarth Press.

Arlow, J. A. (2000) 'Psychoanalysis', in R. J. Corsini and D. Wedding (eds) *Current Psychotherapies* (6th edn, pp. 16–53). Itasca, IL: Peacock.
Bowlby, J. (1958) 'The nature of the child's ties to the mother'. *International Journal of Psychoanalysis*, 52, 137–44.
Freud, S. (1935) *An Autobiographical Study*. London: Hogarth Press.
Freud, S. (1936) *The Problem of Anxiety*. New York: W.W. Norton. Originally published in 1926 under the title *Inhibitions, Symptoms and Anxiety*.
Freud, S. (1949; original edn 1940) *An Outline of Psychoanalysis*. New York: W.W. Norton.

Freud, S. (1950; original edn 1937) 'Analysis terminable and interminable', in S. Freud, *Collected Papers* (Vol. 5). London: Hogarth Press.

Freud, S. (1955a; original edn 1909) *Analysis of a Phobia in a Five-year-old Boy*, in *Standard Edition* (Vol. 10). London: Hogarth Press.

Freud, S. (1955b; original edn 1918) *From the History of an Infantile Neurosis*, in *Standard Edition* (Vol. 17). London: Hogarth Press.

Freud, S. (1958; original edn 1911) *Psycho-analytic Notes on an Autobiographical Account of a Case of Paranoia (Dementia Paranoides)*, in *Standard Edition* (Vol. 12). London: Hogarth Press.

Freud, S. (1959; original edn 1921) *Group Psychology and the Analysis of the Ego*. London: Hogarth Press.

Freud, S. (1960; original edn 1901) *Psychotherapy of Everyday Life*. London: Hogarth Press.

Freud, S. (1961; original edn 1920) *Beyond the Pleasure Principle*. London: Hogarth Press.

Freud, S. (1962a; original edn 1905) *Three Contributions to the Theory of Sex*. New York: E.P. Dutton.

Freud, S. (1962b; original edn 1923) *The Ego and the Id*. London: Hogarth Press.

Freud, S. (1962c; original edn 1930) *Civilization and its Discontents*. New York: W.W. Norton.

Freud, S. (1963; original edn 1905) *Dora: An Analysis of a Case of Hysteria*. New York: Collier Books.

Freud, S. (1964; original edn 1926) *The Question of Lay Analysis*. New York: Anchor Books.

Freud, S. (1973; original edn 1933 (1932)) *New Introductory Lectures on Psychoanalysis*. Harmondsworth: Penguin Books.

Freud, S. (1976; original edn 1900) *The Interpretation of Dreams*. Harmondsworth: Penguin Books.

Freud, S. and Breuer, J. (1956; original edn 1895) *Studies on Hysteria*. London: Hogarth Press.

Fromm, E. (1959) *Sigmund Freud's Mission*. London: George Allen & Unwin.

Hall, C. S. (1954) *A Primer of Freudian Psychology*. New York: Mentor Books.

Jones, E. (1963) *The Life and Work of Sigmund Freud*, edited and abridged in one volume by Lionel Trilling and Steven Marcus. New York: Anchor Books. Also available in a Penguin edition.

Klein, M. (1932) *The Psychoanalysis of Children*. London: Hogarth Press.

Winnicott, D. W. (1953) 'Transitional objects and transitional phenomena: a study of the first not-me possession', *International Journal of Psychoanalysis*, **34**, 89–97.

Jung's Analytical Therapy

*Although we human beings have our own personal
life, we are yet in large measure the representatives,
the victims and the promoters of a collective spirit
whose years are counted in centuries.*

Carl Jung

INTRODUCTION

Do you ever think of yourself or other people as being
predominantly introverted or extroverted? How do you feel
about your persona or social mask? What about your shadow,
the aspects of yourself which you experience difficulty with or
refuse to acknowledge? If a woman, are you aware that you
have an animus, the masculine nature of your unconscious, or
if a man, that you have an anima, the female nature of your
unconscious? Furthermore, are you aware that, underneath,
all human beings share the same collective unconscious?

The two most significant theorists of the unconscious are
Sigmund Freud and Carl Jung. Freud's and Jung's lives over-
lapped; for a time they were close associates, and what Jung
called his 'analytical psychology' has some of its roots in
Freudian psychoanalysis. Nevertheless, as you can sense from
the first paragraph of this chapter, Jung was to develop a very
different psychodynamic theory and practice to that of Freud.
In particular, Jung and Freud diverged in their views of the
unconscious. Whereas Freud emphasized sexual repression,
Jung considered that, at its deepest level, the unconscious
consisted of archetypes, or inborn possibilities for psychological apprehension and representation, which may then be
expressed in universal myths and symbols.

In 1906, Jung and Freud became friends and intellectual
companions. Freud admired Jung's brilliance and regarded
him as his crown prince and heir apparent. In addition, Freud

thought that, by having Jung prominent in the movement, he might avoid the risk of psychoanalysis being viewed as a mainly Jewish activity. Jung had gone through a troubled relationship with his own father and was fiercely intellectually independent. It was an error of judgement on both men's part to think that any 'father–son' relationship could be maintained. In 1913, Jung and Freud parted bitterly, never to meet again in the remaining twenty-six years of Freud's life.

CARL GUSTAV JUNG (1875–1961)

In July 1875, Carl Gustav Jung was born in Kesswil, a small village by Lake Constance in north-eastern Switzerland, the only surviving son of his parents who had lost two previous boys in infancy. Jung was named after his paternal grandfather who, in 1822, had moved from Germany to become professor of surgery at the University of Basel. Jung's father was a Swiss Reform Church pastor and his mother was the daughter of a well-established Basel family. When Jung was 9, the family was completed by the birth of his sister.

Jung was an introverted, sensitive, solitary and lonely child. His parents, Paul and Emilie, had a troubled marriage and, in 1878, they separated temporarily and his mother spent some time in a mental hospital. During his childhood Jung suffered from his mother's depressive invalidism and critical tongue. However, Jung admired his mother and enjoyed her companionship and cooking. Jung also had to contend with his father's irritability, partly connected with his agonizing over his religious faith. Nevertheless, in the autobiography compiled at the end of his life Jung refers to his 'dear and generous father', who never tyrannized over him (Jung, 1961).

The earliest dream Jung remembers was when he was aged between 3 and 4. Jung had a rich inner life of dreams, fantasies and thoughts about the world. When he was 10, Jung carved a manikin out of the end of a ruler; it was about two inches long with frock coat, top hat and shiny black boots. He placed the manikin and an oblong blackish stone from the Rhine in a case and took it to the attic. Whenever Jung felt hurt or stressed he would think of the manikin and, from time to time, visit it in the forbidden attic. Jung regarded this manikin episode, which lasted about a year, as the conclusion of his childhood.

In 1879 the Jungs moved to Klein Hüningen, near Basel. At

age 6 Jung attended the local school and, at age 11, was uprooted from his rustic schoolmates and sent to the Gymnasium at Basel. Jung hated mathematics, was exempted from drawing on the grounds of incapacity, and also loathed gymnastics. Of mathematics he writes: 'But my fear of failure and sense of smallness in face of the vast world around me created in me not only a dislike, but a kind of silent despair which completely ruined school for me' (Jung, 1961, p. 45). For a time Jung suffered from fainting spells connected with school. He also saw himself as two people: a schoolboy who was less intelligent, hard-working and decent than many other boys, and an old man mistrustful of human beings but close to nature, to dreams and to whatever God worked through him.

In reality, Jung was a highly intelligent student who, in 1895, passed his final examinations at the Gymnasium and entered the University of Basel Medical School. During medical school Jung suffered from financial worries, partly stemming from the death of his father in 1896. In 1900 Jung graduated equal first in his medical school class. His medical school thesis was on the psychological foundations of the occult. Jung chose to specialize in psychiatry, which provided a bridge between his scientific, humanities and psychological interests. Shortly after graduation he accepted a post at the Burghölzli Mental Hospital in Zurich.

The director at the Burghölzli was Eugen Bleuler, an expert on schizophrenia, whose influence Jung valued. In 1902, Jung spent several months studying at the Sâlpetrière Hospital in Paris with the famous psychiatrist Pierre Janet. In 1905 Jung became lecturer in psychiatry at the University of Zurich and senior physician at the psychiatric clinic. He also had a private practice which became so successful that, in 1909, he resigned from the Burghölzli. However, he continued to lecture at the University of Zurich until 1913. At the Burghölzli, as well as working with patients, Jung conducted research on word associations and the underlying psychological complexes indicated by how people responded. As mentioned above, Jung also developed a relationship with Freud and became prominent in the psychoanalytic movement.

After his break with Freud, Jung went through a profound mid-life crisis which lasted from 1913 to 1918, and which took him to the edge of insanity. During this period of inner uncertainty and disorientation, Jung continued seeing patients for much of the time. He developed his ideas of the collective unconscious during this period of confrontation with his own unconscious. He writes:

> The years when I was pursuing my inner images were the most important in my life – in them everything essential was decided. It all began then; the later details are only supplements and clarifications of the material that burst forth from the unconscious, and at first swamped me. It was the *prima materia* for a lifetime's work.
>
> (Jung, 1961, p. 225)

Jung was fond of women, who played a crucial role throughout his life. In 1903 he had married the extremely wealthy Emma Rauschenbach. Under Swiss law, at the time Jung married Emma, husbands had complete access to their wives' money and could spend it as they wished without consent. In short, though Jung was always a hard worker, he was financially set up for life independent of his own endeavours.

Despite his wife's disapproval of his behaviour and his growing family, Jung was sexually attracted to other women, probably extending to intimate relationships with one or more of his patients, for example, Sabina Spielrein and Toni Wolff. Toni was able to be of special comfort to him during his near psychotic period so much so that, in 1916, Jung persuaded Emma to accept her as part of a permanent domestic threesome. Jung probably abandoned his philandering at this stage. He encouraged Emma to become a Jungian therapist, and eventually, Toni became one too.

After Jung returned to feeling more normal, there were a number of ongoing and interweaving strands in his life. At his beautiful home by Lake Zurich, though not the warmest and most present of fathers, Jung engaged in family activities with his wife, four daughters and son. In 1922, Jung bought some land at Bollingen, at the upper end of Lake Zurich, and, over the next thirty or so years, developed the 'Tower', a house he built for himself as a retreat from his family. Whereas the family home was the territory of his wife, the only person Jung allowed to stay at Bollingen was Toni Wolff and, in later years, a companion-housekeeper.

Jung continued his large private practice, which he regarded as a valuable source of information for understanding the psyche. Most of Jung's clients were women, almost all were reasonably well-off, and a minority were fabulously wealthy Americans; for instance, one of John D. Rockefeller's daughters and a member of the Mellon banking family. Jung also continued his own inner journey, analysing his dreams, fantasies and visions.

Jung engaged in wide-ranging scholarly activities. In 1921 he published a large work on psychological types. As well as reading widely in philosophy, world literature, mythology and astrology, Jung became increasingly interested in alchemy. He also conducted what might be called fieldwork, by visiting North Africa, Kenya and Uganda, the Pueblo Indians in North America, and India. Jung was immensely interested in the presence and universality of myths and symbols across cultures and in primitive as well as civilized cultures. Based on his scholarly researches, field trips, wide reading and professional and personal experiences, right up to his death Jung was a prolific author across a range of subjects, including psychiatry and psychology, parapsychology, alchemy and religion.

Jung lectured extensively not only in the Germanic but in the English-speaking world. In 1909 he had gone with Freud to Clark University in Massachusetts, where both men received honorary doctorates, and he was to return to America repeatedly in the following thirty years. Jung was also an Anglophile and visited England many times, for example, giving a notable series of lectures at the Tavistock Clinic in 1935. His honorary doctorates included those from Harvard and Oxford universities. In addition, from the early 1930s, Jung regularly attended the annual Eranos conferences on Jungian studies. At these conferences, held at the northern end of Lake Maggiore on the estate of a wealthy woman who had built a conference hall specially for them, Jung tended to be lionized by the largely female participants.

Intimations of Jung's mortality included a severe heart attack in 1944, the death of Toni Wolff in 1953, and his wife's death in 1955. Jung's companion-housekeeper during his final years was Ruth Bailey, an Englishwoman. On 6 June 1961, Jung died after a brief illness.

It is tempting when looking at pictures of Jung to view him as a gentle, spiritual, scholarly sage full of the milk of human kindness. Undoubtedly, Jung had many attractive features as well as a charismatic personality, especially for women.

However, Jung was not without his shadow aspects. He held extreme right-wing Social Darwinist political views and strongly believed that different rules applied to 'beasts' and 'supermen' (McLynn, 1996). For various reasons, he strongly favoured the death penalty. Though probably not anti-Semitic, Jung has been criticized for not speaking out loudly enough against the rise of Nazism. He could be domineering and hectoring at professional meetings and a domestic tyrant at home. Jung could also be a bile-laden person and his relationship with Freud became particularly bitter. In addition, Jung had been a philandering husband, probably including some clients among his lovers.

Like Freud, Jung was an ideas man with an amazing breadth of vision. Some of his ideas have stood the test of time in terms of becoming part of Western psychological consciousness, for example, the concepts of the collective unconscious and extraversion/introversion. In addition, Jung was the founder of an analytical approach to therapy that still claims many adherents.

THEORY

The primordial images and the nature of the archetype took a central place in my researches and it became clear to me that without history there can be no psychology, and certainly no psychology of the unconscious.

Carl Jung

BASIC CONCEPTS

Psychology is first the science of consciousness and then the science of the products of the unconscious psyche. Jung used the term 'psyche' to refer to the mind or soul. He distinguished between three psychic levels of consciousness. In addition, his was a dynamic psychology that paid attention to the distribution of psychic energy between the different psychic levels. Furthermore, Jung presented a typology of different personality types.

Structure of the psyche

Jung goes beyond distinguishing consciousness from uncon-sciousness to divide the latter into its personal and collective elements. Thus the psyche's three levels are: (1) consciousness, (2) the personal unconscious, and (3) the collective uncon-scious. Though Jung did not wish to push the analogy too far, he saw consciousness as an island rising out of a vast sea of unconsciousness.

Consciousness

Jung observes: 'the child develops out of an originally uncon-scious, animal condition into consciousness, primitive at first, and then slowly becoming more civilised' (Jung, 1981, p. 53). Consciousness is an intermittent phenomenon since people enter the unconscious every time they go to sleep. The conscious mind is narrow since it can only hold a few simultaneous contents at a given moment. Furthermore, con-sciousness is transitory and people can only gain an awareness of the external world through a succession of conscious moments.

The **ego** is the indispensable centre of a person's conscious-ness. Sometimes Jung refers to it as the ego-complex. The ego gives a person a sense of identity and continuity. The ego has both external and internal tasks. Its external task is to provide a system of relationship between consciousness and the facts and data coming from the environment. Sensation, thinking, feeling and intuition are four functions by means of which it performs its ectopsychic task. The ego's internal task is to provide a system of relationship between the contents of consciousness and the processes of the unconscious. Jung (1968) states: 'The ego is only a bit of consciousness that floats on an ocean of dark things. The dark things are the inner things' (p. 21).

The personal unconscious

The contents of the personal unconscious are definitely of a personal origin. These contents fall into two main categories. First, material that lost its intensity either because it was forgotten or repressed. Second, material that never possessed sufficient intensity to reach consciousness but has somehow entered the psyche: for instance, some sense impressions. There is nothing peculiar about the contents of the personal unconscious, and its contents might just as well be conscious. People differ in regard to the contents of their personal unconscious: some people are conscious of things which other people are not.

Complexes are an important feature of the personal unconscious. Jung discovered the complex through his research on word associations, finding that complexes disturbed memory and produced blockages in the flow of associations. Complexes are accumulations of associations, sometimes of a traumatic nature, that possess strong emotional content. They possess a tendency to develop a life of their own apart from a person's intentions. One of Jung's sayings was: 'A person does not have a complex; the complex has him.'

The mother complex is an example of a complex. Jung considered that 'the mother always plays an active part in the origin of the disturbance, especially in infantile neuroses or in neuroses whose aetiology undoubtedly dates back to early childhood' (Jung, 1982, p. 113). Typical effects of the mother complex on the son are homosexuality, Don Juanism, and sometimes impotence. In daughters the mother complex can lead to an exaggeration of the feminine side of personality or its neglect. Other examples of complexes include those connected with inferiority, sex, aesthetic beauty and money.

The collective unconscious

Unlike Freud, who saw the unconscious as a receptacle for things which were repressed, Jung believed that the deeper layers of the unconscious lose their uniqueness as they retreat further and further from consciousness. At its deepest levels the unconscious is a vast collective and universal historical storehouse whose contents belong to mankind in general. Whereas the contents of the personal unconscious owe their existence to personal experience, the contents of the collective unconscious have never been in consciousness, but owe their existence to heredity.

Archetypes are inborn possibilities or patterns for representation. Jung borrowed the term 'archetype' from St Augustine. He observes: 'Whereas the personal unconscious consists for the most part of *complexes*, the content of the collective unconscious is made up essentially of *archetypes*' (Jung, 1976a, p. 60). Similar to instinctive patterns for action, archetypes provide instinctive patterns for mental activity. Archetypes are 'primordial images' and 'primordial thoughts' rather than the representations of the images or thoughts themselves. For example, well-known motifs appear in myths, fairy-tales, legends and folklore across a range of cultures and historical periods. Such motifs include the hero, the redeemer, the dragon, the mother, the wise old man and the descent into the cave. Archetypes are evolutionary predispositions or potentials for such motifs rather than the forms in which the contents become expressed.

Symbols are the images by means of which archetypes are expressed. Jung distinguished between a sign and a symbol. If the image denotes a known thing it is a sign. Symbolic images express the best possible formulation of a relatively unknown thing, which for that reason cannot be more clearly or characteristically represented. For example, a triangle with a bare eye enclosed in it is so meaningless that it conjures up a symbolic interpretation.

Archetypes important in shaping the development of personality include the persona, the anima and animus, the shadow and the self.

• *The persona*   The persona is a concept derived from the mask worn by actors in antiquity. At one level, the persona is the individual's system of adaptation or way of coping with the world. At a different level, the persona is not just an individual mask but a mask of the collective psyche, 'a mask that *feigns individuality*, making others and oneself believe that one is an individual, whereas one is simply acting out a role through which the collective psyche speaks' (Jung, 1976b, p. 105).

The persona exists for reasons of personal convenience, but should not be confused with genuine individuality. The persona is exclusively concerned with relation to outer objects, an outer attitude. This outer attitude must be distinguished from an inner attitude, which is the relation to the subject or 'inner object' which is the unconscious.

In reality, individuals may have more than one persona; for example, wearing different masks at work and home.

Furthermore, each profession has its own characteristic persona. However, there is a danger that people become identified with their personas, for instance, the professor with his textbook. Too rigid adherence to a persona can lead people to become alienated from the 'subject', the stirrings, feelings, thoughts and sensations that well up from their unconscious. Identifications with social roles are often fruitful sources of neuroses. Jung regarded it as essential for individuals to be able to distinguish themselves from their personas.

- *The anima and the animus* People are psychologically bisexual. The larger number of male or female genes is the decisive factor in the determination of biological sex. However, the smaller number of opposite sex genes appears to produce a corresponding opposite sex character, which usually remains unconscious. The anima is the personification of the feminine nature in a man's unconscious, whereas the animus is the personification of the masculine nature in a woman's unconscious. Every man or woman carries within themselves an imprint or archetype of all the ancestral experiences of the opposite sex.

  Jung thought that in its primary form the animus is composed of spontaneous, unpremeditated opinions that exercise a powerful influence on the woman's emotional life. Similarly, the anima is composed of feelings which thereafter distort and influence a man's understanding. He wrote: 'as the anima produces *moods*, so the animus produces *opinions*; and as the moods of a man issue from a shadowy background, so the opinions of a woman rest on equally unconscious prior assumptions' (Jung, 1982, pp. 95–6). Jung stressed the importance of people acknowledging their distinction, not only from their persona but from their anima or animus as well. The animus and anima should function as a bridge leading to the images of the collective unconscious. Both men and women should learn to acknowledge and appropriately express the opposite sex characteristics of their personalities and avoid falsely projecting them on to others.

- *The shadow* The shadow archetype reflects the realm of human beings' animal ancestors and, as such, comprises the whole historical aspect of the unconscious. For the most part, the shadow consists of inferior traits of personality that individuals refuse to acknowledge. Though Jung emphasized the darker aspects of the shadow, he acknowledged that it also displayed some good qualities, such as normal instincts, appropriate reactions, realistic insights and creative impulses. The shadow is compensatory to consciousness and its effects can be positive as well as negative.

In general, people do not like looking at the shadow-side of themselves. However, with insight and goodwill, much of the shadow can be assimilated into the conscious personality without too much difficulty. Nevertheless, there are some unconscious projections from the shadow whose recognition meets the most obstinate resistance and which thus prove almost impossible to influence.

- *The self*   The self is the central archetype, the archetype of order. The self, which expresses the unity of personality as a whole, encompasses both conscious and unconscious components. The self is a superordinate construct to the ego which is restricted to being the focal point of the conscious mind. The ego is related to the self like a part to the whole. Jung considered that there was little hope of ever being able to reach even approximate consciousness of the self given the huge and indeterminate amount of unconscious material that belongs to it.

  The main symbol for the unity of the self archetype is the mandala. The word 'mandala' (Sanskrit for 'circle') is a circular form that often contains a quaternity, symmetrical arrangements of the number four and its multiples. The self also appears in dreams, myths and fairy-tales in the figure of a superordinate personality, such as a king, hero, prophet or saviour.

Dynamics of the psyche

Psychodynamics refers to the activity and interrelation of the various parts of an individual's personality or psyche. More specifically, psychodynamics entails the generation and transfer of energy within the structure of the psyche. Jung's ideas on psychodynamics were influenced by his interest in and knowledge of physics, the branch of science dealing with the properties and interactions of matter and energy.

Psychic energy

Jung emphasized the concept of psychic energy, sometimes referred to as libido, as the psychic analogue of physical energy. All the instincts, including hunger, sex and aggression, are expressions of psychic energy. In physics there are different manifestations of energy, such as electricity, heat and light. The same situation occurs in psychology, where energy can appear in various guises. Psychic energy is also provided from the external environment by way of one's senses and feelings. The psyche is a relatively closed energy system. Psychic energy derived from both internal and external sources is continually being shifted and redistributed among the structures of the psyche.

A psychic value is the amount of energy invested in a particular psychic element. When a person places a high value on something, such as an idea or feeling, this means that the idea or feeling exerts a particularly strong influence on them. Complexes, which by definition are strongly emotionally toned, are examples of mental elements with high psychic value.

Opposition

Jung (1961) observed: 'Among other things, the psyche appears as a dynamic process which rests on a foundation of antithesis, on a flow of energy between two poles' (p. 383). Just as in physics all energy proceeds from opposition, so the psyche possesses an inner polarity which is an essential prerequisite for its aliveness. Tension and conflict arising from the clash of opposites is central to Jungian personality dynamics. Consciousness opposes unconsciousness, feminine opposes masculine, ego opposes shadow, and positive aspects of archetypal images oppose their negative elements.

Compensation

The function of compensation is to balance or adjust the energy distributed throughout the psyche. Compensation, for the most part, is an unconscious process that entails an inherent self-regulation of the psychic apparatus. The activity of the unconscious balances the one-sidedness produced by consciousness. Consciousness, because of its selectiveness and need for focus, is bound to become one-sided. As consciousness becomes more and more one-sided, the more antagonistic are the contents arising from the unconscious, so that there is a real opposition between the two. For the most part, unconscious compensation balances rather than opposes consciousness. For example, in dreams the unconscious supplies 'all those contents that are constellated by conscious situation but are inhibited by conscious selection, although a knowledge of them would be indispensable for complete adaptation' (Jung, 1971, p. 420).

Breakthrough of unconscious content

The energy of all unconscious contents, once they are activated, is normally insufficient to propel their content into consciousness. A lowering of energy in the conscious mind that allows unconscious material to break through into consciousness may come about in two ways. First, there may be a malfunctioning of the conscious mind. Just as primitive people can suffer from 'loss of soul', so can civilized people suffer from loss of initiative for no apparent reason. Carelessness, neglected duties, wilful outbursts of defiance can dam up energy so that certain quanta of it, no longer finding a conscious outlet, stream off into the unconscious. Here they activate other compensating contents, which can in turn start exerting a compulsive influence on the conscious mind. Jung (1966) illustrates this point with the common example of extreme neglect of duty combined with a compulsion neurosis.

The second way in which a loss of energy to the conscious mind may come about is through a 'spontaneous' activation of unconscious contents, which then react upon consciousness. During the incubation period of changes in personality, the new development draws off the loss of energy it needs from consciousness. For example, lowering of energy from the conscious mind takes place before the onset of psychosis and a fallow and quiet period preceding creative work. Jung (1966) observed: 'The remarkable potency of unconscious contents, therefore, always indicates a corresponding weakness in the conscious mind and its functions' (p. 181). In the near psychotic period of his life, Jung himself had to struggle with the heightened energy of his unconscious contents in relation to his conscious ego.

The transcendent function

The transcendent function is a psychological function similar to a mathematical function of the same name, which is a function of real and imaginary numbers. In face of the disturbing energy of the unconscious, Jung postulates a synthesizing process, the transcendent function, which can get rid of some of the separation between consciousness and unconsciousness.

The transcendent function is both a process and a method. Jung postulated that there are certain spontaneous *processes* in the unconscious which, by virtue of their symbolism, can compensate for the defects in the conscious mind. In turn these reactions, usually manifested in dreams, are brought to conscious realization through the analytical *method* (Jung, 1971).

The confrontation of two opposed positions can generate a tension charged with energy which creates a living, third thing. Jung (1976c) talked about the transcendent function manifesting itself as 'a movement out of the suspension between opposites, a living birth that leads to a new level of being, a new situation. The transcendent function manifests itself as a quality of conjoined opposites' (p. 298). By means of the transcendent function, consciousness is widened through the confrontation with previously unconscious contents.

The transcendent function is the means by which progress is made towards realizing the unfolding of the individual's original potential for wholeness. However, attaining integration at a new level of consciousness by means of the transcendent function does not always take place. Apart from insufficient skills on the part of therapists, there are many reasons why the synthesizing of opposites to create a new way of being may not take place. These reasons include people having insufficient intelligence to understand the procedure, lacking self-confidence, and being mentally and morally too lazy.

Psychological types

In 1921 Jung published his famous work entitled *Psychological Types*. Here Jung distinguished between attitude-types, based on the habitual direction of an individual's interests, and function-types, based on the individual's most differentiated function of psychological adaptation. For simplicity, we will call them attitudes and functions.

Attitudes: introversion and extraversion

The *introvert*'s predominant, but not exclusive, conscious attitude is one in which the main interest is the withdrawal of psychic energy from the object as though to prevent the object from gaining power over her or him. The introvert thinks, feels and acts as though the subjective is what is most important and the object is of secondary importance. The introverted attitude type is characterized by an orientation in life that particularly values subjective psychic contents. Introverts tend to be reserved, inscrutable and rather shy people.

The *extravert*'s predominant, but not exclusive, conscious attitude is characterized by concentration of interest on the external object. The extravert thinks, feels and acts as though the object were of most importance. This is done so directly and clearly that no doubt can remain about his or her dependence on the object. Extraverts tend to be open, friendly and sociable or they may quarrel with everybody. Nevertheless, extraverts always relate to people in some way and in turn are affected by them.

In sum, introversion is characterized by interest in one's internal world and extraversion is characterized by interest in the external world. However, matters are not that simple, since a conscious extraverted attitude is compensated by an unconscious introverted attitude, and a conscious introverted attitude is compensated by an extraverted unconscious attitude.

Functions: thinking, feeling, sensation and intuition

The four psychological functions are thinking, feeling, sensation and intuition. As a rule one function predominates.

The *thinking* individual is mainly governed by reflective thinking so that important actions proceed, or are intended to proceed, from intellectually considered motives. The *feeling* individual is mainly governed by values placed on things arising from feelings. Here Jung is regarding feeling as an evaluative function. Thinking and feeling individuals are rational types because they are characterized by the primacy of the reasoning and judging functions.

The *sensation* individual is mainly governed by their aware-ness of external facts provided through the function of the senses: seeing, hearing, touching, tasting and smelling. The *intuition* individual is mainly governed by hunches and insights. Intuition is a predominantly unconscious process. The conscious aspect of intuition is to transmit images or perceptions of relations between things that could not be transmitted by the other functions. Sensation and intuition individuals are irrational types because their actions are based on the sheer intensity of perception rather than on any rational judgement.

Combining attitudes and functions to form psychological types

Jung combined attitudes and functions to provide eight main psychological types (see Box 3.1). Though one main attitude and one main function combine in each individual, people categorized within the eight psychological types vary. Further-more, the other attitude and functions are always part of someone's personality.

Box 3.1   Jung's psychological types

The following are brief descriptions of each of the eight main psychological types.

Extraverted-thinking type

This type makes all activities dependent on intellectual functioning oriented to objective data in the form of external facts or generally accepted ideas. Jung cites the scientist Charles Darwin as an example.

Introverted-thinking type

This type makes all activities dependent on intellectual functioning oriented to subjective data. Jung cites the philo-sopher Immanuel Kant as an example.

Extraverted-feeling type

This type consists almost exclusively of women who are guided by feelings that appear adjusted to harmonize with objective situations and general values: for instance, the love choice of a 'suitable' man.

Introverted-feeling type

This type is predominantly guided by subjective feelings and their true motives generally remain hidden. This type mainly consists of women of whom it may be said 'still waters run deep'.

Extraverted-sensation type

This type consists mainly of men for whom anything new that comes within their range of interest is acquired by way of sensations received from the outside. Guided by the intensity of objective influences, this type encompasses the grossly sensual and those whose sensations are aesthetically highly developed.

Introverted-sensation type

This type is guided by the intensity of the subjective sensation. No proportional relationship exists between object and sensation, but one that is unpredictable and arbitrary.

Extraverted-intuition type

For this type intuition as the function of unconscious perception is directed wholly to external objects. This type uses intuition to apprehend the widest range of possibilities in objective situations and to discover what they hold in store.

Introverted-intuition type

The peculiar intuition of this type produces mystical dreamers, seers, artists and cranks. The intensification of intuition may lead this type to be out of touch with tangible reality and to experience difficulty in communicating to others.

ACQUISITION

Jung never developed a rigorous elaboration of the development of the psyche and of human behaviour. A possible reason for this is that he was more interested in researching and understanding the collective unconscious, which he perceived as the inherited foundation of psychological life.

Stages of life

To Jung the arc of life has four stages: childhood, youth, middle age and extreme old age (Jung, 1989). He was particularly interested in the problems of middle age.

Childhood (birth to puberty)

Jung likened children, during the first two or three years of life when they are unconscious of themselves, to being in an animal state. In early infancy the psyche is to a large extent the maternal psyche and soon comprises the paternal psyche as well. Gradually the ego develops as the organizing centre for the child's psychic processes and only when children begin to say 'I' is there any perceptible continuity of consciousness. The conscious mind progressively arises out of the unconscious as fragments of the unconscious are added to consciousness and separated from their previous source in the unconscious (Jung, 1981).

Jung saw the origins of childhood neuroses mainly as symptoms of the mental conditions of parents. He wrote: 'The child is hopelessly exposed to the psychic influence of the parents and is bound to copy their self-deception, their insincerity, their hypocrisy, cowardice, self-righteousness, and selfish regard for their own comfort, just as wax takes up the imprint of the seal' (Jung 1981, p. 79). Jung did not expect parents to commit no faults but to recognize them for what they were, thus creating a more honest psychological atmosphere for their children.

Youth (puberty to 35–40 years)

The human mind's growth keeps pace with a widening range of consciousness and each step forward can be an extremely painful and laborious achievement. During youth the demands of life put an end to childhood, for example, the transitions to marriage and a career. In addition, young people may experience inner psychic difficulties concerned with the sexual instinct or feelings of inferiority. The essential feature of the problems of youth is a clinging to the childhood level of consciousness. Achievement, usefulness and becoming established are ways of proceeding out from the problems of the period of youth. People can adapt what they have been given from the past to the possibilities and demands of the future.

Middle age (35–40 years to extreme old age)

Jung used the analogy of the sun which rises to a peak in the first part of the day and then descends and in the process illuminates itself. Likewise human life does not inexorably expand, but there is an inexorable and deep-seated shift in the psyche towards contraction with the possibility of self-illumination. While the tasks of the first half of life concern the individual's development and entrenchment in the outer world, the tasks of the second half of life are for people to devote serious attention to understanding and developing themselves more fully. Just as neurotic problems in youth spring from people not escaping from their childhood, so neurotic problems in middle age can spring from people not escaping from their youth. Jung did not regard this psychological shrinking from approaching old age to be caused by fear of death, rather than from a basic change in the human psyche taking place around that time. Middle age is a time for contemplation, self-realization and learning to live more in harmony with primordial images and symbols.

Extreme old age

Though childhood and extreme old age are utterly different, Jung regarded them as having one thing in common: submersion into unconscious psychic happenings. The child's mind and ego grow out of unconsciousness. The elderly person sinks again into unconsciousness and progressively vanishes within it. Jung viewed childhood and extreme old age as being stages of life without any conscious problems, and hence they were not his major focus.

Progression and regression

Life requires an ongoing process of psychological adaptation to the reality of the environment. Progression and regression are two important uses of psychic energy. *Progression* is 'the daily advance of the process of psychological adaptation ... a continual satisfaction of the demands of environmental conditions' (Jung, 1983, p. 59). In progression, the psychic value of conscious and unconscious opposites become balanced through regular interaction and mutual influence.

Regression is the backward movement of psychic energy when a frustrating situation dams the energy of the libido: for instance, a thinking attitude may attempt to deal with a situation that can only be solved by feeling. Regression confronts the individual with the problem of the inner psyche as contrasted with outward adaptation to reality. The struggle between opposites would persist but for regression, which raises the psychic value of material of which the individual was only dimly conscious or totally unconscious. Regression can be positive as well as negative with its unconscious contents containing not only psychological slime, but the seeds of new possibilities. For example, if thinking fails as the adapted function, the unconscious material activated by regression will contain the missing feeling function, although still in embryonic, archaic and undeveloped form. Regression occurs regularly in dreams which can reveal important unconscious material.

Individuation

The central concept of Jung's psychology is the process of individuation. Individuation is the process by which the person becomes differentiated as a separate psychological individual, a separate whole as distinct from the collective psychology. However, the process of individuation also raises a person's consciousness of the human community since it makes people aware of the unconscious, which unites all mankind.

The goal of psychic development is the self which, as shown previously, differs from the ego. Individuation may be viewed as coming to selfhood or self-realization. The transcendent function is the means by which individuals are able to bridge part of the gap between consciousness and unconsciousness and live more in harmony with their unconscious processes.

Individuation involves a process of assimilating unconscious content into consciousness. There is a shift of the centre of personality from the ego, which is the centre of consciousness, to the self which moves from being located in the centre of unconsciousness to being at the central point between consciousness and unconsciousness. Creating this new balance between consciousness and unconsciousness allows the personality to rest on a new and more solid foundation.

Although the self-archetype is present from birth, its influence does not become significant until middle age. Individuation proceeds in life's morning through education and appropriate life experiences. However, a major emphasis on realizing the self through the process of individuation might be viewed more as a task of the afternoon of human life.

MAINTENANCE

Jung never systematically identified the factors that contribute to individuals maintaining lower levels of psychic development and individuation than desirable. He differentiated between the tasks of the first part of life, which entailed practical adaptations concerning such matters as relationships and occupation, and the second part of life, which concerned realizing the underlying self. The concept of maintenance should ideally take into account the different factors contributing to problems connected to addressing the tasks of each life stage. To avoid repetition and for the sake of simplicity, the following discussion is restricted to some central, sometimes overlapping, factors.

Rigid persona

People who develop rigid personas develop in a very one-sided fashion and become out of touch with the subjective and unconscious side of themselves. This one-sidedness seeks social adaptation at the expense of inner alienation.

Mass collective consciousness

The collective consciousness in a group, for instance, the Swiss nation, may be one that encourages people to avoid examining themselves and dealing more deeply with problems in life. Allied to this, the collective consciousness may be conducive to people reinforcing one another's rigid personas.

Complexes

Complexes, such as the mother complex, form part of the personal unconscious. Individuals who remain unaware of their complexes are likely to maintain them.

Fear of the shadow

Individuals tend not to like examining what they perceive as undesirable and inferior traits in themselves. People who possess rigid personas may be particularly prone to avoid looking at their shadow-sides.

Fear of the contents of the unconscious

Fear of the shadow is just one aspect of fear of the unconscious. At varying levels of awareness, individuals may fear that their conscious functioning may be overwhelmed by the strength of their unconscious, with its archetypes and symbolic messages. People may possess insufficient courage to face their inner selves. For example, men and women may be reluctant to admit and explore the feminine (anima) and masculine (animus) aspects of themselves, respectively.

Projection

Projection means the expulsion of a subjective content into an object. By means of projections, which are unintentional and purely automatic occurrences, individuals get rid of incompatible aspects of themselves by projecting them on to others. Usually these subjective contents are painful, for instance, aspects of one's shadow. However, projections are sometimes positive, but for reasons of self-depreciation are inaccessible to individuals.

Regression

Earlier, it was mentioned that regression involves the backward flow of psychic energy. Regression only becomes negative when the individual becomes stuck in the unconscious activity and material generated by it, rather than being able to use it for regeneration.

Inability to understand the language of dreams

The issue of understanding dreams is covered in the following section on therapy. Suffice it to say for now that inability to attend to dreams and understand their language and meaning is likely to contribute to maintaining pathology. The corollary of this is that heeding and understanding the language of dreams can foster the process of individuation.

Problems using the transcendent function

The transcendent function is the synthesizing or integrating process whereby unconscious material opposes conscious material to provide a third living thing resembling the conjunction of opposites. Reasons why this synthesizing of opposites to create something new may not take place include ignorance, laziness, and insufficient intelligence and courage.

THERAPY

> *As far as we can discern, the sole purpose of human existence is to kindle a light in the darkness of mere being.*
>
> Carl Jung

THERAPEUTIC GOALS

In his paper entitled 'The aims of psychotherapy', Jung (1966) talks about the psychology of life's morning and the psychology of its afternoon. The main therapeutic goal for youth is normal adaptation to overcome neuroses connected with shrinking back from concrete life tasks. Therapy is mainly focused on attaining specific goals, dealing with complexes, and strengthening consciousness and ego functioning. Jung emphasized the importance for young people, who were still unadapted and yet to achieve anything, to educate their conscious will.

People in the second half of life no longer need to educate their conscious will, but to understand their own inner being and the meaning of their lives. Fully two-thirds of Jung's clients were in the second half of life and about one-third were not suffering from any clinically definable neuroses, but from the senselessness and aimlessness of their lives. Most of these patients were socially well-adapted individuals to whom normalization meant nothing. For such people, the major therapeutic goal was self-realization involving a deeper comprehension of their psyche and incorporating more unconscious material so that a new balance was created between consciousness and unconsciousness.

Jung did not believe in the concept of cure, rather in being better able to engage in the processes of attaining life's tasks and of synthesizing conscious and unconscious material. Until his death, Jung continued his quest for individuation and self-realization by understanding the meaning of the dreams and symbols from his own unconscious.

PROCESS OF THERAPY

Jungian analysis definitely does not follow the medical model of diagnosis, prognosis and treatment. Jung believed that clinical diagnosis was all but meaningless and that the true nature of a neurosis only reveals itself during the course of therapy.

Jung postulated four stages in analytic psychotherapy: confession, elucidation, education and transformation (see Box 3.2). Though each of the stages has a curious sense of finality about it, normal adaptation will usually only be achieved by proceeding through the first three stages. The fourth stage, transformation, fulfils a further need beyond the scope of the other stages, but is not a final truth.

Jungian analysis is very much tailored to each individual. The process of therapy varies depending on such factors as the client's stage of life, their personality characteristics, and the nature of their problems. The four stages of therapy are indicative rather than prescriptive. For instance, clients vary in how much work is required in dealing with the transference

Box 3.2 The four stages of analytical therapy

Stage 1. Confession

The prototype of analytical therapy is confession. The first step in the therapeutic process is to share secrets and reveal inhibited emotions. Cathartic confession restores to the ego contents which should normally be part of it and which are capable of becoming conscious. However, confession should not be regarded as a panacea.

Stage 2. Elucidation

Elucidation is a process of throwing light upon and clearing up the contents elicited by the transference. Partly by analysing clients' dreams, therapists interpret and explain what clients project on to them. The effects of elucidation are that clients gain insight into their personal unconscious and the infantile origins of their projections, and thus become more accepting of their shortcomings.

Stage 3. Education

Elucidation can leave clients intelligent but still incapable children. Education entails helping clients draw out of themselves new and adaptive habits to replace the self-defeating habits of their neurosis. In this stage, therapy moves beyond insight to training clients in responsible actions.

Stage 4. Transformation

For many people completion of the first three stages may be sufficient. However, some people wish to move beyond being normal and adapted persons because their deepest needs are to be healthy in leading 'abnormal' lives. In the transformation stage with such clients, the therapist as well as the client is 'in the analysis'. In the personal relationship between them there are imponderable factors which bring about a mutual transformation, with the stronger and more stable personality deciding the final issue. The personality of the therapist is the curative or harmful factor and the educator must now become the self-educator going through the stages of confession, elucidation and education so that his or her personality does not react unfavourably on the client.

and its projections. Furthermore, the fourth stage of transformation is more appropriate to those facing problems of self-realization in the afternoon of their lives.

With difficult cases, Jung would start with three or four sessions a week. He would commence seeing most clients twice weekly, but once analytic therapy was under way, sessions would be reduced to once a week. Under his direction, Jung would also encourage clients to perform between-session activities, for instance, recording dreams and painting, which would enable them to make a contribution to their common work. Approximately once every ten weeks Jung would break off treatment both to prevent clients from becoming too dependent and to allow time to be a healing factor. A thorough course of analytic therapy could last for some years. Jung believed that, in most instances, very frequent sessions did not shorten the length of treatment. With clients of limited means, Jung would space sessions further apart and get clients to work on their own in the interim.

THE THERAPEUTIC RELATIONSHIP

Jung (1961) wrote: 'Analysis is a dialogue involving two partners. Analyst and patient sit facing one another, eye to eye; the doctor has something to say, but so does the patient' (p. 153). Therapy is different in every case, with each client requiring individual understanding. Furthermore, clients needed to reach their own view of things without therapist compulsion or attempts at conversion.

Jung was very aware that within and between therapists and clients relationships take place on conscious and unconscious levels. Since treatment is a dialectical process in which the therapist participates just as much as the client, the personalities of therapists and clients may be more important to treatment outcomes than what the therapist says or does. Therapists should not hide behind professional façades, but be human enough to allow themselves to be influenced by their clients. Jung (1961) observed, 'Only the wounded physician heals' (p. 156). Nevertheless, boundaries must be observed, including therapists monitoring themselves and questioning how their unconscious experiences situations.

As an example of unconscious contamination, the transference can evoke a counter-transference. Just as patients project unconscious material on to therapists, the reverse might be the case to the detriment of therapeutic outcomes. Jung strongly favoured training analyses so that therapists would be better able to protect clients from their own infections as well as to resist being infected by their clients' problems. Furthermore, Jung favoured ongoing contact with a third person who could monitor the therapist's functioning, observing that even the Pope had a confessor.

The relationship in analytic therapy differs according to the stage of therapy. For example, the relationship established during the confession stage can lay the foundation for the development of a transference relationship. Furthermore, the deeper levels of therapists' personalities are likely to be more involved in the transformation stage than in the earlier stages, which is why Jung stressed the self-education aspects of this stage.

The therapeutic relationship takes place not only face to face, but also in both therapist and client dreams and fantasies. Therapists need to be sensitive to the meaning of any dreams involving their clients. Once, when analysing his dreams, Jung understood the message that he was putting a woman, whom he recognized to be a patient, so high that his neck hurt to see her, as a compensation for the fact that he was looking down on her in therapy. After disclosing the dream and sharing his analysis of it with her, treatment improved (Jung, 1968).

Jung could also confront clients if he deemed it necessary. When one imperious aristocratic lady client threatened to slap him after he had to say something unpleasant to her, Jung jumped up and said, 'Very well, you are the lady. You hit first – ladies first! But then I hit back!' (Jung, 1961, p. 165). The client then slumped back into her chair, observed that no one had ever talked to her like that before, and proceeded to work better in therapy.

THERAPEUTIC INTERVENTIONS

Jung advocated flexibility in adapting the therapy to the client. With people in the morning of life, Jung (1966) generally went along with Freudian and Adlerian approaches since these seemed to bring clients to appropriate levels of adaptation without leaving disturbing after-effects. He also observed: 'We need a different language for every patient. In one analysis I can be heard talking the Adlerian dialect, in another the Freudian' (Jung, 1961, p. 153). Jungian language and dialect appears most appropriate for those in the second half of life.

Analysis of the transference

Transferences are emotionally toned unconscious projections that occur from client to therapist. Projections take place because an activated unconscious content seeks expression. The intensity of the transference is related to the importance of the emotional content to the client. Because they are emotionally toned, transference projections arouse emotions in therapists. Counter-transference takes place when the unconscious contents of a client's projections are identical with the therapist's own unconscious processes. If therapist and client are bound together by mutual unconsciousness, the result can be highly counter-productive for analytical therapy.

Any highly emotional contents of the unconscious can be a matter for projection, including erotic material and activated archetypes. Thus transference projections can come from the personal and collective unconscious. Though transference can be a spontaneous reaction, it usually occurs during analysis. Transference is often a compensation for lack of genuine rapport between therapist and client. Therapists should not actively seek to promote transference projections. Transferences are not necessary for effective analysis, because therapists can obtain all the material they need from dreams anyway.

Transferences take up clients' psychic energy. Once the transference projections are extracted and consciously understood, a corresponding amount of energy will fall back into the client's possession instead of being wasted.

Jung (1968) described four stages of analysis or therapy of the transference. However, it is possible to condense these four stages into two: handling transference projections from the personal unconscious, and handling transference projections from the collective unconscious.

The first main stage involves working through transference projections that are repetitions based on clients' former personal experiences with authority figures. There are basically two tasks. The first task is for clients to realize that they are projecting past negative and positive experiences, with their associated emotions, on to their therapists. The second task is for clients to withdraw the projections from their therapists and assimilate them into their own personalities. Clients need to learn how to assume responsibility for being whole persons, including their good and bad sides. For example, clients who project negative qualities can realize that these qualities represent their shadow-side which they find difficulty in acknowledging because they would rather possess a more positive image of themselves. Clients who project positive qualities can realize that perhaps they should develop these qualities in themselves.

The second main stage of transference analysis comes after the projection of personal images has been worked through and dissolved through conscious realization. A transference may still remain based on impersonal and collective rather than on personal unconscious contents. Clients need to learn to discriminate between the personal and impersonal contents they project on to their therapists. Jung advocated great sensitivity in handling impersonal projections and taking them seriously rather than trying to dissolve their contents. He provides the example of it being a great mistake to say to a client: 'You see, you simply project the saviour image into me. What nonsense to expect a saviour and to make me responsible' (Jung, 1968, pp. 180–1). The saviour archetypal image is everywhere and clients need to keep in touch with their impersonal images.

As part of the second stage of transference analysis, clients can learn to differentiate their personal relationship to the therapist from impersonal archetypal images. Clients can have normal human reactions to their therapists for helping them, but such reactions are human and decent only when not sullied by impersonal factors. Clients need also to realize the importance of their archetypal images, many of which have a religious nature. For some clients, the recognition of impersonal values may mean that they join a church or religious creed.

Therapy of the transference is complete when clients learn to objectify their impersonal images. Detaching consciousness from the object, a major aim of Eastern religious practices, is an essential part of the process of individuation. Clients learn to assume responsibility for their lives and no longer place the guarantees of their happiness on factors outside of themselves.

They attain a condition of detachment in which their centre of gravity becomes themselves rather than external objects on which they depend.

Active imagination

Active imagination is a technique devised by Jung to help people get in touch with unconscious material. Clients begin by concentrating on a starting point. They then allow their unconscious to produce a series of images, which may make a complete story. Box 3.3 provides two examples of active imagination, the second in abbreviated form (Jung, 1968, pp. 190–3).

Box 3.3   Examples of active imagination

Example 1.   Jung as a child

As a little boy, Jung would go to a spinster aunt's house. The house was full of beautiful old coloured engravings, one of which was a picture of his grandfather on his mother's side, a sort of bishop represented as coming out of the house and standing at the top of a little terrace. There were some stairs coming down from the terrace and a footpath leading to the cathedral. Jung would kneel and look at the picture until he 'actively imagined' his grandfather coming down the steps.

Example 2.   The young artist

A young artist client of Jung's looked at a railway station poster about a place in the Bernese Alps and imagined himself in the poster. He walked up the hill and among the cows depicted in the poster and then imagined himself coming to the top and looking down the other side. He walked down the meadow on the other side, over a stile, and then down a footpath that ran round a ravine, and a rock, and then he came to a small chapel with the door ajar. He pushed open the door and saw an altar with flowers and a wooden Mother of God. At the exact moment he looked up at her face, something with pointed ears disappeared behind the altar.

Though not the only starting point, clients can use a dream as a stimulus for active imagination. If clients do not allow conscious reason to interfere, the images can have a life of their own, which is the origin of the term 'active imagination'. After the active imagination process stops, some clients proceed to develop their unconscious images through painting, drawing, sculpting, weaving, dancing or writing.

Jung stressed that active imagination is not a panacea and that he only used it with some clients. He advised against forcing active imagination upon clients. Jung sometimes found using active imagination particularly valuable in the later stages of therapy.

Dream analysis

Dreams are utterances or statements from the unconscious. They are the doors to the innermost secrets of the psyche. Jung thought the idea that dreams were merely wish-fulfilments hopelessly out of date. As well as wishes and fears, dreams 'may contain ineluctable truths, philosophical pronouncements, illusions, wild fantasies, memories, plans, anticipations, irrational experiences, even telepathic visions, and heaven knows what else besides' (Jung, 1968, p. 147). Dreams may also point to solutions to issues and problems and be prescient about future events.

Jung regarded dreams as containing their whole meaning and not having false fronts. Dreams are comparable to texts that appear unintelligible, but the therapist has to discover how to read them. Dreams do not conceal, rather therapists need to discover their language. An understanding of myths and symbols is central to being able to read the language of dreams.

Jung distinguished between various kinds of dreams. Initial dreams are those that occur at the start of analysis and may deal with the client's attitude towards the therapist. For instance, a client predicted a brief and unsuccessful therapeutic contact with the dream '*I have to cross the frontier into another country, but cannot find the frontier and nobody can tell me where it is*' (Jung, 1968, p. 144). Another distinction is between minor dreams which are concerned with relatively unimportant matters and 'big' dreams. Big dreams are numinous, a favourite Jung term for inexpressible, mysterious, terrifying and intensely mysterious experiences. Big dreams are of particular importance. Another distinction is that between single dreams and a series of dreams, with Jung's strong preference being to work with series of dreams.

Tasks of dream analysis

The first task in analysing a dream is to establish its context. Here Jung used a technique he called 'amplification'. Amplification involves the elaboration and clarification of dream images by way of directed association. Rather than free association, therapists must encourage clients' associations that stick as close as possible to the dream images. For example, the dream image of a simple peasant's house may mean different things to different clients. To establish the context of the simple peasant's house, Jung would ask: 'So how does that appear to you?' or 'What are your associations to a simple peasant's house?' In this instance, the client replied: 'It is the lazar-house of St Jacob near Basel' (Jung, 1968, p. 97). From this association, Jung was able to make many connections: for example, the client feeling himself an outcast and being in great danger.

Another example of clarifying context is that of a client, whose writing desk is different, dreaming of a 'deal table'. Jung would keep returning to the image and say: 'Suppose I had no idea what the words "deal table" mean, describe this object and give me its history in such a way that I cannot fail to understand what sort of thing it is' (Jung, 1966, pp. 149–50). Therapist and client need to work on establishing the context for all the images in the dream.

Interpretation is the second task of dream analysis. Since basic ideas and themes can be much more clearly recognized in dream series than in single dreams, clients should keep a careful record of their dreams and of the interpretations made. Jung would also train clients in how to work on their dreams between sessions so that they could come prepared to the next consultation with the dream and its context written out. When interpreting dreams, a basic question for the therapist to address is 'What conscious attitude does it compensate?'

Related to the interpretation of dreams is the third task of dream analysis, assimilation. Jung valued unconscious contents and sought to bring about change in and through the unconscious as well. Assimilation 'means mutual penetration of conscious and unconscious, and not – as is commonly thought and practised – a one-sided evaluation, interpretation, and deformation of unconscious contents by the conscious mind' (Jung, 1966, p. 152). Unconscious contents lose their danger the moment clients begin to assimilate contents that were previously repressed.

Box 3.4   Example of dream analysis

The young man's dream

My father is driving away from the house in his new car. He drives clumsily, and I get very annoyed over his apparent stupidity. He goes this way and that, forwards and backwards, and manoeuvres the car into a dangerous position. Finally he runs into a wall and damages the car badly. I shout out at him in a perfect fury that he ought to behave himself. My father only laughs and then I see that he is dead drunk.

Context of the dream

The young man has a genuinely positive and admiring relationship with an unusually successful father. There was nothing neurotically ambivalent about the relationship.

Jung's interpretation of the dream

The client's relationship with his father is too good and his father is still doing too much for him, so that the client's unconscious is compensating by trying to take the father down a peg. The son's danger is that he cannot see his own reality. The dream forces the son to contrast himself with his father so that he can become conscious of himself.

The client's assimilation of the dream

Jung's interpretation struck home with the client and received his immediate assent. Jung points out that the interpretation damaged no real conscious values for either father or son.

Assimilation requires the assent of the client to the therapist's interpretations. The values of the client's conscious personality must be respected and left intact, because unconscious compensation requires co-operation with an 'integral consciousness'. Box 3.4 provides an abbreviated version of Jung's analysis of a young man's dream (Jung, 1966, pp. 154–5).

Dream symbols are expressions of content not yet consciously recognized or consciously formulated. Symbols can be relatively fixed, but interpretation of their content in the last resort is not definite. Box 3.5 illustrates Jung's interpretation of the symbolism in one of the dreams of a 17-year-old female client (Jung, 1966, pp. 158–60).

The dream illustrated in Box 3.5 was taken from long-term analytical therapy where the goal is the client's progressive

---

Box 3.5   Example of interpreting a dream symbol

The young woman's dream

I was coming home at night. Everything is quiet as death. The door to the living room is half open, and I see my mother hanging from the chandelier, swinging to and fro in the cold wind that blows through the open windows.

Part of the dream's context

Jung was called in after two specialists had made contrary diagnoses of this 17-year-old young woman. One specialist thought she might be in the first stages of progressive muscular atrophy. The other thought she was a case of hysteria.

Jung's interpretation of the dream

The mother symbol refers to the archetype of the place of origin, to nature. The symbol also stands for the instinctive and unconscious life and the body. Jung's interpretation was that the unconscious life is destroying itself or that the dream pointed to a grave organic disease that would have a fatal outcome. This prognosis was soon confirmed.

individuation. In such therapy, over a period of months and years there are successive assimilations of unconscious dream material. This process realizes more of the client's self in the interests of becoming a whole human being.

CASE MATERIAL

Perhaps some indication of Jung's attitude to case material can be gleaned from the following quotation: 'Each individual analysis by itself shows only one part of one aspect of the deeper process, and for this reason nothing but hopeless confusion can result from comparative case histories' (Jung, 1966, p. 161). Case material that illustrates analytic therapy comes from both primary and secondary sources. In his autobiographical *Memories, Dreams and Reflections*, Jung (1961) provides case material, including many dreams, from his own explorations and confrontations with his unconscious. In his 1935 Tavistock Lectures, published as *Analytical Psychology* (1968), Jung provides case examples illustrating active imagination and dream analysis. Numerous further examples of how Jung worked are to be found in the various papers that comprise *The Practice of Psychotherapy* (Jung, 1966). In addition, *Symbols of Transformation* (Jung, 1967) provides lengthy analyses of symbolic material contained in the fantasies of a young American lady, Miss Miller.

Jung was a very original and individualistic therapist with a vast range of scholarship to draw upon. Secondary source case material, such as that provided by Douglas (2000) and Casement (1996), can only go some way to catching the real essence of how Jung himself worked.

FURTHER DEVELOPMENTS

Samuels (1985) divided the development of analytical psychology into three schools: classical, developmental and archetypal. The classical school is that most closely based on Jung's original theory and practice, the topic of this chapter. The developmental school incorporates psychoanalytic ways of thinking and working. The archetypal school focuses on the development of symbols and images in the psyche. Douglas (2000) talks of developments in Jung's work extending into many different areas, including child analysis, group work, art therapy and a hybrid of Jungian psychology and Melanie Klein's object relations theory. The rise of feminism is also leading to a reappraisal of Jung's ideas about masculine and feminine characteristics.

In 1922 a Jung club was established in London, and in 1946, a Society of Analytical Psychology (SAP) was founded in Britain. There is an International Association of Analytical Psychology which, as of 1 December 1999, had 2305 members. Particularly in the Western world, interest in Jungian psychology remains strong. Jung has been called a 'homo religiosus' (Casement, 1996) or 'theologian manqué' (McLynn, 1996). His work has continuing appeal to many of those who are dissatisfied with the narrowness of scientific psychology and who seek to understand human beings in their wholeness.

SUMMARY

- *The psyche's three levels are: consciousness, the personal unconscious and the collective unconscious.*
- *Consciousness or awareness is transitory. The centre of consciousness is the ego. The ego has the external task of providing a system of relationship between consciousness and input from the environment and the internal task of providing a system of relationship between consciousness and unconscious processes.*
- *The contents of the personal unconscious are personal to the individual. Complexes, such as the mother complex, are accumulations of associations, sometimes of a traumatic nature, that possess strong emotional content. Complexes are an important feature of the personal unconscious.*
- *The contents of the collective unconscious are a universal historical storehouse made up essentially of archetypes. Archetypes are primordial images or primordial thoughts that appear in myths, for example, the hero or the redeemer, and are represented by symbols, such as the mandala.*
- *Important archetypes include the persona, anima and animus, shadow and self. The persona, or mask, is the individual's system of adaptation or way of coping with the world. The persona can also be a mask of a collective psyche. The anima is the personification of the feminine nature in a man's unconscious, whereas the animus is the*

personification of the masculine nature in a woman's unconscious.

- For the most part, the shadow represents inferior traits of personality that individuals are reluctant to acknowledge. The self, which is a superordinate construct to the ego, expresses the unity of the personality as a whole and encompasses both conscious and unconscious components.
- Psychic energy is the psychic analogue of physical energy. Two important aspects of Jungian psychodynamics are opposition, the flow of energy between two poles, and compensation, a largely unconscious process that for the most part balances rather than opposes consciousness.
- The transcendent function is a synthesizing process whereby the tension between consciousness and unconsciousness creates a living third thing that allows for a new level of consciousness.
- The introverted attitude is characterized by an orientation in life that particularly values subjective psychic contents, whereas the extraverted attitude reflects a focus on the external object or world. Thinking and feeling are rational functions, whereas sensing and intuiting are irrational functions. Jung combined attitudes and functions to provide eight main psychological types.
- There are four stages of life: childhood, youth, middle age and extreme old age, with the inner challenges of middle age being of particular interest to Jung.
- Progression is the forward movement of psychic energy to advance the process of psychological adaptation, whereas regression is the backward movement of psychic energy.
- Individuation is the process by which the person becomes differentiated as a separate psychological individual and learns to live more in harmony with unconscious content.
- Ways in which individuals maintain levels of adaptation that may be lower than desirable include rigid personas, complexes, fears of the contents of the unconscious, projection and regression.
- Therapeutic goals differ according to the individual's stage of life and particular circumstances. Therapy for people in life's morning focuses more on attaining specific goals of adaptation, whereas goals for life's afternoon focus more on realizing the self.
- Though not intended as a strait-jacket, there are four stages

of analytic therapy: confession, elucidation, education and transformation.

- *The relationship between therapist and client involves a human dialogue, with each client requiring individual understanding. Therapists and clients relate to each other on both conscious and unconscious levels. The nature of the relationship varies according to that stage of therapy.*

- *Analysis of the transference involves first handling projections from the personal unconscious and then those from the collective unconscious. Counter-transference takes place when the client's unconscious contents activate material in the therapist's unconscious.*

- *Active imagination entails clients concentrating on a starting point or stimulus and then actively imagining themselves participating in a flow of images which take on a life of their own.*

- *Therapists need to learn the language of their clients' dreams. Three tasks of dream analysis are: establishing the context of the dream, interpreting it, and the client being able to assimilate the interpretation. In long-term therapy clients successively assimilate interpretations of unconscious dream material as part of the process of individuation.*

- *The theory and practice of analytic therapy continue to develop. In addition to members of professional societies affiliated to the International Association of Analytical Psychology, numerous other people, both professional and lay, are interested in analytic therapy and its focus on the development of the whole person.*

REVIEW AND PERSONAL QUESTIONS

Review questions

1. Describe consciousness and the ego.
2. Describe the personal unconscious and its complexes.
3. Describe the collective unconscious and its archetypes.
4. What are Jungian psychodynamics and how do they differ from Freudian psychodynamics?
5. What are Jung's views on psychological types?
6. What are the four stages of life and how do the tasks of life's morning and afternoon differ?

7. How do people maintain levels of adaptation lower than desirable?
8. Describe the goals and process of analytic therapy.
9. Describe Jung's ideas on the analysis of the transference.
10. Describe as best you can how Jung approached the task of dream analysis.

Personal questions

1. Do Jung's ideas of the personal unconscious and the collective unconscious resonate in terms of your own life? If so, please elaborate.
2. Me and my shadow. What are some aspects of your shadow and what do you intend to do about them?
3. What do you consider is your personality type and why?
4. Try using Jung's method of active imagination.
5. Take one of your dreams and, to the best of your ability, apply Jung's methods of dream analysis to it.
6. What goals would you set for yourself if you were to be a client in Jungian therapy?

ANNOTATED BIBLIOGRAPHY

C. G. Jung (1968) *Analytical Psychology: Its Theory and Practice.* New York: Vintage Books.

This book presents the five lectures, plus discussion, that Jung gave at the Tavistock Clinic in London in 1935. Topics covered include the structure of the mind, word association and psychological types, and the methods of active imagination, dream analysis and the analysis of the transference. This book provides an excellent concise introduction to analytical psychology.

C. G. Jung (1966) *The Practice of Psychotherapy* (2nd edn). London: Routledge (Vol. 16 in *The Collected Works of C. G. Jung*).

This book is divided into two parts. Part I, entitled 'General problems of psychotherapy', contains nine papers, including one on the aims of psychotherapy. Part II, entitled 'Specific problems of psychotherapy', contains Jung's ideas on the therapeutic value of abreaction, the practical use of dream analysis, and the psychology of transference. Some useful case study material is included in an appendix entitled 'The realities of practical psychotherapy'.

C. G. Jung (1961) *Memories, Dreams and Reflections*. London: Fontana Press.

Jung regarded his life as a story of the realization of the unconscious. In this book compiled at the end of his life Jung tells his personal myth, an inner journey structured around the following chapter headings: first years, school years, student years, psychiatric activities, Sigmund Freud, confrontation with the unconscious, the work, the tower, travels, visions, on life after death, and late thoughts. Some controversy exists over the extent of Jung's secretary's contribution to this book rather than its being a solely primary source.

C. G. Jung. (1971) *Psychological Types*. London: Routledge (Vol. 6 in *The Collected Works of C. G. Jung*).

This book was originally published in 1921 after Jung's fallow period. It starts with a scholarly discussion of the notion of psychological types drawing on material from literature, aesthetics, religion and philosophy as well as from psychology. Jung then presents his ideas on attitudes, functions and psychological types. The book ends with an appendix containing four papers on psychological typology.

Hall, C. S. and Nordby, B. J. (1973) *A Primer of Jungian Psychology*. New York: New American Library.

A valuable and relatively short secondary source book about Jungian theory. However, there is little mention of the practice of analytical therapy. Good coverage of the structure, dynamics and development of personality, the psychological types and of symbols and dreams.

REFERENCES

All Jung's writings can be found in the eighteen volumes of *The Collected Works of C. G. Jung*, published in Britain by Routledge, London, and in America by Princeton University Press, Princeton, NJ.

Casement, A. (1996) 'Psychodynamic therapy: the Jungian approach', in W. Dryden (ed.) *Handbook of Individual Therapy*. London: Sage, pp. 77–102.
Douglas, C. (2000) 'Analytical psychotherapy', in R. Corsini and D. Wedding (eds) *Current Psychotherapies* (6th edn). Itasca, IL: Peacock, pp. 99–132.
Hall, C. S. and Nordby, B. J. (1973) *A Primer of Jungian Psychology*. New York: New American Library.

Jung, C. G. (1961) *Memories, Dreams and Reflections*. London: Fontana Press.

Jung, C. G. (1966) *The Practice of Psychotherapy* (2nd edn). London: Routledge (Vol. 16 in the CW).

Jung, C. G. (1967) *Symbols of Transformation* (2nd edn). Princeton, NJ: Princeton University Press (Vol. 5 in the CW).

Jung, C. G. (1968) *Analytical Psychology: Its Theory and Practice*. New York: Vintage Books.

Jung, C. G. (1971) *Psychological Types*. London: Routledge.

Jung, C. G. (1976a) 'The concept of the collective unconscious', in J. Campbell (ed.) *The Portable Jung*. London: Penguin Books, pp. 59–70.

Jung, C. G. (1976b) 'The relations between the ego and the unconscious', in J. Campbell (ed.) *The Portable Jung*. London: Penguin Books, pp. 70–138.

Jung, C. G. (1976c) 'The transcendent function', in J. Campbell (ed.) *The Portable Jung*. London: Penguin Books, pp. 273–300.

Jung, C. G. (1981) *The Development of Personality: Papers on Child Psychology, Education and Related Subjects*. London: Routledge.

Jung, C. G. (1982) *Aspects of the Feminine*. London: Ark Paperbacks.

Jung, C. G. (1983) 'Fundamental concepts of libido theory', in A. Storr (ed.) *The Essential Jung*. Princeton, NJ: Princeton University Press, pp. 59–64.

Jung, C. G. (1989) *Aspects of the Masculine*. Princeton, NJ: Princeton University Press.

McLynn, F. (1996) *Carl Gustav Jung: A Biography*. London: Bantam Press.

Samuels, A. (1985) *Jung and the Post-Jungians*. London: Routledge & Kegan Paul.

4

Person-centred Therapy

*It seems to me that at bottom each person is asking,
'Who am I really? How can I get in touch with this
real self, underlying all my surface behaviour? How
can I become myself?'*

Carl Rogers

INTRODUCTION

Have you ever felt that you would like to find yourself and be
more truly your own person? Are you able to experience your
feelings and act autonomously or are you still mainly a
creation of your parents and of the influence of significant
others in your background? Carl Rogers was the originator of
an approach to counselling and therapy that aimed to help
clients fulfil their unique potential and become their own
persons. His approach was partly an attempt to get away
from the interpretive psychodynamic therapies described in
Chapters 2 and 3. In addition, Rogers was trying to emanci-
pate people from the overbearing influence that parents of his
time often had on the thoughts, feelings and actions of their
offspring. In the early part of the twentieth century when
Rogers was growing up, parents exercised much more power
in the home than they do now at the start of the twenty-first
century. Rogers' person-centred therapy challenged authoritarian tendencies in both therapy and parenting and championed the rights of clients to discover their own directions.

On 11 December 1940, Rogers gave a presentation at the
University of Minnesota entitled 'Some newer concepts in
psychotherapy' which is the single event most often identified
with the birth of client-centred therapy (Raskin and Rogers,
2000). In 1974, Rogers and his colleagues changed the name
from 'client-centred' to 'person-centred'. They believed that
the new name would more adequately describe the human

values and the mutuality underlying their approach and would apply to contexts other than counselling and psychotherapy. However, Thorne observes: 'Rogers never completely jettisoned the term client-centred therapy. He uses client-centred and person-centred interchangeably when talking about counselling and psychotherapy but *always* employs the term "the person-centred approach" when referring to activities outside the one-to-one therapy situation' (B. Thorne, personal communication, 15 March 1994).

Rogers regarded himself as having one seminal idea. The central hypothesis of the person-centred approach is that every person has within himself or herself 'vast resources for self-understanding, for altering his or her self-concept, attitudes, and self-directed behaviour – and that these resources can be tapped only if a definable climate of facilitative psychological attitudes can be provided' (Rogers, 1986a, p. 197). Empathy, congruence and unconditional positive regard are the three therapist-offered facilitative conditions that Rogers regarded as necessary and sufficient for therapeutic change (Rogers, 1957).

This chapter is drawn mainly from Rogers' writings. However, he encouraged colleagues and associates to develop it, and consequently regarded his theory as a group enterprise (Rogers, 1959). In addition, Rogers was influenced by psychologists like Combs, Snygg and Maslow. I incorporate the ideas of Rogers' collaborators when it adds to or clarifies his position.

CARL ROGERS (1902–87)

Carl Ransom Rogers was born in Illinois, USA, the fourth of six children. His father was a civil engineer and contractor who had a successful construction business. A rather sickly boy, Rogers lived his childhood in a close-knit family in which hard work and a highly conservative, almost fundamentalist Protestant Christianity were almost equally revered. Rogers was a shy boy who was teased a lot at home. Included among reasons for the teasing were that he was rather a bookworm and extremely absent-minded; in fact, his family called him 'Professor Moony' after a famous comic-strip character (Cohen, 1997).

When Rogers was 12 his parents bought a farm and this

became the family home. Rogers regarded his parents as masters of the art of subtle, loving control. He shared little of his private thoughts and feelings with them because he knew these would have been judged and found wanting. Until Rogers went to college he was a loner who read incessantly and adopted his parents' attitude towards the outside world, summed up in the statement: 'Other persons behave in dubious ways which we do not approve in our family' (Rogers, 1980, p. 28). Such dubious ways included playing cards, going to the cinema, smoking, dancing, drinking and engaging in other even less mentionable activities. He was socially incompetent in other than superficial contacts and, while at high school, had only two dates with girls. He relates that his fantasies during this period were bizarre and would probably have been classified as schizoid by a psychological diagnostician.

Rogers entered the University of Wisconsin to study agriculture, but later switched to history, feeling that this would be a better preparation for his emerging professional goal of becoming a minister of religion. His first real experience of fellowship was in a group at university who met for a YMCA class. When he was 20, Rogers went to China for an international World Student Christian Federation Conference and, for the first time, emancipated himself from the religious thinking of his parents, a fundamental step towards becoming an independent person. At about this time Rogers fell in love, and, on completing college, married Helen Elliott, an artist. The marriage lasted until she died in 1979.

In 1924, Rogers went to Union Theological Seminary, but after two years moved to Teachers College, Columbia University, where he was exposed to the instrumentalist philosophy of John Dewey, the highly statistical and Thorndikean behavioural approaches of Teachers College, and the Freudian orientation of the Institute for Child Guidance where he had an internship. Along with his formal learning he was starting to understand relationships with others better, and was beginning to realize that, in close relationships, the elements that 'cannot' be shared are those that are the most important and rewarding to share.

Rogers received his MA from Columbia University in 1928 and then spent twelve years in a community child guidance clinic in Rochester, New York. In 1931, he received his Ph.D.

from Columbia University and in 1939 published his first book, entitled *The Clinical Treatment of the Problem Child*. During this period Rogers felt that he was becoming more competent as a therapist, not least because his experience with clients was providing him with valuable learning and insights which contributed to a shift from diagnosis to listening. Furthermore, such a relationship approach met his own needs, since, stemming from his early loneliness, the therapy interview was a socially approved way of getting really close to people without the pains and longer time-span of the friendship process outside therapy.

In 1940, Rogers accepted a position as a professor of psychology at Ohio State University and two years later published *Counseling and Psychotherapy*, the contents of which were derived primarily from his work as a counsellor rather than as an academic psychologist. After initial poor sales, the book became well known because it offered a way to work with veterans returning from the Second World War. From 1942, Rogers had undertaken consultancies relating to the war effort, including training counsellors. After leaving Ohio State University, Rogers spent a brief spell as director of counselling for the United Services Organization, a service-man's welfare organization. From 1945 to 1957 Rogers was professor of psychology and executive secretary of the university counselling centre at the University of Chicago, where non-directive, or client-centred therapy, as it came to be called, was further developed and researched. In 1951, Rogers published *Client-Centered Therapy*, which contained a theoretical statement as well as a series of chapters related to client-centred practice.

In 1957, Rogers was appointed professor of psychology and psychiatry at the University of Wisconsin, where he examined the impact of the client-centred approach on hospitalized schizophrenics. In 1959, Rogers published by far the most thorough statement of his theoretical position (Rogers, 1959) and in 1961, *On Becoming a Person*, one of his most commercially successful books. From 1962 to 1963 Rogers was a fellow at the Center for Advanced Study in the Behavioral Sciences at Stanford University. In 1964 he went to the Western Behavioral Sciences Institute at La Jolla, California, as a resident fellow. Then, in 1968 with some colleagues, Rogers formed the Center for Studies of the Person at La Jolla, where he was a resident fellow until his death. During the latter part of his career Rogers developed a great interest in the application of person-centred ideas to group work, community change, and preventing 'nuclear, planetary suicide', and ran many large-scale workshops around the world (Kirschenbaum and Henderson, 1990). In addition, as Rogers grew older, having earlier firmly rejected his Christian past, he realized he had underestimated the mystical or spiritual dimension in life.

From the age of 13 Rogers had viewed himself as a scientist. He was a committed researcher and pioneered the use of tape-recorders to study counselling and therapy processes. In 1956, he received the American Psychological Association's Award for Distinguished Scientific Contributions. Rogers was also an author with a deep commitment to clear and cogent communication. When he was 75, he observed: 'Yet there is, I believe, a much more important reason for my writing. It seems to me that I am still – inside – the shy boy who found communication very difficult in interpersonal situations' (Rogers, 1980, p. 80). As well as those already mentioned, his books include: *Freedom to Learn*; *Encounter Groups*; *Becoming Partners*; *Carl Rogers on Personal Power*, and *A Way of Being*. A chronological bibliography of Rogers' books and articles published in the period 1930 to 1980 is listed at the end of *A Way of Being*.

Although the years since 1940 were very successful for Rogers and his ideas, they also contained professional and personal struggles. Two professional struggles were those with psychiatry and with behavioural psychology. Rogers fought for psychologists, as contrasted with psychiatrists, to be allowed to practise psychotherapy and to have administrative responsibility over 'mental health' work. He also constantly highlighted the philosophical and practical issues involved in a humanistic or person-centred as against a behavioural view of human beings.

On a more personal level, Rogers continued to strive to become a more real, open and growing person. He struggled, with varying degrees of success, with some personal crises and difficulties. During his Chicago period, with counselling help, he worked through a crisis arising from a 'badly bungled therapeutic relationship' (Rogers, 1980, p. 39) with 'a particularly demanding and highly disturbed female client' (Thorne,

1992). In the 1970s, Rogers faced the strains of his wife's long illness – from 1972 she was intermittently in a wheelchair and in 1979 she died. In the last years of her life, there was much pain in his relationship with Helen. Nevertheless, Rogers movingly talks of how he was able to express his appreciation and love for her two days before she died (Rogers, 1980).

Towards the end his life Rogers was increasingly aware of his 'capacity for love, my sensuality, my sexuality' (Rogers, 1980, p. 96) and wished to have loving relationships outside of marriage. In August 1975, Rogers met and fell in love with a much younger divorcee called Bernice Todres, but the relationship was never sexually consummated. In December 1979 this only intermittently satisfactory and episodic relationship finally ended. In the 1970s Rogers was drinking heavily, consuming over 12 oz of vodka a day, which contributed to his putting on weight. At one stage, his daughter Natalie was so worried about his drinking that she is said to have suggested he book himself into a de-tox clinic (Cohen, 1997).

Rogers was a complex mixture of high intelligence, high energy, ambition, competitiveness, Protestant work ethic, strength, vulnerability, charisma, idealism, altruism, self-centredness, caring, shyness, sensitivity, warmth, and ability to touch others deeply. Arguably, as his career developed, Rogers allowed the need to become and maintain the professional persona of Carl Rogers to get in the way of his becoming a more highly developed person. Clearly very conscious of his place in the history of American counselling and therapy, Rogers left the United States Library of Congress 140 boxes of his papers as well as tapes and films of his work.

Even as an old man, Rogers was still prone to blame his parents for making him feel that he did not deserve to be loved (Cohen, 1997). A wounded theorist, Rogers was influenced by his own early emotional deprivations to design a counselling approach to overcome their effects and hence to meet his own companionship and growth needs. Other sources of learning included his clients and the stimulus provided by younger colleagues. Rogers claimed that serendipity or 'the faculty of making fortunate and unexpected discoveries by accident' had also been important (Rogers, 1980, p. 64). Rogers enjoyed gardening and finding the right conditions for plants to grow. As with plants, so with people. While regarding the following saying from Lao-Tse as an over-simplification, Rogers considers that it sums up many of his deeper beliefs about human growth.

> If I keep from meddling with people, they take care of themselves,
> If I keep from commanding people, they behave themselves,
> If I keep from preaching at people, they improve themselves,
> If I keep from imposing on people, they become themselves.

THEORY

I have formed some philosophical impressions of the life and goal toward which the individual moves when he is free.

Carl Rogers

BASIC CONCEPTS

In 1951 Rogers presented his theory of personality and behaviour as the final chapter of *Client-Centred Therapy*. Eight years later, in an edited publication entitled *Psychology: A Study of Science*, he presented an updated version which he regarded as his major and most rigorous theoretical statement and 'the most thoroughly ignored of anything I have written' (Rogers, 1980, p. 60). Later, with collaborators, Rogers restated his theory, but did not alter it (e.g., Raskin and Rogers, 2000). Rogers thought that this and any theory should be a stimulus for further creative thinking rather than a dogma of truth.

Perceptual or subjective frame of reference

Combs and Snygg (1959) state that, broadly speaking, behaviour may be observed from either the point of view of outsiders or the point of view of the behavers themselves. It is sometimes stated that the former is viewing behaviour from the external frame of reference while the latter is viewing behaviour from the internal, subjective or perceptual frame of reference. Rogers writes of his fundamental belief in the subjective, observing that 'Man lives essentially in his own personal and subjective world, and even his most objective functioning, in science, mathematics, and the like, is the result of subjective purpose and subjective choice' (Rogers, 1959, p. 191). It is this emphasis on the subjective, perceptual view of clients which has led to the term 'client-centred'. The perceptions of clients are viewed as their versions of reality.

Later, Rogers was again to stress that the only reality people can possibly know is the world which they individually perceive and experience at this moment. The notion that there is a 'real world', the definition of which can be agreed upon by everyone, is a luxury that the human race cannot afford, since it leads to false beliefs, like faith in technology, which have brought our species to the brink of annihilation. His alternative hypothesis is that there are as many realities as there are people. Furthermore, people are increasingly 'inwardly and organismically rejecting the view of one single, culture-approved reality' (Rogers, 1980, p. 26).

Actualizing tendency

The actualizing tendency is the single basic motivating drive. It is an active process representing the inherent tendency of the organism to develop its capacities in the direction of maintaining, enhancing and reproducing itself. The actualizing tendency is operative at all times in all organisms and is the distinguishing feature of whether a given organism is alive or dead. The organism is always up to something. In addition, the actualizing tendency involves a development towards the differentiation of organs and functions.

Rogers observes, from his experiences with individual and group counselling and from his attempts to provide students in classes with 'freedom to learn', that 'the most impressive fact about the individual human being seems to be the directional tendency toward wholeness, toward actualization of potentialities' (Rogers, 1977, p. 240). Furthermore, he cited support for the actualizing tendency both in his observations of the natural world, for instance, the behaviour of seaweed and of children learning to walk, and in empirical research, be it on sea urchins, rats, human infants or brain-damaged war veterans. The cornerstone of both Rogers' therapeutic and political thinking was that, because of their actualizing tendency, people move towards self-regulation and their own enhancement and away from control by external forces.

The actualizing tendency is basically positive. It represents Rogers' trust in the wisdom of the organism and its constructive directional flow towards the realization of each individual's full potential. People have the capacity to guide, regulate and control themselves, provided certain definable conditions exist. The person-centred approach posits a unitary diagnosis that all psychological difficulties are caused by blockages to this actualizing tendency and, consequently, the task of therapy is to release further this fundamentally good motivating drive. Maslow (1970) reiterates this assessment of people's basic nature when he writes that the human being does seem to have instinct remnants and that clinical and other evidence suggests that those weak instinctoid tendencies are good, desirable and worth saving.

Often, however, people appear to have two motivational systems: their organismic actualizing tendency and their conscious self. Maslow (1962) writes of the basic conflict in human beings between defensive forces and growth trends and observes that the actualizing tendency may involve both deficiency and growth motivations. However, given a certain emotional environment, growth motivations will become increasingly strong.

Organismic valuing process

The concept of an organismic valuing process is central to the idea of a real or true and unique self. A person's organismic valuing process relates to the continuous weighing of experience and the placing of values on that experience in terms of its ability to satisfy the actualizing tendency. For instance, the behaviour of infants indicates that they prefer those experiences, such as curiosity and security, which maintain and enhance their organism and reject those, such as pain and hunger, which do not. This weighing of experience is an organismic rather than a conscious symbolic process. The source of the valuing process or values placed on the various experiences clearly seems to be in the infants, who react to their own sensory and visceral evidence. As people grow older, their valuing process is effective in helping them to achieve self-actualizing to the degree that they are able to be aware of and perceive the experiencing which is going on within themselves.

Experience and experiencing

Rogers uses the term 'sensory and visceral experience' in a psychological rather than a physiological sense. Perhaps another way of stating sensory and visceral experience is the undergoing of facts and events, which are potentially available to conscious awareness, by the organism's sensory and visceral equipment. People may be unaware of much of their experiencing. For instance, when sitting, you may not be aware of the sensation in your buttocks until your attention is drawn to it. Another example is that you may not be aware of the physiological aspects of hunger because you are so fascinated by work or play. However, this experience is potentially available to conscious awareness. The total range of experience at any given moment may be called the 'experiential', 'perceptual' or 'phenomenal' field. Rogers stressed that physiological events such as neuron discharges or changes in blood sugar are not included in his psychological definition of experience.

The verb 'to experience' means that the organism is receiving the impact of any sensory or visceral experiences which happen at that moment. Experiencing a feeling includes receiving both the emotional content and the personal meaning or cognitive content 'as they are experienced inseparably in the moment' (Rogers, 1959, p. 198). Experiencing a feeling fully means that experiencing, awareness and expression of the feeling are all congruent.

Perception and awareness

Perception and awareness are virtually synonymous in person-centred theory. When an experience is perceived, this means that it is in conscious awareness, however dimly, though it need not be expressed in verbal symbols. Another way of stating this is that 'perceiving' is 'becoming aware of stimuli or experiences'. Rogers viewed all perception and awareness as transactional in nature, being a construction from past experience and a hypothesis or prediction of the future. Perception or awareness may or may not correspond with experience or 'reality'. When an experience is symbolized accurately in awareness, this means that the hypothesis implicit in the awareness will be borne out if tested by acting on it. Many experiences may not be symbolized accurately in awareness because of defensive denials and distortions. Other experiences, such as sitting on a chair, may not be perceived, since they may be unimportant to the actualizing tendency.

Awareness, or conscious attention, is one of the latest evolutionary developments of the human species. One way in which Rogers regarded it was as 'a tiny peak of awareness, of symbolizing capacity, topping a vast pyramid of non-conscious organismic functioning' (Rogers, 1977, p. 244). Box 4.1 attempts to illustrate this. When a person is functioning well, awareness is a reflection of part of the flow of the organism at that moment. However, all too often people are not functioning well, and organismically they are moving in one direction while their aware or conscious lives are struggling in another.

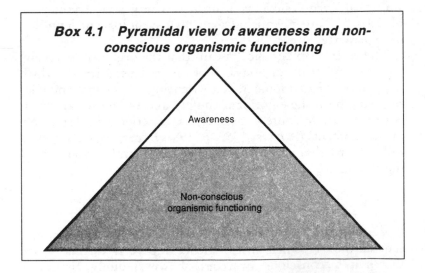

Box 4.1   Pyramidal view of awareness and non-conscious organismic functioning

Awareness

Non-conscious organismic functioning

ACQUISITION

Person-centred theory may become clearer to the reader by maintaining a distinction between self and self-concept. The self may be viewed as the real, underlying, organismic self expressed in popular sayings such as 'To thine own self be true' and 'To be that self which one truly is'. People's self-concepts are their perceptions of themselves, which do not always correspond with their own experiencing or organismic selves. Thus, ideally the actualizing tendency refers to self-actualizing where aspects of self and of self-concept are synonymous or congruent. However, where self and self-concept are incongruent, the desire to actualize the self-concept may work against the deeper need to actualize the organismic self. In Rogers' writings the above distinction is always implicit, if not always explicit.

Early development of self-concept

The self-concept is the self as perceived and the values attached to these perceptions, or what a person refers to as 'I' or 'me'. Initially, the self-concept may be made up largely of self-experiences, events in the phenomenal field discriminated by the individual as 'I', 'me' or 'self', even though in a pre-verbal way. For instance, infants who discover their toes may incorporate the fact that they have toes into their self-concept, and infants who are hungry may incorporate into their self-concepts the fact that they negatively value hunger. As young people interact with the environment, more and more experience may become symbolized in awareness as self-experience. Not least through interaction with significant others who treat them as a separate self, they develop a self-concept which includes both their perceptions about themselves and the varying positive and negative values attached to these self-perceptions.

Conditions of worth

A need for positive regard from others is a learned need developed in early infancy. Positive regard means here the perception of experiencing oneself as making a positive difference in the experiential field of another. It is likely that on many occasions young people's behaviour and experiencing of their behaviour will coincide with positive regard from others and hence meet their need for positive regard. For instance, smiling at parents may reflect a pleasurable experience as well as generating positive regard.

However, on other occasions, young people may feel that their experiencing conflicts with their need for positive regard from significant others. Rogers gives the example of the child who experiences satisfaction at hitting his baby brother, but who experiences the words and actions of his parents as saying 'You are bad, the behaviour is bad, and you are not loved or lovable when you behave this way'. An outcome of this may be that the child does not acknowledge the pleasurable value of hitting his baby brother emanating from his own experience, but comes to place a negative value on the experience because of the attitudes held by his parents and his need for positive regard. Thus, instead of an accurate symbolization of the experience, such as 'While I experience the behaviour as satisfying, my parents experience it as unsatisfying', there may come a distorted symbolization, such as 'I perceive this behaviour as unsatisfying' (Rogers, 1951, p. 500). Such values, which are based on others' evaluations rather than on the individual's own organismic valuing process, are called 'conditions of worth'. Conditions of worth are prevalent because all too often 'individuals are culturally conditioned, rewarded, reinforced, for behaviors that are in fact perversions of the natural directions of the unitary actualizing tendency' (Rogers, 1977, p. 247).

The concept of conditions of worth is important because it means that people develop a second valuing process. The first is the organismic valuing process which truly reflects the actualizing tendency. The second is a conditions of worth process, based on the internalization or 'introjection' of others' evaluations, which does not truly reflect the actualizing tendency but may serve to impede it. However, people possess a false awareness in regard to this second valuing process, since they feel that decisions based on it are in fact based on their organismic valuing process. Thus experiences may be sought or avoided to meet false rather than real needs.

Self-actualizing, when it takes the form of self-concept actualizing based on conditions of worth, is by no means always a good thing. Rogers advocated self-actualizing based on individuals' organismic valuing process that genuinely reflects their unique actualizing tendency. This distinction can be an area of great confusion for students.

Family life

The adequacy of the self-concepts of parents affects the ways in which they relate to their children. Thomas Gordon, a contributor to Rogers' 1951 book *Client-centered Therapy*, has emphasized that the level of self-acceptance or self-regard of parents may be related to their degree of acceptance of the behaviour of their children, though this is not something which is static. Box 4.2 is a representation, albeit over-simplified, of the possible effects of parents on their children. Rogers observed that parents are able to feel unconditional positive regard for a child only to the extent that they experience unconditional self-regard. By 'unconditional positive regard' Rogers meant prizing a child even though the parent may not value equally all of his or her behaviours. The greater the degree of unconditional positive regard that parents experience towards the child, the fewer the conditions of worth in the child and the higher the level of its psychological adjustment. Put simply, high-functioning parents create the conditions for the development of high-functioning children. In 1970, Gordon published *Parent Effectiveness Training* based on person-

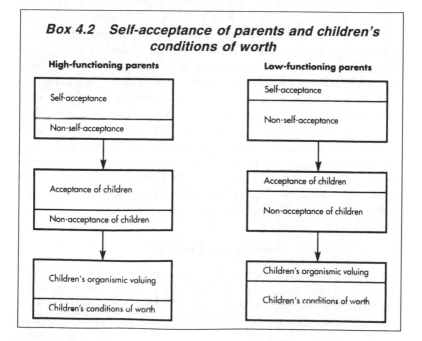

Box 4.2 Self-acceptance of parents and children's conditions of worth

High-functioning parents	Low-functioning parents
Self-acceptance	Self-acceptance
Non-self-acceptance	Non-self-acceptance
Acceptance of children	Acceptance of children
Non-acceptance of children	Non-acceptance of children
Children's organismic valuing	Children's organismic valuing
Children's conditions of worth	Children's conditions of worth

centred principles. This book attempts to teach parents how to listen to and talk with their children, thus helping the attitude of prizing to be communicated to them.

Effect of conditions of worth on self-concept

People differ in the degree to which they internalize conditions of worth depending not only on the level of unconditional positive regard they are offered by significant others, but also on the empathic understanding and congruence shown to them. In addition, the extent of their need for positive regard influences their vulnerability to introjecting conditions of worth. For some, their self-concepts will develop so as to allow much of their experience to be accurately perceived. However, even the most fortunate are likely to internalize some conditions of worth, and the less fortunate are fated to internalize many.

Some common examples of conditions of worth are: 'Achievement is very important and I am less of a person if I do not achieve', 'Making money is very important and, if I do not make much money, then I am a failure', and 'Sexual fantasies and behaviours are mostly bad and I should not like myself for having them'. Thus conditions of worth entail not only internalized evaluations of how people should be, but also internalized evaluations of how they should feel about themselves if they perceive that they are not the way they should be. Rogers believed that it is common for most people to have their values largely introjected, held as fixed concepts and rarely examined or tested. Thus, not only are they estranged from their experiencing, but their level of self-regard is lowered and they are unable to prize themselves fully. Furthermore, by internalizing conditions of worth, they have internalized a process by which they come to be the agents of lowering their own level of self-regard or, more colloquially, of 'self-oppression'.

Marriage and education

The person-centred view is that the conditions for the development of adequate self-concepts and those for remedying inadequate self-concepts are essentially the same. Both contain the characteristics of good and loving interpersonal relationships. Implicit in this is the notion that significant experiences for the development of adequate and, regrettably, also of inadequate self-concepts are neither restricted to childhood and adolescence nor to family life.

Rogers saw contributions to the development of adequate self-concepts as potentially available in many other human situations. Most people are less self-actualizing than desirable because they are cluttered up with conditions of worth. Rogers increasingly turned his attentions to the problems of the less disturbed. Relationships between partners, whether marital or otherwise, can have growth-inducing properties in which conditions of worth dissolve and the level of self-regard increases. In *Becoming Partners*, Rogers (1973) gave a moving case study involving Joe's steady and healing concern for and trust in Irene's potential, despite her initial self-conception that 'I don't let you see this little, black, rotten, ugly ball I have buried down inside that's really me, that's unlovable and unacceptable' (Rogers, 1973, p. 100).

Rogers also turned his attention to the under-realized potential of educational institutions for creating emotional climates for the development of healthy self-concepts. He particularly favoured significant experiential learning which was self-initiated and reflected the concerns of students rather than those of teachers or administrators (Rogers, 1969). In addition, he focused on the politics of interpersonal and intergroup relationships and saw his faith in the actualizing tendency as indicating a more democratic sharing of power and control (Rogers, 1977).

MAINTENANCE

For practising counsellors and therapists the question is not so much how clients become the way they are, as what currently causes them to maintain behaviour which does not meet their real needs. The concept of maintenance, or of how maladjusted behaviour and perceptions are perpetuated, often in the face of conflicting evidence, is critical to a full understanding of person-centred theory and practice. Person-centred theory may be viewed as a theory of human information processing or of the processing of experiences into perceptions. This is a process in which, especially for those who are disturbed, conditions of worth play a large part.

Processing of experience

Rogers observed that when experiences occur in people's lives there are four possible outcomes. First, like the sensation of sitting, they may be ignored. Second, they may be accurately perceived and organized into some relationship with the self-concept either because they meet a need of the self or because they are consistent with the self-concept and thus reinforce it. Third, their perception may be distorted in such a way as to resolve the conflict between self-concept and experiencing. For instance, students with low academic self-concepts may receive some positive feedback about their essays and perceive that 'The teacher did not read it properly', or 'The teacher must have low standards'. Fourth, the experiences may be denied or not perceived at all. For example, people may have had their self-concepts deeply influenced by strict moral upbringings and thus be unable to perceive their cravings for sexual satisfaction.

Box 4.3 represents the processing of experience by low-

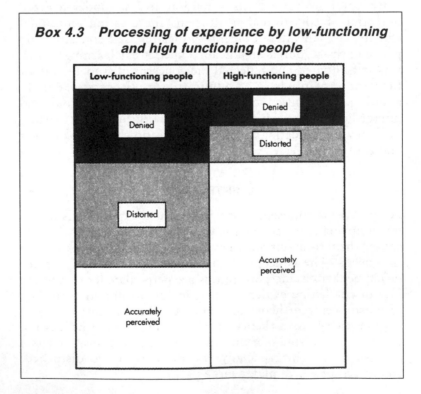

Box 4.3   Processing of experience by low-functioning and high functioning people

functioning and high-functioning people. I previously mentioned that people have two valuing processes: their own organismic valuing process and an internalized process based on conditions of worth. Low-functioning people are out of touch with their own valuing process for large areas of their experiencing. In these areas their self-concepts are based on conditions of worth which cause them to distort and deny much of their experiencing. On the other hand, high-functioning people have fewer conditions of worth and are thus able to perceive most of their experiences accurately.

Both high-functioning and low-functioning people are motivated by the actualizing tendency. In addition, they possess a general tendency towards self-actualization, or actualization of that portion of the organism's experience symbolized in the self. The self-concepts of high-functioning people allow them to perceive most significant sensory and visceral experiences and thus their self-actualizing entails no significant blockages to their actualizing tendency. However, with low-functioning people a split occurs and 'the general tendency to actualize the organism may work at cross purposes with the subsystem of that motive, the tendency to actualize the self' (Rogers, 1959, p. 197). Low-functioning people engage in a process of self-actualizing insufficiently based on their organism's own valuing process. Consequently, while high-functioning people are able to interact with others and their environments on the basis of largely realistic information, low-functioning people do not have that capacity to any great extent.

Incongruence between self-concept and experience

When experiences are accurately symbolized and included in the self-concept, there is a state of congruence between self-concept and experience or, stated another way, between the self-concept and the organismic valuing process. When, however, experience is denied and distorted, there exists a state of incongruence between self-concept and experience. This state of incongruence may exist where experiences are positive as well as where they are negative. Counselling and therapy clients tend to have low self-concepts and frequently deny and distort positive feedback from outside as well as inhibit positive feelings from within.

Threat, anxiety and subception

Rogers uses the concept of subception or pre-perception to explain the mechanism by which sensory and visceral experiences relevant to the actualizing tendency may be denied or inaccurately perceived. He quotes McCleary and Lazarus' finding that 'Even when a subject is unable to report a visual discrimination he is still able to make a stimulus discrimination at some level below that required for conscious recognition' (1949, p. 178). Subception involves a filtering of experience in such a way that experiences contradictory and threatening to the self-concept may be excluded or altered. Thus the organism may discriminate the meaning of an experience without using the higher nerve centres involved in conscious awareness or perception. The process of subception is the mechanism of defence of the self-concept in response to threats to its current structure or set of self-conceptions.

Anxiety is a state of uneasiness or tension which is the response of the organism to the 'subception' that a discrepancy or incongruence between self-concept and experience may enter perception or awareness, thus forcing a change in the currently prevailing self-concept. The term 'intensionality' is used to describe characteristics of the individual who is in a defensive state. Intensional reactions include seeing experience in absolute and rigid terms, over-generalization, confusing facts and evaluation, and relying on abstractions rather than on reality testing.

Breakdown and disorganization

This section relates to serious disturbance. The self-concepts of very low-functioning people block their accurate perception of large areas of their significant sensory and visceral experience. If, however, a situation develops in which a significant experience occurs suddenly, or very obviously, in an area of high incongruence, the process of defence may be unable to operate successfully. Thus, not only may anxiety be experienced to the extent to which the self-concept is threatened, but, with the process of defence being unsuccessful, the experience may be accurately symbolized in awareness. People are brought face-to-face with more of their denied experiences than they can handle, with an ensuing state of disorganization and the possibility of a psychotic breakdown. Rogers mentioned that he had known psychotic breakdowns to occur when people sought 'therapy' from many different sources simultaneously and also when clients were prematurely faced with material revealed under the influence of sodium pentathol. Once acute psychotic behaviours have been exhibited, the defensive processes may work to protect people against the pain and anxiety generated by the perception of the incongruence.

Importance of self-concept

A person's self-concept, especially certain self-perceptions which are viewed as central, has been demonstrated to be fundamental to understanding how psychological maladjustment is maintained. The self-concept is so important to people because it is the constellation of their perceptions about themselves and, as such, the means by which they interact with life in such a way as to meet their needs. Effective self-concepts allow people to perceive their experiences realistically, whether they originate within their organisms or in their environments; in other words, such self-concepts allow them open access to their experiences.

Ineffective self-concepts may be maintained tenaciously for a number of reasons. First, as with effective self-concepts, ineffective self-concepts are perceived as the means of need gratification and the source of personal adequacy. Second, ineffective self-concepts contain within them many conditions of worth which may have been functional at one stage of people's lives, but which have outgrown any usefulness they once possessed. Nevertheless, because they originate from people's need for positive regard, they may be deeply embedded in the structure of their self-concepts as a kind of 'emotional baggage'. Third, the more deeply embedded such conditions of worth have become the more tenaciously they are maintained, since to alter them would involve the anxiety of perceiving the incongruence between these self-perceptions and experiencing. Fourth, the conditions of worth have the effect of lowering people's sense of worth and thus making it less likely that they will have the confidence to acknowledge and face their areas of incongruence. There is a threshold area for both high-functioning and low-functioning people in which they may be able to assimilate incongruent perceptions into their self-concepts. This threshold area appears to be narrower and more tightly defined for low-functioning people.

Characteristics of self-concept

Since the idea of self-concept, sometimes expressed as 'self-structure', 'perceived self', 'phenomenal self', or just 'self', is so fundamental to person-centred theory, I briefly review some of its characteristics.

Content areas

People's self-concepts are unique complexes of many different self-conceptions which constitute their way of describing and distinguishing themselves. Some content areas of people's self-concepts include bodily, social, sexual, feelings and emotions, tastes and preferences, work, recreation, intellectual activity, and philosophy and values. People vary in the importance they attach to these various areas and also in the kinds of self-conceptions they have in them. For instance, the shape of their nose may be felt as important by one person while another may be scarcely aware of it. The self-concept may be described in self-referent statements such as 'I am a good carpenter', 'I like ice-cream' and 'Meeting new people makes me nervous'.

Structure or process

The self-concept may be viewed as a structure made up of different self-conceptions related to each other in various ways. The self-concept is also the means or process by which people interact with the environment and by which they ignore, deny, distort or accurately perceive experience.

Central-peripheral

Combs and Snygg (1959) distinguish between the phenomenal self, the organization or pattern of all those aspects which people refer to as 'I' or 'me', and the self-concept, those perceptions about self which are most vital to people themselves and which may be regarded as their very essence. For all people, some self-conceptions are much more central than others, and everyone has their unique way of ordering self-conceptions as central or peripheral, even though this is often more implicit than explicit.

Congruence-incongruence

Many self-conceptions may match the reality of people's experiencing, in which case there is congruence between self-conception and experience. Other self-conceptions may be different in varying degrees from the reality of their experiencing, in which case a state of incongruence exists.

Conditions of worth

Incongruence implies that a self-conception is based on a condition of worth rather than on the organism's own valuing process. For example, an incongruent self-conception for a person may be 'I want to be a doctor', whereas a congruent self-conception may be 'I want to be an artist'. Being a doctor may be based on values internalized from parents, whereas being an artist represents the organism's own valuing process.

Subception and defence

This is an area of self-concept as a process. Experiences may be denied or distorted by the process of subception. This process defends existing self-conceptions by preventing the person from perceiving incongruence and hence possibly changing both self-conceptions and behaviour.

Intensionality-extensionality

Intensionality describes characteristics of a self-concept in a defensive state, for example, rigidity and absence of adequate reality testing. Extensionality describes characteristics of a mature self-concept, such as seeing experience in limited, differentiated terms and testing inferences and abstractions against reality.

Level of self-regard

Another way of expressing 'level of self-regard' is 'the degree to which individuals prize themselves'. Rogers stated that when people's self-concepts were such that no self-experience could be discriminated as more or less worthy of positive regard than any other, they were experiencing unconditional positive self-regard. 'Level of self-acceptance' is another way of stating 'level of self-regard'.

Real-ideal

Whereas real self-conceptions represent my perceptions of how I am, ideal self-conceptions represent my conceptions of how I would most like to be. Both real and ideal self-conceptions form parts of people's self-concept complex.

THERAPY

> *The person-centred approach, then is primarily a way of being that finds its expression in attitudes and behaviours that promote a growth-promoting climate. It is a basic philosophy rather than simply a technique or method.*
>
> Carl Rogers

THERAPEUTIC GOALS

The question of goals in person-centred therapy can be addressed in two ways: first, the goals of individual clients in therapy, and second, overall goals reflecting the human potential for growth. Clients in person-centred therapy are responsible for having their own purposes and goals. Therapists do not tell clients where they should be going or how to get there. At the start of therapy there is no process of assessment and goal-setting. Rather, clients may come with some goals and then, within the context of a safe therapeutic relationship, may choose to reveal further goals and, as therapy progresses, still different goals may emerge. Much of person-centred therapy focuses on helping clients become more in touch with their feelings and organismic valuing process. During this process clients may evolve a greater sense of what truly are their goals. For some clients, working through to what are personal goals, as contrasted with goals that are 'hand-me-downs' from significant others, may take many therapy sessions.

Much of the time, Rogers saw overall goals in terms of characteristics of the fully functioning person (Rogers, 1959, 1961). However, Rogers also wrote a later statement on the qualities of the person of tomorrow who can live in a vastly changed world (Rogers, 1980). He considered that a paradigm shift was taking place from old to new ways of conceptualizing the person. Box 4.4 presents characteristics, albeit overlapping, of the fully functioning person and the person of tomorrow.

Box 4.4   Characteristics of the fully functioning person and the person of tomorrow

The fully functioning person	The person of tomorrow
Open to experience and able to perceive realistically	Openness to the world, both inner and outer
Rational and not defensive	Desire for authenticity
Engaged in existential process of living	Scepticism regarding science and technology
Trusts in organismic valuing process	Desire for wholeness as a human being
Construes experience in extensional manner	The wish for intimacy
Accepts responsibility for being different	Process persons
Accepts responsibility for own behaviour	Caring for others
Relates creatively to the environment	Attitude of closeness towards nature
Accepts others as unique individuals	Anti-institutional
Prizes himself or herself	Trusts the authority within
Prizes others	Material things unimportant
Relates openly and freely on the basis of immediate experiencing	A yearning for the spiritual
Communicates rich self-awareness when desired	

Here I identify six main dimensions or themes concerning goals in Rogers' writings, including the scale he developed with some colleagues to measure process changes in psychotherapy (Walker *et al.*, 1960). Clients might come into therapy at differing levels on these dimensions and then, during the course of successful therapy, move forward to higher levels of functioning.

Openness to experience

A self-concept which allows all significant sensory and visceral experiences to be perceived is the basis for effective functioning. Rogers frequently used the term 'openness to experience' to describe the capacity for realistic perception and observed that 'There is no need for the mechanism of "subception" whereby the organism is forewarned of experiences threatening to the self' (Rogers, 1959, p. 206). Openness to experience makes for more efficient behaviour in that people have a wider perceptual field and are able to behave more often from choice than from necessity. Openness to experience may also increase the possibility of spontaneity and creativity, since people are less bound by the strait-jacket of conditions of worth. In other words, openness to experience enables people to engage in an existential process of living where they are alive, able to handle change, and alert to the range of their choices for creating their lives.

Rationality

A feature of openness to experience is that it allows for rationality. When people are in touch with their actualizing tendency their behaviour is likely to be rational in terms of maintaining and enhancing their organism. Rogers thought it tragic that most people's defences kept them out of touch with how rational they could be. What was earlier described as extensionality rather than intensionality is a characteristic of this rationality.

Personal responsibility

The term 'personal responsibility' refers to people taking responsibility *for* their self-actualizing and not just feeling responsible *to* others. This covers Rogers' ideas of individuals' trust in their organismic valuing process, trust of the authority within, acceptance of responsibility for their own behaviour, and also acceptance of responsibility for being different from others. Personally responsible people, within the existential parameters of death and destiny, are capable of taking control of their lives and of self-actualizing. The person-centred philosophy in many aspects is one of self-control, self-help and personal power, hopefully within the context of caring relationships. Acknowledgement of personal responsibility is a central part of the self-concepts of effective people.

Self-regard

Self-regard is another important part of the self-concepts of effective people. One way of expressing this is that a person possesses a high degree of unconditional self-regard, or self-acceptance. It is a self-regard based on their organismic valuing process rather than on the praise and needs of others. People with a high degree of unconditional self-regard will prize themselves, even though they may not prize all their behaviours and attributes.

Capacity for good personal relationships

Self-acceptance means that people are less likely to be defensive and hence more likely to accept others. The capacity for good personal relationships incorporates Rogers' notions of accepting others as unique individuals, prizing others, relating openly and freely to them on the basis of immediate experiencing, and having the capacity, when appropriate, to communicate a rich self-awareness. These relationships are characterized by mutual concern for both people's self-actualizing. Rogers considered congruence, genuineness or 'realness' to be probably the most important element in the ordinary interactions of life, while empathy has the highest priority where the other person is anxious and vulnerable.

Ethical living

Person-centred theory is based on a view that people, at their core, are trustworthy organisms. This shows itself in the social relations of self-actualizing people in at least two ways. First, they are capable of a wide identification with other human beings, so they are likely to seek others' self-actualizing along with their own. Consequently, they are careful not to infringe the rights of others while pursuing their own ends. Second, they appear to be able to distinguish sharply between ends and means and between good and evil. Qualities which are likely to contribute to such people's ethical living are: trust in internal rather than in external authority; an indifference to material things, such as money and status symbols; an attitude of closeness to and reverence for nature; and a yearning and seeking for spiritual values that are greater than the individual.

PROCESS OF THERAPY

The process of person-centred therapy is built on a basic trust of the client's ability, within a growth-promoting climate, to actualize her or his human potential. Right from the beginning Rogers would encourage clients to assume responsibility for the contents of the therapy sessions. Therapy starts with an invitation indicating that the therapist will be an interested listener to whatever the client wants to share. The following is Rogers' opening statement from a demonstration interview conducted in his later years (Raskin and Rogers, 2000).

> I don't know what you might want to talk about, but I'm very ready to hear. We have half an hour, and I hope that in that half an hour we can get to know each other as deeply as possible, but we don't need to strive for anything, I guess that's my feeling. Do you want to tell me whatever is on your mind?

There is no formal assessment in person-centred therapy since all clients are viewed as being out of touch with their actualizing tendency on account of their conditions of worth. If therapists were, from their own external frames of reference, to assess clients, they would risk replicating the circumstances that had led clients to acquire and maintain their conditions of worth. In addition, therapists avoid any interpretations or placing external constructions on what the client reveals. Rather, they act as companions as clients share whatever seems important at the time. In particular, Rogers would assist clients to express, experience and explore feelings, be they positive, negative, ambivalent or confused, at a rate comfortable to them.

Rogers would define his and the client's role not only through his opening remarks but also by how he listened carefully to what clients communicated without trying to judge or influence their stream of talk in any direction other than their own. Furthermore, Rogers would refuse to let clients place him in roles that allowed him to assume responsibility for directing and leading them. For example, if a client said: 'What do you think I should do?' Rogers would show acceptance and understanding of the client's feeling of really wanting an answer about what to do without usurping the client's authority and supplying the answer. In such situations Rogers might indicate that, without having the answers himself, he hoped he could assist the client to find an answer than was right for him or her. The initial session would end without any attempt to summarize the session or tie up loose ends before closing. Therapist and client would respectfully take their leave of one another.

Person-centred therapy is a process which goes on between as well as within sessions. Though no formal homework is set, clients usually continue the process of therapy by means of their thoughts, feelings and actions between sessions. Subsequent sessions start with clients being allowed to assume responsibility about where to begin: for instance, with an opening remark such as 'Where would you like to start today?' Again, Rogers would attempt to provide a growth-promoting climate as clients attempted to get in touch with and experience their own feelings, explore the circumstances of their lives, and settle upon goals and directions that seemed appropriate for them. The same growth-promoting climate allows clients, when ready, to address the issue of terminating therapy and how best to lead their lives afterwards.

A more poetic impression of the process of person-centred therapy can be gathered from one of Rogers' favourite sayings from Lao-Tse.

> It is as though he listened
> and such listening as his enfolds us in a silence
> in which at last we begin to hear
> what we are meant to be.

THE THERAPEUTIC RELATIONSHIP

The therapist in the relationship

How is a growth-promoting relationship achieved? Person-centred therapy does not rely on techniques or on doing things to clients. Rogers believed that in therapy 'it is the *quality* of the interpersonal encounter with the client which is the most significant element in determining effectiveness' (Rogers, 1962, p. 416). Person-centred therapy is a process that can intensely involve the thoughts and feelings of both clients and their therapists. There is a coherence between how person-centred therapists see the origins of clients' self-alienation and inner schisms and how they can assist them to grow and become healed. Person-centred therapists try to provide the attitudinal conditions that are the antidote to the emotional deprivations their clients have experienced.

What are the conditions for client growth and reintegration? In 1957, Rogers presented his six necessary and sufficient conditions for therapeutic personality change. He stated that the following conditions had to exist and continue over a period of time for constructive personality change to occur; also, that 'No other conditions are necessary' (Rogers, 1957, p. 96). First, two people need to be in psychological contact. Second, the client is in a state of incongruence and is vulnerable or anxious. Third, the therapist 'is congruent or integrated in the relationship'. Fourth and fifth, the therapist experiences 'unconditional positive regard for the client', and 'an empathic understanding of the client's internal frame of reference and endeavours to communicate this to the client' (p. 96). Sixth, the therapist is minimally successful in communicating empathic understanding and unconditional positive regard to the client. Rogers regarded congruence, unconditional positive regard and empathy as 'the attitudinal conditions that foster therapeutic growth' (Rogers and Sanford, 1985, p. 1379). He stressed that they were not all-or-nothing conditions, but exist on continua.

Congruence

Other words for congruence are genuineness, realness, openness, transparency and presence. Congruence is the most basic of the attitudinal conditions. Therapists need to be in touch with the feelings they experience, have them available to awareness, and 'to live these feelings, be them in the relationship, and ... communicate them if appropriate' (Rogers, 1962, p. 417). Therapists should encounter their clients in direct person-to-person contact. They should avoid an intellectual approach in which clients are treated as objects. Congruent therapists are not playing roles, being polite and putting on professional facades.

Rogers acknowledged that no one fully achieves congruence all the time. Imperfect human beings can be of assistance to clients. It is enough for therapists, in particular moments in immediate relationships with specific persons, to be completely and fully themselves with their experiences accurately symbolized into their self-concepts.

Congruence does not mean that therapists 'blurt out impulsively every passing feeling' (Rogers, 1962, p. 418). Nor does it mean that they allow their sessions to become therapist-centred rather than client-centred. However, it can mean that they take the risk of sharing a feeling or giving feedback that might improve the relationship because it is genuinely expressed. An example is that of therapists sharing their experience of fatigue rather than trying to cover it up. Such openness may restore the therapist's energy level and allow the client to see that they are dealing with a real person. Another example is that Rogers believed that, if he felt persistently bored with a client, he owed it to the client and their relationship to share the feeling. He would own the bored feeling as located in himself rather than make it into an accusatory statement. He would also communicate his discomfort at sharing the feeling and state that he would like to be more in touch with the client. Rogers strove to overcome the barrier between them by being real, imperfect and sharing his genuine feeling. He would hope that the client could use this as a stepping stone to speak more genuinely.

Another insight into congruence may be obtained from what Rogers says about the concept of presence. In therapy, both therapists and clients can attain altered states of consciousness in which they feel they are in touch with and grasp the meaning of the underlying evolutionary flow (Rogers, 1980, 1986a). There can be a mystical and spiritual dimension in counselling and therapy. Rogers considered he was at his best as a therapist when he was closest to his inner intuitive self and 'when perhaps I am in a slightly altered state of consciousness. Then simply my *presence* is releasing and helpful to the other' (Rogers, 1980, p. 129). In such a state, behaviours which may be strange, impulsive and hard to justify rationally turn out to be right. Rogers wrote: 'it seems that my inner spirit has reached out and touched the inner spirit of the other. Our relationship transcends itself and becomes a part of something larger. Profound growth and healing and energy are present' (Rogers, 1980, p. 129).

Unconditional positive regard

Other terms used to describe this condition include non-possessive warmth, caring, prizing, acceptance and respect. Unconditional positive regard relates to Rogers' deep trust in his clients' capacity for constructive change if provided with the right nurturing conditions. Rogers stressed the importance of the therapist's attitude towards the worth and significance of each person. The therapist's own struggles for personal integration are relevant to unconditional positive regard since they can only be respectful of clients' capacities to achieve constructive self-direction if that respect is an integral part of their own personality make-up.

Unconditional positive regard involves the therapist's willingness for clients 'to *be* whatever immediate feeling is going on – confusion, resentment, fear, anger, courage, love, or pride' (Rogers, 1986a, p. 198). This respect is equivalent to the love expressed by the Christian concept of 'agape', without any romantic or possessive connotations. Rogers makes the analogy between the kind of love parents can feel for their children, prizing them as people regardless of their particular behaviour at any moment. Therapists do not show positive regard for their clients – *if*: *if* they are smarter, less defensive, less vulnerable and so on. Person-centred theory explains the need for clients to seek therapy because in their pasts they were shown positive regard – *if*.

There are boundaries to showing unconditional positive regard, for instance, if a client were to physically threaten a therapist. Further, unconditional positive regard does not mean that therapists need, from their frames of reference, to approve of all their clients' behaviours. Rather, unconditional positive regard is an attitude and philosophical orientation, reflected in therapist behaviour, that clients are more likely to move forward if they feel prized for their humanity and they experience an emotional climate of safety and freedom in which, without losing their therapist's acceptance, they can show feelings and relate events.

Empathy

Other terms for empathy include accurate empathy, empathic understanding, empathic responsiveness, an empathic way of being, an empathic stance, and an empathic attitude. Rogers (1957) wrote: 'To sense the client's private world as if it were your own, but without ever losing the "as if" quality – this is empathy' (p. 99). There are various facets to an empathic way of being with clients. Therapists need to 'get into the shoes' and 'under the skin' of their clients to understand their private subjective worlds. They need to be sensitive to the moment-by-moment flow of experiencing that goes on both in clients and themselves. They need the capacity to pick up nuances and sense meanings of which clients are scarcely aware. With tact, sensitivity and awareness of what clients can handle, they need to communicate their understandings of their sensings of clients' worlds and personal meanings.

Therapists should communicate their commitment to understanding their clients' worlds by frequently checking the accuracy of their understandings and showing their willingness to be corrected. Empathy is an active process in which therapists desire to know and reach out to receive clients' communications and meanings (Barrett-Lennard, 1998). An empathic attitude creates an emotional climate in which clients can assist their therapists to understand them more accurately.

Responding to individual client statements is a process of listening and observing, resonating, discriminating, communicating and checking your understanding. Needless to say, the final dimension is that the client has, to some extent, perceived the therapist's empathy. Even better is that the therapist's empathy has enabled the client to be more in touch with the flow of her or his experiencing. Box 4.5, taken from a demonstration film (1965) with Rogers as the therapist, illustrates this process. The client, Gloria, is talking about

Box 4.5   Dimensions of the empathy process

Gloria's statement

I don't know what it is. You know when I talk about it it feels more flip. If I just sit still a minute, it feels like a great big hurt down there. Instead, I feel cheated.

Rogers' responding processes

Observing and listening: Observes and listens to the client's verbal, vocal and bodily communication.

Resonating: Feels some of the emotion the client experiences.

Discriminating: Discriminates what is really important to the client and formulates this into a response.

Communicating: 'It's much easier to be a little flip because then you don't feel that big lump inside of hurt.' Communicates a response that attempts to show understanding of the client's thoughts, feelings and personal meanings. Accompanies verbal with good vocal and bodily communication.

Checking: In this instance, Gloria quickly made her next statement which followed the train of her experiencing and thought. However, Rogers could either have waited and allowed Gloria space to respond or enquired if his response was accurate.

Gloria's perception of Rogers' responding

How Gloria reacted indicated she perceived that Rogers showed excellent empathy and that she was able to continue to get more in touch with her experiencing.

how her father could never show he cared for her the way she would have liked.

Though the next example of empathy comes from an encounter group (Rogers, 1975, p. 3), the empathic process it demonstrates holds true when working with individual clients. A man has been making vaguely negative statements about his father. First, the facilitator enquires whether he might be angry with his father. When the man says he doesn't think so, the facilitator says 'Possibly dissatisfied with him?', to which the man rather doubtfully responds 'Well, yes, perhaps.' The facilitator then enquires whether the man is disappointed in his father, to which he quickly responds, 'That's it! I *am* disappointed that he's not a strong person. I think I've always been disappointed in him ever since I was a boy.'

In this example the facilitator is not interpreting the client, nor would Rogers. Rather, the facilitator progressively checks out his understanding to grasp exactly what the man wishes to say. Gendlin (1988) mentions how Rogers would take in each correction until the client indicated 'Yes, that's how it is. That's what I feel' (p. 127). Characteristically this statement would be followed by a silence in which the client fully received the empathic understanding. Very often during these silences, clients would get in touch with something deeper.

A word now about what empathy is not. True empathy has no judgemental or diagnostic quality about it. In addition, empathy is most definitely not a 'wooden technique of pseudo-understanding in which the counselor "reflects back what the client has just said"' (Rogers, 1962, p. 420). In his 1975 article on empathy, Rogers observed how at first he found it helpful to believe that the best response was to 'reflect' feelings back to clients, but that later on in his career the word 'reflect' made him cringe. Still unhappy with the term 'reflection of feelings', Rogers later suggested that therapists' mirroring responses would be better labelled as 'Testing Understanding' or 'Checking Perceptions' (Rogers, 1986b). To Rogers, empathy was an attitude, a very special form of companionship, a gentle and sensitive way of being with clients. However well intended, mechanical reflections form no part of offering empathy.

The client in the relationship

Here, I draw parallels between how the presence of the three therapist attitudinal conditions of congruence, unconditional positive regard and empathy can promote the growth of client congruence, unconditional positive regard and empathy.

Congruence

Given the right growth-promoting emotional climate, clients will feel less need to be defensive and to look for external regard. Though painful at times, they may progressively take more risks in disclosing themselves to their therapists. Therapists who accept clients and prize their rights to be their true selves allow them to share parts of themselves that they may find embarrassing, abnormal or frightening. They also give clients the opportunity to share parts of themselves that they like, without being negatively judged for such disclosures. As the therapy relationship develops, a mutuality of congruence can develop between therapist and client with each making it easier for the other to be real in the relationship. For some clients, the relationship can transcend itself into becoming a profound spiritual experience in which they, like their therapists, attain an altered state of consciousness. A further outcome of successful person-centred therapy is that clients become more congruent in their outside relationships.

Unconditional positive regard

Here I refer to clients' regard for themselves rather than for their therapists. Clients generally lack self-esteem. Rogers (1975) suggested a number of ways in which an empathic attitude may raise clients' level of regard. First, having the hidden and unacceptable parts of themselves understood and accepted dissolves clients' alienation and helps connect them to the human race. Second, being cared for and valued for their true selves allows clients to think, 'this other individual trusts me, thinks I'm worthwhile. Perhaps I *am* worth something. Perhaps *I* could value *myself*. Perhaps I could care for myself' (p. 7). Third, not being judged by their therapists may lead clients to judge themselves less harshly, thus gradually increasing the possibility of self-acceptance. In addition, as clients gain in self-esteem, they are likely to shift their locusof-evaluation from other people's standards and beliefs to their own. Thus, they become less vulnerable to the damaging effects of conditions of worth.

Empathy

The three therapist attitudinal conditions make it easier for clients to be empathic to themselves both inside and outside of therapy. At varying rates, clients' self-concepts can allow more of their experiencing into awareness. Having their feelings sensitively listened to provides clients with the opportunity to experience and explore these feelings and so understand themselves better. Furthermore, clients learn the importance of listening on their own to their feelings as a guide to their actions and future directions. The more empathic clients are able to be to themselves, the more likely they are to experience and show empathy to their therapists and other people, thus improving the quality of their relationships with them.

THERAPEUTIC INTERVENTIONS

Person-centred therapy is unique among the therapies covered in this book in that Rogers considered a growth promoting relationship characterized by the attitudinal conditions necessary and sufficient for client change to occur. The same attitudinal conditions are relevant when dealing with clients' feelings towards therapists. Rogers considered that some client feelings towards their therapists were understandable responses to therapist behaviour, whereas other feelings were projections 'transferred' from previous relationships. Even in dealing with clients' transference feelings, there was no call for special interventions, such as interpreting the transference. Rogers observed, whether the feelings be therapist-caused or transference reactions, 'If the therapist is sensitively understanding and genuinely acceptant and non-judgemental, then therapy will move forward through these feelings' (Rogers, 1990, p. 130).

CASE MATERIAL

Rogers was very diligent in providing case material and researching the processes and outcomes of person-centred therapy. Readers are encouraged to explore primary sources to get a feel for how Rogers worked. The following are some suggestions about where to look. In *Counseling and Psychotherapy*, Rogers provides a transcript and some commentary for each of his eight sessions with Herbert Bryan, a young man in his late twenties whom he regarded as definitely neurotic (Rogers, 1942). In *On Becoming a Person*, Rogers provides two excerpts from the case of Mrs Oak, a housewife in her late thirties who was experiencing difficulties in marital and family relationships (Rogers, 1961). Rogers' work with Gloria is both on film (Rogers, 1965) and written up as a case example (Raskin and Rogers, 2000). Raskin and Rogers also provided an example of the first and final thirds of a demonstration interview conducted by Rogers in 1983 illustrating the process of therapy, followed by a brief commentary. Elsewhere, Rogers presented excerpts and commentary from another demonstration interview with a woman called Jan, conducted before a workshop of 600 participants in Johannesburg, South Africa (Rogers, 1986a).

FURTHER DEVELOPMENTS

Person-centred therapy has been presented here in relation to individual work. However, Rogers' interests and influence were much more extensive. Rogers championed the use of person-centred principles in encounter groups, classroom teaching, management, and peace and conflict resolution.

Rogers has also influenced other people to develop his ideas. For example, in Britain Dave Mearns has been addressing the concept of *relational depth* between therapists and clients and how best to train for it (Mearns, 1997). The Canadian psychologist David Rennie has developed what he terms an experiential approach to person-centred therapy (Rennie, 1998). Rennie's approach revolves around clients' and therapists' *reflexivity*, which he defines as self-awareness and agency within that self-awareness. Rennie's approach goes beyond empathic responding to focus on both client and therapist processes. Two elements of process work are process *identification* – 'I notice that you seem to have come to a halt'; and process *direction* – 'I don't know if it would be useful or not, but one thing you could try would be to see if you can make contact with the feeling of *being* stuck' (Rennie, 1998, p. 119).

Rogers' influence pervades the work of therapists of other theoretical orientations: for example, today all competent cognitive and cognitive-behavioural therapists heavily emphasize the quality of the relationship when assessing clients and delivering interventions. Rogers has also influenced many therapists who describe themselves as eclectic. For example, some eclectic therapists might use a person-centred approach as the treatment of choice for some clients either at the start of or throughout therapy. Furthermore, eclectic therapists can also integrate a more client-focused approach into how they apply interventions derived from many other theoretical positions. However, for many person-centred therapists such eclecticism or integration of person-centred ideas and practices constitutes a violation of the person-centred approach as a coherent functional philosophy.

The development of person-centred therapy and therapists proceeds by means of journals and training centres. Journals devoted to Rogers' approach include *The Person-Centered Journal* and *Person-Centred Practice*. Training opportunities for developing person-centred counselling and therapy skills are provided in numerous countries throughout the world (Barrett-Lennard, 1998).

SUMMARY

- *Person-centred or client-centred theory emphasizes the importance of people's subjective self-concept, which consists of the ways in which they perceive and define themselves.*
- *The actualizing tendency inherent in the organism to maintain and enhance itself is people's single motivating drive.*
- *Very early on in life human beings start to develop a self-concept. Many of the self-conceptions which form the self-concept are likely to be based on the organism's own valuing process. However, other self-conceptions reflect internalized conditions of worth or the values of others treated as if they were based on the organism's own valuing process. Thus a conflict arises between the actualizing tendency and the self-concept, which is a subsystem of the actualizing tendency, in that conditions of worth impede accurate perception of both inner and outer experiences.*
- *Subception is the mechanism by which the organism dis-*

criminates experience at variance with the self-concept. Depending on the degree of threat inherent in the experience, the organism may defend its self-concept by denying the experience or distorting its perception. People are psychologically well to the extent that their self-concepts allow them to perceive all their significant sensory and visceral experiences.

- *Six key characteristics of the self-concepts of fully functioning or self-actualizing persons are: openness to experience, rationality, personal responsibility, self-regard, capacity for good personal relations, and ethical living.*
- *Clients in person-centred therapy are responsible for finding and formulating their own goals and directions. Such goals may emerge and become clearer during therapy.*
- *The process of person-centred therapy emphasizes clients taking responsibility for the contents of therapy sessions and working on material that has personal meaning for them.*
- *The central assumption of person-centred therapy is that if therapists provide clients with certain growth-promoting attitudinal conditions then constructive personality change will occur.*
- *The person-centred therapist provides to all clients the same attitudinal conditions of congruence, unconditional positive regard and empathy.*
- *The impact of these attitudinal conditions on clients leads them to possess more congruence, self-regard and empathy. In short, clients are in the process of becoming individuals and regulating their own lives.*
- *Further developments in person-centred therapy include elaborating the concept of relational depth and focusing on process identification and direction.*

REVIEW AND PERSONAL QUESTIONS

Review questions

1. Critically review Rogers' concept of the actualizing tendency. What evidence might support or negate Rogers' views about the concept?
2. What does Rogers mean by organismic valuing process?

3. What does Rogers mean by the terms experience, experiencing and awareness?
4. What are conditions of worth and how do they develop?
5. Specify how low-functioning people process their experiences differently from high-functioning people.
6. With reference to a person's self-concept and experience, what does Rogers mean by the term incongruence? Provide an example.
7. Why does Rogers present how to conduct therapy in terms of growth-promoting attitudinal conditions rather than techniques?
8. Describe each of the three therapist-offered growth-promoting attitudinal conditions.
9. In what ways do clients change both during and at the end of successful person-centred therapy?
10. What do you consider the strengths and weaknesses of Rogers' model of the person?
11. What do you consider the strengths and weaknesses of Rogers' model of therapy?

Personal questions

1. Are you aware of any of your conditions of worth? If so, what are they and how did you acquire each of them?
2. Examine a past or current relationship which you think has helped or is helping you to attain a more adequate self-concept. What characteristics of the other person were or are helpful?
3. Examine a past or current relationship which you think has hindered you from attaining a more adequate self-concept. What characteristics of the other person were or are harmful?
4. Assess yourself on each of the following attributes of fully functioning or self-actualizing people: openness to experience, rationality, personal responsibility, self-regard, capacity for good personal relationships, and ethical living.
5. If you conduct therapy, how congruent are you and how do you know?
6. If you conduct therapy, how well do you offer unconditional positive regard and how do you know?
7. If you conduct therapy, how empathic are you and how do you know?

8. What relevance, if any, has the theory and practice of person-centred therapy for how you conduct therapy?
9. What relevance, if any, has the theory and practice of person-centred therapy for how you live?

ANNOTATED BIBLIOGRAPHY

Rogers, C. R. (1959) 'A theory of therapy, personality, and inter-personal relationships, as developed in the client-centred framework', in S. Koch (ed.) *Psychology: A Study of Science* (Study 1, Vol. 3, pp. 184–256). New York: McGraw-Hill.

Rogers regarded this chapter as one of his most significant publications. He worked for three or four years on it and was proud of its thoroughness and rigour. He endeavoured to make every major statement in it something that could be tested by research. This chapter is the major reference for readers wishing to understand Rogerian theory.

Rogers, C. R. (1951) *Client-centered Therapy*. Boston, MA: Houghton Mifflin.

This book describes the attitudinal orientation of the counsellor, the therapeutic relationship experienced by the client, the process of counselling, and various issues and applications of the client-centred approach. The book concludes with an important nineteen-proposition statement of Rogers' theory of personality and behaviour.

Rogers, C. R. (1957). 'The necessary and sufficient conditions of therapeutic personality change'. *Journal of Consulting Psychology*, **21**, 95–103.

Also regarded by Rogers as one of his most significant publications, this article presents and discusses six conditions for effective counselling practice. It elaborates the counsellor conditions of congruence, unconditional positive regard and empathic understanding.

Rogers C. R. (1961) *On Becoming a Person*. Boston, MA: Houghton Mifflin.

Another publication regarded by Rogers as one of his most significant. Rogers acknowledged the book as certainly his most popular and thought it had spoken to people all over the world. The book comprises seven parts: speaking personally; how can I be of help?; the process of becoming a person; a philosophy of persons; the place of research in psychotherapy; what are the implications for living?; and the behavioural sciences and the person.

Rogers C. R. (1975) 'Empathic: An unappreciated way of being'. *The Counseling Psychologist*, 5, 2–10.

This paper, reprinted in *A Way of Being*, is Rogers' re-evaluation of the attitudinal condition of empathy. It is his major statement on the subject.

Rogers, C. R. (1980) *A Way of Being*. Boston, MA: Houghton Mifflin.

A collection of fifteen papers written between 1960 and 1980, this book is divided into four parts: personal experiences and perspectives; aspects of a person-centred approach; the process of education – and its future; and looking ahead – a person-centred scenario. This book is written in the same reader-friendly style as *On Becoming a Person*.

Kirschenbaum, H. and Henderson, V. L. (eds) (1990) *The Carl Rogers Reader*. London: Constable.

The portable Rogers. Rogers had begun to work on a selection of his writings before his death in 1987. This book contains thirty-three selections from Rogers' life work of books and articles divided into nine sections: speaking personally; the therapeutic relationship; the person in process; theory and research; a human science; education; the helping professions; a philosophy of persons; and a more human world.

Raskin, N. J. and Rogers, C. R. (2000) 'Person-centered therapy', in R. J. Corsini and D. Wedding (eds) *Current Psychotherapies* (6th edn, pp. 133–67). Itasca, IL: Peacock.

An authoritative overview of the theory and practice of person-centred therapy based on a chapter originally written by Rogers.

Mearns, D. and Thorne, B. (1999) *Person-centred Counselling in Action* (2nd edn). London: Sage.

Engagingly written, this best-selling text introduces person-centred theory and practice in a way that clearly and sensitively brings to life the processes going on within and between counsellors and clients. The book's eight chapters are: the person-centred approach; the counsellor's use of the self; empathy; unconditional positive regard; congruence; 'beginnings'; 'middles'; and 'endings'.

REFERENCES

Barrett-Lennard, G. T. (1998) *Carl Rogers' Helping System: Journey and Substance*. London: Sage.

Cohen, D. (1997) *Carl Rogers: A Critical Biography*. London: Constable.

Combs, A. W. and Snygg, D. (1959) *Individual Behavior* (rev. edn). New York: Harper and Row.

Gendlin, E. T. (1988) 'Carl Rogers (1902–1987)'. *American Psychologist*, **43**, 127–8.

Gordon, T. (1970) *Parent Effectiveness Training: The Tested New Way to Raise Responsible Children*. New York: Wyden.

Kirschenbaum, H. and Henderson, V. L. (eds) (1990) *The Carl Rogers Reader*. London: Constable.

McCleary, R. A. and Lazarus, R. S. (1949) 'Autonomic discrimination without awareness'. *Journal of Personality*, **18**, 171–9.

Maslow, A. H. (1962) *Toward a Psychology of Being*. Princeton, NJ: Van Nostrand.

Maslow, A. H. (1970) *Motivation and Personality* (2nd edn). New York: Harper and Row.

Mearns, D. (1997) *Person-centred Counselling Training*. London: Sage.

Mearns, D. and Thorne, B. (1999) *Person-centred Counselling in Action* (2nd edn). London: Sage.

Raskin, N. J. and Rogers, C. R. (2000) 'Person-centered therapy', in R. J. Corsini and D. Wedding (eds) *Current Psychotherapies* (6th edn, pp. 133–67). Itasca, IL: Peacock.

Rennie, D. L. (1998) *Person-centred Counselling: An Experiential Approach*. London: Sage.

Rogers, C. R. (1939) *The Clinical Treatment of the Problem Child*. Boston, MA: Houghton Mifflin.

Rogers, C. R. (1942) *Counseling and Psychotherapy*. Boston, MA: Houghton Mifflin.

Rogers, C. R. (1951) *Client-centered Therapy*. Boston, MA: Houghton Mifflin.

Rogers, C. R. (1957) 'The necessary and sufficient conditions of therapeutic personality change'. *Journal of Consulting Psychology*, **21**, 95–103.

Rogers, C. R. (1959) 'A theory of therapy, personality, and interpersonal relationships, as developed in the client-centred framework', in S. Koch (ed.) *Psychology: A Study of Science* (Study 1, Vol. 3, pp. 184–256). New York: McGraw-Hill.

Rogers C. R. (1961) *On Becoming a Person*. Boston, MA: Houghton Mifflin.

Rogers, C. R. (1962) 'The interpersonal relationship: the core of guidance'. *Harvard Educational Review*, **32**, 416–29.

Rogers, C. R. (1969) *Freedom to Learn*. Columbus, OH: Charles E. Merrill.

Rogers, C. R. (1970) *Encounter Groups*. London: Penguin Books.

Rogers, C. R. (1973) *Becoming Partners: Marriage and its Alternatives*. London: Constable.
Rogers, C. R. (1974) 'In retrospect: forty-six years'. *American Psychologist*, 29, 115–23.
Rogers C. R. (1975) 'Empathic: an unappreciated way of being'. *The Counseling Psychologist*, 5, 2–10.
Rogers, C. R. (1977) *Carl Rogers on Personal Power*. London: Constable.
Rogers, C. R. (1980) *A Way of Being*. Boston, MA: Houghton Mifflin.
Rogers, C. R. (1986a) 'A client-centered/person-centered approach to therapy', in I. Kutash and A. Wolf (eds) *Psychotherapist's Casebook: Theory and Technique in the Practice of Modern Therapies* (pp. 197–208). San Francisco: Jossey Bass. Reproduced in Kirschenbaum and Henderson (eds) (1990) *The Carl Rogers Reader*, pp. 135–52.
Rogers, C. R. (1986b) 'Reflection of feelings'. *Person-Centred Review*, 1, 375–7.
Rogers, C. R. (1990) 'Reflection of feelings and transference', in H. Kirschenbaum and V. Henderson (eds) *The Carl Rogers Reader* (pp. 127–34). London: Constable.
Rogers, C. R. and Sanford, R. A. (1985) 'Client-centered psychotherapy', in H. I. Kaplan, B. J. Sadock and A. M. Friedman (eds) *Comprehensive Textbook of Psychiatry* (4th edn, pp. 1374–88). Baltimore, MA: William & Wilkins.
Thorne, B. (1992) *Carl Rogers*. London: Sage.
Walker, A. M., Rablen, R. A. and Rogers, C. R. (1960) 'Development of a scale to measure process changes in psychotherapy'. *Journal of Clinical Psychology*, 16, 79–85.

Rogers on film

Rogers, C. R. (1965) 'Client-centred therapy', in E. Shostrom (ed.) *Three Approaches to Psychotherapy*. Santa Ana, CA: Psychological Films.

5

Gestalt Therapy

*Every individual, every plant, every animal has only
one inborn goal – to actualise itself as it is.*

Fritz Perls

INTRODUCTION

Gestalt therapy, according to Perls, its main originator, is an existential approach 'not just occupied with dealing with symptoms or character structure, but with the total existence of a person' (Perls, 1969a, p. 71). Towards the end of his life Perls wrote that he considered gestalt therapy to be one of the three then-existing types of existential therapy: the two others being Frankl's logotherapy and Binswanger's daseins therapy. Clients who come for gestalt therapy are in states of existential crisis and need to learn to take responsibility for their existences. Perls considered that all other existential philosophies borrowed concepts from other sources: for example, Binswanger from psychoanalysis, Tillich from Protestantism, and Sartre from Communism. Gestalt therapy is the only existential approach which has support in its own formation since gestalt formation, the emergence of needs, is a primary biological phenomenon. He observed: 'Gestalt therapy is a philosophy that tries to be in harmony, in alignment with everything else, with medicine, with science, with the universe, with what *is*' (Perls, 1969a, p. 17).

FRITZ PERLS (1893–1970)

Friederich (Frederick or Fritz) Soloman Perls was born in Berlin, the son of a Jewish travelling salesman of Palestinian wines. He grew up with his two sisters in a disturbed family in which his parents had many bitter fights, both verbal and physical. Perls' mother used carpet-beating rods on him but he claims she did not break his spirit, rather he broke the carpet-beaters. He saw his father as a hypocrite who preached one thing and lived another and who progressively isolated himself from his family. Perls wrote: 'Basically I hated him and his pompous righteousness, but he could also be loving and warm. How much my attitude was influenced by my mother's hatred of him, how much she poisoned us children with it, I could not say' (Perls, 1969b, pp. 250–1). During his puberty years, a period during which he was initiated into both sex and acting, Perls was the black sheep of his family. Throughout his life he was a rebel rather than a complier, a man with a very quick eye for others' phoniness and pseudo-authenticity, and somewhat of an exhibitionist himself. His early experiences of rejection and insecurity may have deeply influenced his later life.

Perls' ideas were largely formed in the Austro-Germanic world. On leaving high school, he enrolled as a medical student at Berlin University. At the start of the First World War, Perls had been declared physically unfit for active service. However, by 1916 fitness requirements were much lower and Perls interrupted his medical studies to serve as a medical officer, including a spell in the trenches from 1916 to 1917. In 1918 Perls returned to being a student at the universities of Freiburg and Berlin, and in 1920 he received his MD from the latter institution.

In 1926 Perls moved to Frankfurt, where he accepted a post as assistant to the gestalt psychologist Kurt Goldstein at the Frankfurt Neurological Institute. Also in 1926, Perls met Laura Posner, whom he was to marry in 1929. Together they shared a strong interest in gestalt psychology. Perls considered he had a peculiar relationship with the gestalt psychologists, admiring much of their work, but unable to go along with them when they became logical positivists. He did not read any of their textbooks, but had read some papers by Lewin, Wertheimer and Kohler. He observed: 'Most important for me was the idea of the unfinished situation, the incomplete gestalt' (Perls, 1969b, p. 62). The academic gestaltists never accepted Perls and he did not regard himself as a pure gestaltist.

For some years, Perls had been undergoing training as a Freudian psychoanalyst. He moved to Vienna in 1927 and a year later completed his analytical training. On returning to

Germany, Perls worked as a certified Freudian psychoanalyst from 1928 to 1933, mainly in Berlin.

In addition to gestalt psychology and Freudian psychoanalysis there were numerous other influences on Perls. He had a love of acting and, early in his life, studied under Max Reinhardt, the noted director of the Deutsche Theater. Reinhardt insisted that his students observe very closely how people express emotions through their voices and gestures (Clarkson and Mackewn, 1993). Perls was also interested in Reich's idea of character armour, whereby repressions and resistances became total organismic functions. Later influences were to include Moreno, with his ideas on therapy by means of psychodrama, American humanistic psychology and Eastern religion, especially Zen Buddhism.

In 1933, with the rise of Hitler, Perls fled from Germany to Holland. Apart from his being a Jew, Fritz and Laura Perls had to leave Germany suddenly to avoid being rounded up by the Nazis because of their left-wing political activism. At the time of his departure his analyst was Wilhelm Reich and his supervisors were Otto Fenichel and Karen Horney. Perls wrote: 'From Fenichel I got confusion; from Reich, brazenness; from Horney, human involvement without terminology' (Perls, 1969b, p. 39). In 1934, on the recommendation of Ernest Jones, Freud's friend and biographer, accompanied by wife and young daughter, Renate, Perls moved to Johannesburg as a training analyst. In 1935, despite Perls wanting her to abort her pregnancy, Laura give birth to their son Stephen, who was to regard Fritz as a distant and disengaged father very much wrapped up in his own world (Perls, 1993).

Fritz and Laura Perls soon had successful private practices and, in 1935, they established the South African Institute for Psychoanalysis. From 1942 to 1945, Perls worked as a South African army medical officer and psychiatrist near Pretoria in the war against the Nazis. During his South African years Perls was influenced by the holism of Jan Smuts, the South African general, prime minister and philosopher. Smuts wrote about the way individuals and the universe are actively 'whole-making' and introduced the idea from physics that everything has a field and that objects and organisms must be considered in relation to their fields (Smuts, 1987). In 1942 Perls' first book *Ego, Hunger and Aggression* was published in South Africa, the British edition being published in 1947 with the subtitle *A Revision of Freud's Theory and Method*. Several chapters in this book were written by Perls' wife Laura, an important collaborator in the founding of gestalt therapy (Yontef and Jacobs, 2000).

In 1946 Perls emigrated to the United States and established a private practice in New York City. Laura and their by now two children joined him in the autumn of 1947. In 1951 Perls published *Gestalt Therapy: Excitement and Growth in the Human Personality*, a book co-authored with Ralph Hefferline, professor of psychology at Columbia University, and Paul Goodman, a social philosopher and writer. Some view Goodman, an uninhibited radical bisexual, as the third co-founder of gestalt therapy (Clarkson and Mackewn, 1993).

In 1952 Perls established the New York Institute of Gestalt Therapy and, in 1954, the Cleveland Institute for Gestalt Psychotherapy. Between 1952 and 1956, Perls had increasing differences of opinion with Laura Perls and Paul Goodman about directions for gestalt therapy. In 1957, partly for health reasons due to a recently diagnosed heart condition, Perls moved to the milder climate of Miami and was never again to live with Laura for any length of time. In Miami, Perls became the friend and lover of Marty Fromm, even as she continued to be in therapy with him (Clarkson and Mackewn, 1993).

In 1960 Perls moved to the West Coast of the United States and, in 1964, joined the staff of the Esalen Institute at Big Sur, California, as resident associate psychiatrist. During this period, Perls began doing gestalt demonstrations on stage in front of increasingly large groups, including illustrating his hot seat technique. However, Perls realized that large group gestalt demonstrations were not gestalt therapy proper. In May 1969, Perls moved to Cowichan on Vancouver Island in British Columbia where he was establishing a gestalt community. Here he was very happy and finally at peace with the world. In December 1969 Perls left Cowichan for what was to be the last time, went to Europe, but was clearly unwell on his return. After a brief illness Perls died in a Chicago hospital of a heart attack on 14 March 1970 at the age of 76. During his final illness, Laura had flown to join him, only to find Perls sometimes confiding in her and sometimes shouting at and ignoring her.

In 1969, Perls had published *Gestalt Therapy Verbatim* and the autobiographical pot-pourri of prose, poetry and psychology entitled *In and Out of the Garbage Pail*. At the time of his death Perls was working on two books: *The Gestalt Approach* and *Eye Witness to Therapy*; these were published posthumously in 1973 as a single book entitled *The Gestalt Approach & Eye Witness to Therapy*.

Perls had extensive experience of personal relations including many affairs. In his autobiographical book *In and Out of The Garbage Pail*, Perls admits to many compulsions including smoking and leching. He also wrote poems and painted. While Perls may have not always possessed the amount of responsibility (response-ability or freedom of choice) for which his therapeutic approach strives, he appears to have been a tremendously vital and charismatic person. The gestalt prayer of this restless gypsy was:

> I do my thing, and you do your thing
> I am not in this world to live up to your expectations
> And you are not in this world to live up to mine.
> You are you, and I am I,
> And if by chance, we find each other, it's beautiful.
> If not, it can't be helped.
>   (Perls, 1969a, inside front cover page)

THEORY

The basic premise of Gestalt psychology is that human nature is organised into patterns or wholes, that it is experienced by the individual in these terms, and that it can only be understood as a function of the patterns or wholes of which it is made.

                                             Fritz Perls

BASIC CONCEPTS

Perls (1973) wrote in his introduction to *The Gestalt Approach & Eyewitness to Therapy* that gestalt theory was grounded in experience and observation, had changed with years of practice and application and was still growing. The following presentation is almost exclusively based on Perls' own writings, some in conjunction with collaborators.

Though others have developed gestalt therapy after Perls' death, no other really major figure has emerged since then.

Gestalt

The German noun *Gestalt* means form or shape, and among the meanings of the verb *gestalten* are to shape, to form, to fashion, to organize and to structure. Other terms for gestalt are pattern, configuration or organized whole. The major thrust of the experimental work of the gestalt psychologists was to show that human beings do not perceive things in isolation but organize them through their perceptual processes into meaningful wholes (for example, a row of dots may be perceived as a straight line).

People's visual fields are structured in terms of 'figure' and 'background' or 'ground'. Whereas 'figure' is the focus of interest (an object or pattern, etc.), 'ground' is the setting or context. Perls and his colleagues (Perls *et al.*, 1951) noted that the interplay between figure and ground was dynamic. For instance, the same ground may with differing interests and shifts of attention give rise to different figures. In addition, a given figure may itself become ground in the event that some detail of its own becomes figure.

The holistic doctrine

The human organism is a unified whole. In particular, Perls objected to the old mind–body split. The emergence of psychosomatic medicine made the close relationship between mental and physical activity increasingly apparent. In fact mental activity seemed to be an activity of the whole person carried out at a lower energy level than those activities called physical. Human beings are wholes engaging in fantasizing, play-acting and doing. For instance, people's actions provide clues as to their thoughts and their thoughts provide clues concerning what they would like to do. In short, people do not have organisms but *are* organisms engaged in activities of the same order which are often wrongly dichotomized into mental and physical activities.

Another erroneous dichotomy is that between self and external world. Individuals are not self-sufficient but can only exist in an environmental field. Environments do not create individuals nor do individuals create environments. Rather, each is what it is because of its relationship to the other and the whole. For instance, in the example of a person seeing a tree, there is no sight without something to be seen, nor is anything seen if there is no eye to see it.

There are numerous other false dichotomies such as those between emotional (subjective) and real (objective); infantile and mature; biological and cultural; love and aggression; and conscious and unconscious. For instance, regarding the split between infantile and mature, it is often lack of certain childhood traits which devitalizes adults while other traits called infantile may be the introjections of adult neuroses. A consistent theme of the gestalt approach is to search for the overall pattern rather than for false dichotomies.

Contact boundary and contact

Earlier, I mentioned that Perls disdained the split between self and the external world, considering that the organism and the environment stood in a relationship of mutuality to one another. The contact boundary is the boundary between organism and environment and it is at this boundary that psychological events take place. Perls and his colleagues (1951) considered that 'psychology studies the operation of the contact-boundary in the organism/environment field' (p. 229). Such 'contact' or 'being in touch with' involves both sensory awareness and motor behaviour. The organism's sensory system provides it with a means of orientation, with the motor system providing a means of manipulation. Both orientation and manipulation take place at the contact boundary. In healthy functioning, once the system of orientation has performed its function, the organism manipulates itself and the environment in such a way that organismic balance is restored and the gestalt is closed.

All thoughts, feelings and actions take place at the contact boundary. In healthy functioning, people have an effective contact withdrawal rhythm or means of meeting psychological events at the contact boundary. Contacting the environment represents forming a gestalt, whereas withdrawal is either closing a gestalt completely or mobilizing resources to make closure possible. More simply, contact and withdrawal may respectively be viewed as acceptance and rejection of the environment. The components of contact and withdrawal are almost invariably present, but the neurotic person has a reduced capacity to discriminate between the appropriateness of these dialectical elements and consequently behaves with reduced effectiveness, as will be seen in the later section on interruptions of contact.

Homeostasis and balance

The basic tendency of every organism is to strive for balance. The organism is continuously faced with imbalance that is disturbing through either external (demands from the environment) or internal (needs) factors. Life is characterized by a continuous interplay of balance and imbalance in the organism. Homeostasis or organismic self-regulation is the process by which the organism satisfies its needs by restoring balance when faced with a demand or need which upsets its equilibrium. Health constitutes the appropriate operation of the homeostatic process, whereas sickness means that for too long a time the organism has remained in a state of disequilibrium, of being unable to satisfy its needs. Death constitutes a total breakdown of the homeostatic process.

Though psychological and physiological are interrelated, the organism may be perceived as having psychological as well as physiological contact needs. A simple example of a physiological need is that, for the organism to be in good health, the water content of the blood must be kept at a certain level, neither too low nor excessive. If, for instance, the water content of the blood falls too low the individual feels thirst, with its symptoms of dry mouth and restlessness and the wish to restore the imbalance by drinking. A possible example of a more psychological need is that of mothers to keep their children happy and contented. Consequently, even when sleeping, they may be very sensitive to the cries and whimpers of their offspring.

The homeostatic process also operates where several needs are experienced simultaneously. However, here a selective process takes place based on the organism's need for survival and for self-actualization; with the simultaneous experiencing of many needs, the individual attends to the dominant survival and self-actualization need before attending to the others. Put another way, the dominant need or the need which presses most sharply for satisfaction becomes the foreground figure while the other needs recede, at least momentarily, into the background. Perls (1969a) wrote about doing away with the whole of instinct theory and simply considering the organism as a system that needs balance if it is to function properly. Though practically people have hundreds of unfinished situations in them, the most urgent situation always emerges. Individuals, in order to be able to satisfy their needs (to complete or to close incomplete *Gestalten*) must be able both to sense what they need and to manipulate themselves and their environments to obtain what is necessary.

Life is basically an infinite number of unfinished situations or incomplete gestalts, with one gestalt no sooner being completed than another comes up. The homeostatic process is the means by which the organism maintains itself, 'and the only law which is constant is the forming of gestalts – wholes, completeness. A gestalt is an organic function. A gestalt is an ultimate experiential unit' (Perls, 1969a, p. 16). With the introduction of the concept of the homeostatic process, it was possible to see gestalt formation as a primary biological drive, with the gestalt being the basic experiential unit having such properties as figure and ground and completeness or incompleteness.

The self and self-actualization

The self is the system of contacts at the contact boundary at any given moment. The self exists where there are boundaries of contact, and its activity is that of forming figures and grounds. The self always integrates the senses, motor co-ordination and organic needs. It is the integrator or artist of life and though it 'is only a small factor in the total organism/ environment interaction ... it plays the crucial role of finding and making the meanings that we grow by' (Perls *et al.*, 1951, p. 235).

The self consists of the identifications and alienations at the contact boundary. For instance, individuals may identify with their families but feel alien to people from different countries. Inside the boundary tends to be perceived as good and outside as bad. Self-actualization may be viewed as the expression of appropriate identifications and alienations. Healthy functioning involves identifying with one's forming organismic self, not inhibiting one's creative excitement, yet alienating what is not organismically one's own. Sickness involves restricting one's areas of contact through alienating parts of one's forming organismic self by means of false identifications.

Perhaps a more accessible way of stating this is to make a distinction between self-actualizing based on the existential principle that 'a rose is a rose is a rose', and self-image actualizing in which people live for their image of how they should be rather than how they are. Perls (1969a) considered: 'Every external control, even *internalised* external control – "you should" – interferes with the healthy working of the organism. There is only one thing that should control: the *situation*' (p. 20). If people understand the situations they are in, and let these situations control their actions, they learn how to cope with life. An even more simple view of Perls' ideas on self-actualization may be gained from his dictum: 'So lose your mind and come to your senses' (Perls, 1970a, p. 38).

Excitement

Human beings secure their energy from the food and air they take in. Perls emphasized vitality and the need to integrate the social being and the animal being. He used the word 'excitement' to describe the energy we create, because it coincides with the physiological function of excitation. This life force or *élan vital* is at the heart of the gestalt approach. Perls observed: 'Now normally the *élan vital*, the life force, energizes by sensing, by listening, by scouting, by describing the world – how is the world there. Now this life force first mobilizes the center – *if* you have a center. And the center of the personality is what used to be called the soul: the emotions, the feelings, the spirit' (Perls, 1969a, p. 68).

Excitement varies according to the task on the basis of hormonal differentiation: for instance, it gets tinged with some other substance, for example, adrenalin for anger, or sexual hormones for erotic contact. Much of our excitement goes into energizing the motor system because the muscles link people with the environment. Even for most emotional events, emotion is transferred into movement. However, some excitement goes into energizing the senses. Healthy people allow their excitement to get to their senses and muscles, but unfortunately many people allow much of their excitement to be drained off into their fantasy life, into their computer (unproductive thinking), and into self-image actualization. Perls (1969a) considered that modern human beings live in a state of low grade vitality in which the average person at most lives only 5 to 15 per cent of their potential and the person who has even 25 per cent of their potential available is considered a genius.

Emotion

Emotion, which is the organism's direct evaluative experience of the organism/environment field, is immediate rather than being regulated by thoughts and verbal judgements. Emotion is a continuous process since all instances in people's lives carry some feeling tone of pleasantness or unpleasantness. Excitement is modified into specific emotions according to the situation that has to be met, and the emotions mobilize the sensory and motor system so that needs may be satisfied. Gestalt therapy attaches great importance to the emotions which are not only essential as energy or excitement regulators but are also 'unique deliveries of experience which have no substitute – they are the way we become aware of our concerns, and, therefore, of what we are and what the world is' (Perls *et al.*, 1951, p. 96).

ACQUISITION

Aggression, assimilation and introjection

An aggressive attitude towards experience is necessary if it is really to be assimilated or made the organism's own. An analogy may be made between the aggression required for eating and that required for assimilating experience. Food needs to be destroyed or destructured before what is valuable to the organism can be retained and undesirable substances can be eliminated. Undesirable substance which is not eliminated may be poisonous and detrimental to the organism. Every organism in an environmental field grows by incorporating, digesting or destructuring, and assimilating or absorbing selectively new matter whether it be food, lectures or parental influence. Loving parents are likely to provide their children with experiences which they will assimilate, since they are relevant to their own needs as they grow from environmental support to self-support.

Not all experience, however, goes through the destructuring and assimilation process required for healthy functioning. Introjections are experiences which are swallowed as a whole rather than being properly digested. The outcome of introjection is that undesirable as well as desirable substances have been retained, thus weakening the organism. Hateful parents are likely to provide their children with experiences which have to be introjected or taken in whole, even though they are contrary to the needs of the organism.

Frustration and manipulation

The young baby is virtually totally dependent on its mother, but as time goes by the child learns to communicate, to crawl and walk, to bite and chew, and to accept and reject. In short the child learns to realize some part of its potential for existence. Growth comes about through learning to overcome frustrations by mobilizing one's innate resources to manipulate the environment in order to satisfy needs. The term 'manipulation' refers to a person's ways of mobilizing and using the environment in order to satisfy needs. Both healthy and unhealthy organisms manipulate the environment, with healthy organisms manipulating it on an underlying basis of self-support, whereas unhealthy organisms are seeking environmental rather than self-support.

Perls wrote: 'Without frustration there is no need, no reason to mobilize your resources, to discover that you might be able to do something on your own, and in order not to be frustrated, which is a pretty painful experience, the child learns to manipulate the environment' (Perls, 1969a, p. 35). Perhaps it would be more accurate to say that with the right kind of frustrations the child learns to manipulate the environment in such a way as to meet its needs and restore effective organismic balance. However, with lack of frustration (the spoilt child) or with frustrations which block or are beyond the child's coping capacity, the outcome is likely to be that the child starts to mobilize the environment by playing phoney roles and games: for instance, playing stupid, playing helpless, playing weak and flattering. These false manipulations cause individuals to alienate parts of themselves, be it their eyes, ears or genitals.

Interruptions of contact

Human beings are forced to learn much more through education than by using their biologically based instincts. Consequently much of the animal's intuition as to what is the 'right' procedure is either missing or blocked. Instead there is a whole range of composite fantasies, handed down and modified through the generations, as to what constitutes the 'right' procedures. These procedures perform largely support functions for social contacts (namely manners and ethics) and have the disadvantage of not necessarily being biologically based. Consequently there are frequent interruptions in the contact provided by ongoing organismic processes which, if left alone, would be conducive to self-support. Examples of such interruptions are 'Don't touch that' or 'Don't do this'. Even withdrawals may be interrupted, as in the example 'You stay here now, keep your mind on your homework and don't dream'. People often incorporate their parents' interruptions as introjections in their own lives, for example, 'Grown men don't cry'. Unhealthy organisms or neurotics are self-interrupters who need to become aware both of the fact that they are interrupting themselves and what they are interrupting.

Suppression of emotion

Suppression of emotion is a major way in which adults interrupt the contact of their children. Such adults, who have frequently been brought up in environments in which 'the authorities' were afraid of emotion, tend to suppress the emotions of their children and thus prevent such emotions from undergoing natural development and differentiation. This is mainly achieved through an overemphasis on the 'external world' and the demands of 'reality' and a belittling of organismic needs and emotions. The outcome of this is that children 'adjust' to such unremitting pressure by dulling their body-sense and losing some of their vitality. However, because emotions are inherent to the organism, this suppression of emotions does not eliminate 'undesirable' emotions; rather, it disturbs 'the intricate organism/environment field by setting up a great number of situations which, *unless avoided, are immensely emotion-arousing!'* (Perls *et al.*, 1951, p. 97).

MAINTENANCE

Though Perls often used the terms 'neurosis' and 'neurotic', he considered that problems of poor gestalt formation and closure were extremely widespread. In this section I examine the gestalt view of how people maintain their contact deficiencies. Needless to say, an individual's difficulties are compounded by living in a culture or environment where self-image actualizing rather than self-actualizing is common.

Zones of awareness

There are three zones or layers of awareness: outer, self and intermediate (see Box 5.1). Perls sometimes used the Indian word *maya* to describe the intermediate zone or DMZ. *Maya* means illusion or fantasy and is a kind of dream or trance. More colloquial and crude is Perl's use of the term 'mind-

---

Box 5.1   The three zones of awareness

The outer zone (OZ)

This zone consists of awareness of the world, of those objects, facts and processes that are available to everyone.

The self zone (SZ)

This zone is the place within the skin, our authentic organismic selves.

The intermediate zone (DMZ)

This zone, which is located within the self zone, is often called 'mind' or consciousness which prevents people from good contact or being 'in touch' with themselves or the world. The DMZ is a zone of fantasy activity which consumes excitement and leaves little energy over for being in touch with reality.

f**king' to describe the activity of the DMZ which hinders people from coming to their senses.

Anxiety and stage fright

Gestalt theory has both a physiological and psychological definition of anxiety. The physiological definition is: 'Anxiety is the experience of breathing difficulty during any blocked excitement' (Perls *et al.*, 1951, p. 128). The idea underlying this definition is that heightened energy mobilization, with the need for more air (an increase in the rate and amplitude of breathing), occurs whenever there is strong concern and contact. As such it is a healthy way of being in erotic, aggressive, creative and other sorts of exciting or energy mobilizing situations. A less healthy response is to control, interfere with and interrupt the excitement by trying to continue breathing at the rate that was adequate prior to it. This leads to a narrowing of the chest to force exhalation in order to create a vacuum into which fresh air can rush. Anxiety, derived from the Latin word *angustia* meaning narrowness, is the product of an emergency measure caused by the conflict between excitement and control.

The psychological definition of anxiety is that it is 'the gap between the now and the later' or 'stage fright' (Perls, 1969a, pp. 32–3). As such it is the result of the fantasy activity of the DMZ. This fantasy activity is rehearsing for a future that people do not really want to have because they are afraid of it. Perls wrote: 'We fill in the gap where there should be a future with insurance policies, status quo, sameness, *anything* so as not to experience the possibility of openness towards the future' (Perls, 1969a, pp. 48–9). People who are in the now and have access to their senses are unlikely to be anxious because their excitement can flow immediately into the kind of spontaneous, creative and inventive activity which achieves solutions to unfinished situations. They are not blocked from good contact with themselves and the environment by *maya* or fantasies, prejudices, apprehensions and so on. They are prepared to take reasonable risks in living. Perls distinguished between catastrophic fantasies which entail too much precaution, and anastrophic fantasies which entail too little. He believed some people managed a balance between catastrophic and anastrophic fantasies, thus having both perspective and rational daring.

Neurosis

Neurotic individuals allow society to impinge too heavily on them. They cannot clearly distinguish their own needs and see society as larger than life and themselves as smaller. Society may consist of any one of a number of groups, for example, the family, the state, the social circle and co-workers. When the neurotic and one or more of these groups simultaneously experience different needs, the neurotic is incapable of distinguishing which need is dominant and thus can make neither a good contact nor a good withdrawal. Consequently one or more of the contact boundary disturbances of neurosis seem the most effective way to maintain balance and a sense of self-regulation in situations where the odds appear to be overwhelmingly adverse.

Perls distinguished between health, psychosis and neurosis. In health, people are in touch with the realities both of themselves and the world. In psychosis, people are out of touch with reality and in touch with *maya*, especially fantasies about megalomania and worthlessness. In neurosis a continual fight is taking place between *maya* and reality.

Contact boundary disturbances

The neuroses, which entail significant contact boundary disturbances, operate primarily through four mechanisms, albeit interrelated. These neurotic boundary disturbances are 'nagging, chronic, daily interferences with the processes of growth and self-recognition' (Perls, 1973, p. 32). However, not all disturbances in the organism/environment search for balance are evidence of or produce neurosis. Introjection, projection, confluence and retroflection are the four mechanisms of contact boundary disturbance.

Introjection

I have already mentioned introjection as the process by which material from outside is swallowed whole rather than digested properly with the valuable elements being assimilated and the

undesirable or toxic elements discarded. Introjects, or undi-
gested thoughts, feelings and behaviour, are the results of the
process of introjection. Introjection may be viewed as the
tendency to 'own' as part of the self what is actually part of
the environment. Two outcomes of introjection are: first, that
the introjects prevent individuals from getting in touch with
their own reality because all the time they are having to
contend with these foreign bodies; and second, that the
introjects may be incompatible with one another and thus
contribute to personality disintegration.

Projection

This is the reverse of introjection in that it is the tendency to
'own' as part of the environment what actually is part of the
self. Projection can take place on two levels: in relation to the
outer environment and in relation to the self. Perhaps most
commonly, projection involves shifting those parts of ourselves that we dislike and devalue on to others rather than
recognizing and dealing with the tendencies in ourselves.
Projections are associated with introjects because people
usually devalue themselves in relation to introjected self-
standards, whose unacceptable derivatives in terms of self-
evaluations are then projected on to the environment.

Projection in relation to the self takes place when people
disown as part of themselves areas in which certain impulses
arise. For instance, people may say of their anger 'It took
control of me', whereby the anger is given an objective
existence outside of themselves so that they can make it
responsible for their troubles and avoid full recognition of
the fact that *it* is part of *him* or *her*.

Confluence

With confluence, the individual lacks any distinction or
experiences no boundary at all between self and environment.
People who are unaware of the contact boundaries between
themselves and others are neither able to make good contact
with them nor, where appropriate, to withdraw. A feature of
confluence is demanding likeness and refusal to tolerate
differences. Two examples of confluence are marital partners

and parents who, respectively, refuse to see their spouses and children as different from themselves.

Retroflection

In retroflection, the individual fails to discriminate self and others accurately by treating themselves the way they originally wanted to treat other people or objects. For instance, the harassed mother at the end of a long day in which everything has gone wrong may turn her destructive impulses against herself. Retroflection means literally 'to turn sharply back against'. When people retroflect they redirect their activity inward and substitute themselves instead of the environment as the targets of their behaviour. Retroflection is not necessarily neurotic. In certain situations it may be to the individual's advantage to suppress particular responses. However, retroflection is pathological when it is chronic, habitual and out of control.

Perls was sensitive to the use of language both in representing and helping to sustain contact boundary disturbances. For example: in introjection the personal pronoun 'I' is used when the real meaning is 'they'; in projection the pronouns 'they' or 'it' are used when the real meaning is 'I'; in confluence the pronoun 'we' is used when there may really be differentness; and retroflection uses the reflexive 'myself' as in the statement 'I am ashamed of myself'.

The following is Perl's (1973) succinct summary of the lack of discrimination, interferences and interruptions entailed in the four main contact boundary disturbances: 'The introjector does as others would like him to do, the projector does unto others what he accuses them of doing to him, the man in pathological confluence doesn't know who is doing what to whom, and the retroflector does to himself what he would like to do to others' (p. 40).

Layers of neurosis

Perls (1969a, 1970a) came to see the structure of neurosis as consisting of five layers, each of which is described in Box 5.2. A major feature in the maintenance of neuroses is that people are not willing to undergo the pain of the impasse, the feeling of being stuck and lost. An example involving the later layers

Box 5.2   *The five layers of neurosis*

The cliché layer

For example, the meaningless tokens of meeting such as a handshake or 'Good morning'.

The Eric Berne or Sigmund Freud layer

The layer where people engage in the counter-productive manipulations of phoney roles and games (e.g. the bully, the very important person, the cry-baby, the nice little girl, the good boy).

The impasse

When the role-playing layer is worked through, the therapist and client come to the third layer called the impasse or sometimes the sick-point. This layer is characterized by a phobic attitude manifested in avoidance and flight from authentic living. In particular suffering is avoided, especially the suffering of frustration.

The death or implosive layer

Behind the impasse is the death or implosive layer, which appears either as fear of death or a feeling of not being alive. Here people implode by contracting and compressing themselves.

The explosion

The explosion is the final neurotic layer. There are four basic kinds of explosions from the death layer: into grief, if a person works through a loss which has not been assimilated; into orgasm for sexually blocked people; into anger; and into joy. The explosions, which may be mild depending on the amount of energy invested in the implosive layer, connect with the authentic, organismic person.

of neurosis is that of a young woman who had recently lost her child and who needed to be able to face her nothingness and her grief in order to be able to come back to life and make real contact with the world.

THERAPY

From the point of view of psychotherapy, when there is good contact – e.g., a clear bright figure freely energized from an empty background – then there are not peculiar problems concerning the relations of 'mind' and 'body' or 'self' and 'external world'.

Fritz Perls

THERAPEUTIC GOALS

Clients come to gestalt therapy because they are in existential crises. Perls had a rather cynical view of their motivation, stating: 'Anybody who goes to a therapist has something up his sleeve. I would say roughly 90% don't go to a therapist to be cured, but to be more adequate in their neuroses' (Perls, 1969a, p. 79). Gestalt therapy goals revolve around the client's movement from environmental support to self-support. Beginning clients are mainly concerned with solving problems. Gestalt therapists assist clients to support themselves not only in solving current problems, but in living more authentically. In order to be self-supporting, clients need to be in touch with their organismic existential centres (I am what I am). People who are in touch with their organismic selves or with their senses are self-actualizing or self-supporting.

The process of self-actualizing involves an effective balance of contact and withdrawal at the contact boundary and the ability to use energy or excitement to meet real rather than phoney needs. Furthermore, self-actualizing involves being able to withstand frustration until a solution emerges. Self-supporting people take responsibility for their existences and possess *response-ability* or freedom of choice. They are able appropriately to use aggression to assimilate their experiences and they are largely free from the neurotic contact boundary disturbances of introjection, projection, retroflection and confluence. They also possess relatively little self-destructive unfinished business since they are good at forming and closing strong gestalts.

Yontef and Jacobs (2000) observe that the only goal of gestalt therapy is awareness. Clients require awareness both in particular areas – awareness of content – and also of the processes or automatic habits by which they block awareness – awareness of process. This latter self-reflective kind of awareness, sometimes called 'awareness of awareness', enables clients to use their skills in awareness to rectify disturbances in the awareness process.

PROCESS OF THERAPY

It is important to distinguish how Perls worked towards the end of his life and the practice of ongoing individual gestalt therapy. Perls was a showman who conducted gestalt therapy in workshops which included, as an adjunct at Esalen, communal baths. He required six elements for his performance: '(1) My skill, (2) Kleenex, (3) The hot seat, (4) The empty chair, (5) Cigarettes, (6) An ashtray' (Perls, 1969b, p. 227). Perls viewed all therapy interviews as experimental. Therapists need to try things out to help clients become aware of how they are now functioning as persons and organisms. Sometimes he would do mass experiments or exercises, but generally he worked with a series of single people, or sometimes couples, in front of the group.

In ongoing individual gestalt therapy, assessment is done as part of the therapeutic process rather than as an initial diagnostic procedure. Clients need to be willing to work within the gestalt therapy framework and feel that their therapist is someone whom they can trust. In the initial session therapists are likely to discuss details of fees, cancellation of sessions policy and other pertinent practical matters.

Gestalt therapists' offices are designed to be friendly and comfortable and avoid having desks or tables between therapists and clients. Where possible, space is available for movement and experimentation. In addition, every effort is made to ensure privacy both in terms of sound-proofing and safeguarding records.

Sessions are usually once weekly which gives clients time to digest what happened in the previous session. Though more frequent sessions are possible, gestalt therapists take care to encourage self-support rather than dependency by not becoming too available. Individual therapy is often combined with group therapy, couples therapy, family therapy, workshops and with meditation or biofeedback training.

Evaluation of therapeutic process and outcomes occurs as part of therapy and both therapist and client participate. Beginning clients may be most concerned with solving problems and relief from psychological discomfort. Therapists encourage their clients to assume responsibility for self-support in addressing their problems and resultant discomfort. Initially, clients may talk about their problems but show little insight into the how of their behaviour. As therapy progresses, clients become more aware both of how they behave and of how unaware they have been hitherto. As therapy continues, client and therapist may pay more attention to general personality issues and the patterns and conditions which contribute to clients' insufficient awareness. The idea is that increasingly clients carry their higher levels of awareness into their everyday lives and maintain and build upon them after therapy ends.

THE THERAPEUTIC RELATIONSHIP

There are at least two ways of looking at the therapist–client relationship in gestalt therapy: that of Perls in his demonstrations and workshops and that of other important practitioners, for instance, Laura Perls, Gary Yontef and James Simkin. The relationship and style of Perls' Esalen workshops is often called 'Perlsism' or 'Perlsian gestalt' to differentiate it from the relationship and style of therapy practised by those other leading gestalt therapists.

Perls was a charismatic and dominating personality who, once he became well known, may have attracted clients who felt they might benefit from his confronting approach. Though ostensibly he advocated a democratic dialogue between therapist and client, the reality was that much of the time he was controlling the therapeutic process. Perls' son Stephen was to observe that his father did not know how to relate to another person on an equal basis (Perls, 1993). Fritz Perls' relationships with clients contained the paradox of advocating personal responsibility at the same time as assuming major responsibility for the therapeutic process himself.

At his best Perls was so concerned with helping clients that he would not allow them to sabotage their growth by being phoney, an important word in his vocabulary. A contemporary phrase for Perls' relationships with clients is 'tough love'. Other leading practitioners have conducted gestalt therapy within the context of more equal or horizontal therapist–client relationships.

All gestalt therapists regard the therapeutic relationship as a 'working' rather than a 'talking' relationship. Yontef and Simkin observe: 'When one moves from talking about a problem or being with someone in a general way to studying what one is doing, especially being aware of how one is aware, one is working' (1989, p. 341). In this working relationship, both therapists and clients are self-responsible: therapists for the quality of their presence and self-awareness, their knowledge and skills in relating to the client, and for maintaining an open and non-defensive stance; and clients for their commitment to working to become more in charge of their lives through developing greater self-awareness. Furthermore, therapists are responsible for not colluding in clients' manipulations to get them to do what clients fear they cannot do for themselves. Instead, therapists should relate to clients in a warm, respectful, direct and honest manner.

THERAPEUTIC INTERVENTIONS

The use of gestalt therapy interventions 'hinges on questions of *when, with whom*, and *in what situation*' (Shepherd, 1970, p. 324). In 'Perlsian' therapy, he would be likely to intervene without much, if any, consultation. With most gestalt therapists, appropriate interventions are decided upon in an ongoing dialogue between therapist and client. Such interventions are considered as experiments. A major purpose of encouraging clients to experiment with different ways of thinking and acting is to collect information to achieve genuine understanding rather than mere changes in behaviour. Repeatedly, clients are encouraged to 'Try this and see what you experience' (Yontef and Jacobs, 2000). Creativity from therapists and clients in setting up and carrying out appropriate experiments is highly valued.

Awareness technique

Gestalt therapy is an experiential rather than a verbal or interpretive approach. Assessment data about how clients interrupt their contact with life are collected as therapists and clients work together. Gestalt therapy demands that clients experience themselves as fully as possible in the here and now both in order to understand their present manipulations and contact boundary disturbances and to re-experience the unfinished business of past problems and traumas.

Perls (1973) regarded the simple phrase 'Now I am aware' as the foundation of the gestalt approach. The 'now' because it keeps therapists and clients in the present and reinforces the fact that experience can only take place in the present. The 'aware' because it gives both therapists and clients the best picture of clients' present resources. Awareness always takes place in the present and opens up possibilities for action.

Clients are asked to become aware of their body language, their breathing, their voice quality and their emotions as much as of any pressing thoughts. There follow some examples of Perls directing Gloria the client's attention to her non-verbal behaviour taken from the *Three Approaches to Psychotherapy* film series (Dolliver, 1991, p. 299; Perls, 1965).

> 'What are you doing with your feet now?'
> 'Are you aware of your smile?'
> 'You didn't squirm for the last minute.'
> 'Are you aware that your eyes are moist?'
> 'Are you aware of your facial expression?'

One way of following up a client's awareness report is for the therapist to say 'Stay with it' or 'Feel it out'. Such instructions can encourage clients to more fully experience and work through feelings to completion. For example, staying with moist eyes may lead to further experiencing and then identifying the reasons for feeling sad, and to crying.

Exaggeration, which may focus either on movement and gesture or on verbal statements, is another way of heightening clients' awareness of how they communicate. In each instance, clients are asked progressively and repeatedly to exaggerate their behaviour. Examples of exaggeration requests from Perls' interview with Gloria are as follows (Dolliver, 1991, p. 300; Perls, 1965).

'Can you develop this movement?'
'Develop it as if you were dancing.'
'Now exaggerate this.'
'What you just said, talk to me like this.'
'Do this more.'

Yet another way of heightening clients' awareness of their here-and-now communication is to ask them to use the phrase '*I take responsibility for it*'. For instance, 'I am aware that I am moving my leg and I take responsibility for it.'

When using awareness techniques, therapists may self-disclose and provide here-and-now feedback about how they see the client communicating. Furthermore, therapists can judiciously share how they are affected by the client communicating that way.

Since clients are self-interrupters they often find it difficult to remain in the here and now. The awareness technique is really a concentration technique, sometimes called focal awareness, by which clients learn to experience each now and each need and also how their feelings and behaviour in one area are related to feelings and behaviour in other areas. Thus they come to an awareness not only of the fact that they are interrupting their contact with themselves and the world, but also of what they are interrupting and how they are doing it through the neurotic mechanisms of introjection, projection, etc. Clients are also asked to do some homework which consists of reviewing the session in terms of a systematic application of the awareness technique.

Sympathy and frustration

Empathizing with clients is insufficient since the therapists are withholding themselves and at worst allowing confluence. Sympathy alone spoils clients. What is needed is a combination of sympathy and frustration. Clients must be frustrated in their efforts to control the therapist by neurotic manipulation and instead learn to use their powers of manipulation to meet their real needs. The therapist focuses on getting clients to become more aware and not to become phobic when they start to feel uncomfortable.

Perls provided situations in which his clients experienced being stuck in frustration and then frustrated their avoidances still further until they were willing to mobilize their *own* resources. He repeatedly frustrated clients until they were face-to-face with their blocks, inhibitions, and ways of avoiding having eyes, ears, muscles, authority and security in themselves. Frustration often leads to the discovery that the phobic impasse does not exist in reality but in fantasy, in that clients have been preventing themselves from using their own available resources through catastrophic expectations. Furthermore, frustration helps clients to express their needs and requests directly rather than to cover them over with neurotic manipulations. The imperative is the primary form of communication, and clients who can actually state what they need and mean what they state have made the most important step in their therapy.

Eliciting fantasies

A limitation of the awareness technique is its slowness. In order to speed up therapy, Perls made considerable use of fantasizing, be it verbal, written down or acted out as a drama. There follows an example taken from the *Three Approaches to Psychotherapy* film series in which Perls encourages Gloria to describe a fantasy (Dolliver, 1991, p. 300; Perls, 1965).

> 'Can you describe the corner you'd like to go to?'
> 'Imagine you are in this corner and you are perfectly safe. Now what would you do in that corner?'
> 'What should I do when you are in that corner?'

During the interview, Perls also asked Gloria to describe her fantasies about him (Dolliver, 1991, p. 301).

> 'Now what can I do to you?'
> 'How old must I be?' (for Gloria to scold him)
> 'How should I be? Give me a fantasy. How could I show my concern for you?'
> 'What would I do? How would I conceal my feelings?'

Dolliver observes that whenever Gloria offered Perls feedback about her experience of him, Perls always regarded it as a transference fantasy representing her projected attributes.

Drama techniques

'Monotherapy', perhaps better termed monodrama, is a form of psychodrama with a difference. In monotherapy, instead of involving other people as well as the client in the drama, the client creates his own stage and plays all the roles under his own direction and expression.

In the *shuttle* technique clients are asked to shuttle their attention from one area to another. For instance, a client can shuttle between the visualization of a memory and the organismic reliving of it in the here and now. Another example involves getting clients to shuttle between their feelings in and about an incident and their projections in the incident. For example, a client who feels angry with a colleague for 'apple-polishing' his boss may shuttle to experiencing his own needs and desires for approval from the boss. A further example is that of getting clients to shuttle between talking and listening to themselves. After each sentence, clients are asked: 'Are you aware of this sentence?' The purpose here is to help clients stop compulsive talking which interrupts their experiencing of themselves and listening to others.

Drama and fantasy work can involve both the *hot seat* and the *empty chair*. The hot seat is occupied by the individual with whom at any time the counsellor is working in front of the group. The empty chair is a second chair which is a 'projection-identification gimmick ... waiting to be filled with fantasized people and things' (Perls, 1969b, p. 224). Essentially it is a method of highlighting the shuttling process by getting clients to change chairs as they shuttle between parts of themselves or between different people in a drama.

Topdog–underdog dialogues are one of the main examples of the use of the shuttle technique involving both fantasy work and the empty chair. Perls considered that in their fantasies many people played self-torture games in which they were fragmented into an inner conflict between controller (topdog) and controlled (underdog). The topdog (or super-ego) is righteous, authoritarian, full of 'shoulds' and 'should nots', perfectionistic and manipulates with threats of catastrophe if his demands are not carried out. The underdog (or intra-ego) is cunning and manipulates by being wheedling, defensive, apologetic, playing the cry-baby and so on. Typical underdog statements are 'Mañana', 'I try my best' and 'I have such good intentions'. Through shuttling between these polarities, clients are helped to understand the structure of their behaviour and also to bring about a reconciliation between these two fighting clowns by becoming more in touch with their organismic selves.

Dreamwork

Perls (1970b) regarded dreams as the royal road to integration. Dreams are existential messages, not just unfinished situations, current problems or symptoms. Especially if the dreams are repetitive, a very important existential issue for the client is likely to be involved. There are four stages of dreamwork (see Box 5.3).

Responsibility language

Perls was interested in semantics and he was conscious of how clients could interfere with self-support through poor use of language (Levitsky and Perls, 1970; Perls, 1970a). Using verbs that acknowledge choice and personal agency is one example of using responsibility language: for example, rephrasing 'I can't do that' to 'I *won't* do that'. In addition, clients can be alerted to use the personal pronoun 'I' rather than 'It' or 'They' and to send messages directly to their therapists and to others. Furthermore, if clients ask the kind of questions which manipulate the environment for support, therapists can encourage them to change those passive questions into more active and self-supporting statements.

CASE MATERIAL

Perls' book *Gestalt Therapy Verbatim* (1969a) is primarily made up of verbatim transcripts from his large-scale weekend dreamwork seminars between 1966 and 1968 and from an intensive four-week Gestalt Therapy workshop in 1968, all of which were held at Esalen. Perls presents his work with a number of different clients from the seminars and the workshop. In addition, the *Eyewitness* part of *The Gestalt Approach & Eyewitness to Therapy* (1973) contains transcripts taken from his conducting therapy films that Perls

---

Box 5.3   *The four stages of dreamwork*

Stage 1.   Sharing the dream

The client relates the dream.

Stage 2.   Retelling the dream in the present tense

The client retells the dream or a section of it as a drama by changing the past tense into the present tense, for example, 'I was climbing a mountain' becomes 'I am climbing a mountain'. Perls would ask clients to say their dreams, or parts of their dreams, again 'in the *present tense*: as if you were dreaming it *now*?' (Perls, 1970b, p. 205).

Stage 3.   Talking to the different actors in the dream

The client becomes the stage director, and sets the scene and talks to the different actors in the dream or a section of it. For example, when working with Mary Anne's dream, Perls introduced the action element with the statement: 'Now let's start acting it out. Tell this to the man. Talk to the man – express your resentment' (Perls, 1970b, p. 206). Fourth, the client is encouraged to become the different actors, the props and all that is there. Clients do not have to work with a whole dream for, even if they reidentify with just one or a few items in the dream, the exercise is valuable.

Stage 4.   Conducting a dialogue between different elements in the dream

The fourth stage of dreamwork may be facilitated by the empty chair technique to allow for dialogues between the different people, objects or parts of the self that are encountering each other. These dreamwork encounters provide opportunity for two things: the integration of conflicts and reidentification with those parts of the self that are alienated, especially the assimilation of projections. Dreamwork is an excellent way of finding the holes in a client's personality. These tend to be manifested as voids and blank spaces which are accompanied by nervousness and confusion.

considered had great teaching potential. In the 'gestalt therapy' film in the earlier *Three Approaches to Psychotherapy* series, Perls introduces his approach, conducts a brief interview with Gloria and then summarizes his impressions of the session (Perls, 1965).

Another example of gestalt therapy is that of Laura Perls working first with a 25-year-old black woman and then with a 47-year-old Central European Jewish refugee (Perls, 1968). Joen Fagan (1974) presents transcripts with commentary for three sessions with Iris, who had agreed to be videotaped and had no previous experience with gestalt therapy. Simkin presents a case example with a transcript excerpted from a demonstration film with Peg who had originally been seen in a gestalt training workshop, where she worked on the grief and anger she felt towards her husband who had committed suicide (Yontef and Simkin, 1989). In the same chapter, Simkin presents selected excerpts from a condensed transcript of a gestalt therapy workshop with six volunteers in which he illustrates some gestalt techniques.

Clarkson (1999) illustrates the various stages of long-term gestalt therapy with a progressive case example where the client is Gary, a university lecturer. At the start of therapy, Gary had been in an unsatisfactory relationship with Jessica for the previous two of the six years they had lived together. Yontef and Jacobs (2000) present a case example in the form of an excerpt taken from the fourth year of therapy with Miriam, whose world was characterized by extreme isolation.

FURTHER DEVELOPMENTS

I have already mentioned that many other leading gestalt therapists developed more horizontal relationships with clients than did Perls. Since Perls' death, the practice of gestalt therapy has altered in many other ways and continues to develop (Clarkson, 1999; Mackewn, 1994; Parlett and Hemming, 1996; Yontef and Jacobs, 2000). Contemporary gestalt therapists are more supportive, compassionate and kind. There is less emphasis on frustration and abrasively confronting clients who are perceived as manipulative. When using confrontation, gestalt therapists take great care not to humiliate or re-traumatize clients by triggering unnecessary shame in them.

Therapists are less likely to pose as experts and more likely to reveal their humanity, including their fears, defensiveness and confusion. Gestalt therapists are encouraged to make 'I' statements to enhance their contact with clients and clients' focusing. In describing how she works, Laura Perls (1970c) provides examples of disclosing her awareness and feelings, sharing personal problems and life experiences, and using physical contact. Her guiding principle is to use such disclosures only if they might help clients take their next steps.

Many contemporary gestalt therapists attempt to exemplify Buber's concept of the 'I–Thou' relationship in which two unique people encounter and openly respect one another's essential humanity (Buber, 1958). 'I–Thou' relationships are here-and-now person-to-person encounters in which therapist and client are open to being changed by the other (Clarkson, 1997). Such relationships may be contrasted with 'I–It' relationships in which others are treated as objects to be used and manipulated.

Contemporary gestalt therapy tends to be highly individual with a different therapy being tailor-made for each client. Therapists and clients creatively generate and carry out appropriate experiments as therapy progresses. Clarkson (1999) provides a good example of how one leading gestalt therapist works. She presents a seven-stage cycle of gestalt formation and production: sensation, awareness, mobilization, action, final contact, satisfaction, and withdrawal. The cycle's last six stages are then used as a framework for illustrating the gestalt therapy process. Clarkson suggests some appropriate experiments for each stage.

Another development is that, drawing on gestalt therapy's empty chair technique, Greenberg and his colleagues have devised an empty chair dialogue intervention geared to the resolution of 'unfinished business' with significant others (Greenberg et al., 1993). Such unresolved negative feelings can contribute to anxiety and depression as well as being transferred into other relationships where they are inappropriate. This intervention, 'in which the client engages in an imaginary dialogue with the significant other, is designed to access restricted feelings allowing them to run their course and be restructured in the safety of the therapy environment' (Pavio and Greenberg, 1995, p. 419).

Some gestalt therapists may openly use psychoanalytic formulations to describe character structure (Yontef, 1988). In addition, when conducting groups, though some gestalt therapists still use Perls' working with individuals in front of the group style, the trend is for gestalt therapists to make greater use of the interactions between and contributions from group members than Perls did. A further development is that gestalt therapy techniques have been integrated into other approaches; for example, gestalt techniques and experiments are commonly used in conjunction with transactional analysis (Dusay and Dusay, 1989; James and Jongeward, 1971).

Gestalt therapy has training institutes in every major city of the United States and in most countries of Europe and South America as well as in Australia. Training standards for gestalt therapists in Britain are among the most stringent in the United Kingdom Council for Psychotherapy (Parlett and Hemming, 1996). In Britain there are several hundred psychotherapists who primarily identify themselves as gestalt therapists (Clarkson, 1999). There are national gestalt therapy associations in many countries and the International Gestalt Therapy Association is a new group attempting to form a more international governing structure.

SUMMARY

- *Fritz Perls, its main originator, regarded gestalt therapy as an existential approach. Gestalt means form, shape, pattern or configuration. The human organism is a unified whole which can only exist in an environmental field. Consequently mind–body and person–environment splits are erroneous.*
- *The contact boundary is the boundary between organism and environment and it is here that psychological events take place.*
- *Life is characterized by a continuous process of balance and imbalance in the organism, with homeostasis being the process whereby the organism satisfies its needs by restoring balance. No sooner is one gestalt completed than another comes up.*
- *Perls emphasized vitality and the need to integrate the social being and the animal being. The word 'excitement' is used*

to describe the energy people create. This life force or élan vital *is at the heart of the gestalt approach.*

- *Healthy functioning involves identifying with one's forming organismic self and keeping in touch with one's senses. An aggressive attitude towards experience is necessary if it is to be destructured and then assimilated as one's own.*

- *People need frustrations in order to learn to mobilize their own resources to manipulate the environment. However, children often experience interruptions from significant others which interfere with their capacity for self-support and cause them to suppress their emotions.*

- *Between the self zone and the outer zone is an intermediate zone consisting of maya or fantasy activity. Anxiety or stage fright is the result of this fantasy activity. In neurosis there is a continuous fight between reality and maya.*

- *The four main neurotic mechanisms or contact boundary disturbances are introjection, projection, retroflection and confluence.*

- *The structure of neurosis consists of five layers: the cliché layer; the Eric Berne or Sigmund Freud layer of manipulative roles and games; the impasse; the death or implosive layer; and the explosion.*

- *Goals for therapy include heightened awareness, self-support rather than environmental support, being in touch with one's senses and existential centre, response-ability or freedom of choice, and the ability to form and close strong gestalts.*

- *Towards the end of his life Perls worked primarily in groups, and a distinction can be made between 'Perlsian' therapy in a workshop format and ongoing individual gestalt therapy.*

- *The relationship in gestalt therapy is an active working rather than a passive talking relationship. Other leading gestalt therapy practitioners conduct therapy within the context of a more horizontal relationship than appears to have been the case with Perls.*

- *Change involves focusing on the how of clients' contact boundary disturbances in the now. Experientially engaging clients so that they can become more aware of how they communicate and interfere with their communication in the here and now is central to the practice of gestalt therapy.*

- Perls would frustrate clients so that they experienced being stuck in their frustration and then he frustrated their avoidances still further until they were willing to mobilize their own resources.
- Drama and fantasy work in gestalt therapy can involve the shuttle technique, where clients shuttle between different aspects of themselves and their situations, and the hot seat and empty chair.
- The four stages of gestalt dreamwork are: sharing the dream; retelling the dream in the present tense; talking to the different actors in the dream; and conducting a dialogue between different elements in the dream.
- Clients are encouraged to use personal responsibility language: for example, using verbs that acknowledge choice, the personal pronoun 'I', and making statements rather than asking questions.
- Gestalt therapy developments include a more horizontal therapist–client relationship, less emphasis on frustrating clients, more therapist self-disclosure, more emphasis on forming authentic 'I–Thou' therapeutic relationships, creative use of experiments to individualize and enhance the therapeutic process, development of the empty chair technique to resolve unfinished business with significant others, use of psychoanalytic formulations to describe character structure, and integrating gestalt techniques with those from other approaches, such as transactional analysis.
- Gestalt therapy continues to develop its national and international governing structures and training programmes.

REVIEW AND PERSONAL QUESTIONS

Review questions

1. What did Perls mean by gestalt formation?
2. Why did Perls consider it important for people to take an aggressive attitude to experience?
3. In growing up, what is the role of frustration?
4. Describe each of Perls' three layers of awareness.
5. Describe each of the following mechanisms of contact boundary disturbance: introjection, projection, retroflection, and confluence.
6. What are the goals of gestalt therapy?

7. How and why do gestalt therapists use awareness techniques?
8. How and why do gestalt therapists use sympathy and frustration?
9. How and why do gestalt therapists use drama techniques?
10. What is the purpose of dreamwork and what are its four stages?
11. What is 'Perlsian' gestalt therapy and how does it differ from the way some of Perls' collaborators and many contemporary therapists practise gestalt therapy?

Personal questions

1. What specific events in your life may have influenced you to come to your mind and lose your senses?
2. Assess how you relate to your environment in terms of each of Perls' mechanisms of contact boundary disturbance: introjection, projection, confluence and retroflection.
3. What are the phoney roles and games you use to obtain environmental support rather than rely on self-support?
4. Sit in a comfortable chair and, for the next three minutes, say to yourself 'Now I am aware ...' each time you become aware of your body language, your breathing, your emotions, and any pressing thoughts. For example, 'Now I am aware I'm uncrossing my legs.'
5. Spend the next three minutes focusing on your response-ability for your life by staying in the now and saying to yourself about all your current behaviour '... and I take responsibility for it.'
6. Use the shuttle technique and change chairs as you shuttle between different parts of yourself or between yourself and another person.
7. What is your fantasy of how it would be like for you to be in the hot seat being in therapy with a gestalt therapist like Fritz Perls?
8. What relevance, if any, has the theory and practice of gestalt therapy for how you conduct therapy?
9. What relevance, if any, has the theory and practice of gestalt therapy for how you live?

ANNOTATED BIBLIOGRAPHY

Perls, F. S., Hefferline, R. F. and Goodman, P. (1951) *Gestalt Therapy: Excitement and Growth in the Human Personality.* London: Souvenir Press.

This book contains an introduction and two volumes. Volume 1 is a series of eighteen experiments: experiments 1 to 11 focus on contacting the environment, technique of awareness, and directed awareness; experiments 12 to 18 focus on retroflection, introjection, and projections. Volume 2 is a major statement of gestalt theory consisting of three parts: introduction; reality, human nature, and society; and theory of the self. This detailed book is for serious students and therapists.

Perls, F. S. (1969a) *Gestalt Therapy Verbatim.* New York: Bantam Books.

This book consists of three parts: talk, dreamwork seminar, and intensive workshop. The talk and dreamwork seminar parts are selected and edited material from audiotapes made at weekend dreamwork seminars conducted by Perls at the Esalen Institute, Big Sur, California between 1966 and 1968. The intensive workshop part is taken from audiotapes of a four-week intensive workshop conducted in 1968. The talk part of the book provides an easily readable introduction to gestalt theory.

Perls, F. S. (1969b) *In and Out of the Garbage Pail.* New York: Bantam Books.

As the book's cover says, 'Joy. Sorrow. Chaos. Wisdom. The free-floating autobiography of the man who developed Gestalt Therapy.' A pot-pourri of self-disclosure by means of prose and poetry. This book is a good way to meet Perls, the man.

Perls, F. S. (1973) *The Gestalt Approach & Eyewitness to Therapy.* New York: Bantam Books.

This book is a combination of two projects that Perls was working on at the time of his death. *The Gestalt Approach* is Perls' final statement of his theory and was written because he regarded his two previous theoretical works *Ego, Hunger and Aggression* and *Gestalt Therapy* as too outdated and difficult to read. *Eyewitness to Therapy* provides descriptions of gestalt therapy in action.

Clarkson, P. (1999) *Gestalt Counselling in Action* (2nd edn). London: Sage.

This book starts by introducing gestalt theory and the fundamentals of gestalt practice. A seven-stage cycle of gestalt formation and production is presented and, using the cycle as a framework, the practice of gestalt counselling is reviewed. This engaging and well-written book is a rich source of ideas about how to integrate experiments into gestalt practice.

Yontef, G. and Jacobs, L. (2000) 'Gestalt therapy', in R. J. Corsini and D. Wedding (eds) *Current Psychotherapies* (6th edn, pp. 303–39). Itasca, IL: Peacock.

This chapter provides a good overview of contemporary gestalt therapy. However, the annotated bibliography at the end of the chapter does not contain a single book written by Perls.

REFERENCES

Buber, M. (1958; original edn 1937) *I and Thou* (2nd edn). Edinburgh: T. and T. Clark.
Clarkson, P. (1997) 'Variations on I and thou'. *Gestalt Review*, 1(1): 56–70.
Clarkson, P. (1999) *Gestalt Counselling in Action* (2nd edn). London: Sage.
Clarkson, P. and Mackewn, J. (1993) *Fritz Perls*. London: Sage.
Dolliver, R. H. (1991) 'Perls with Gloria re-viewed: gestalt techniques and Perls' practices'. *Journal of Counseling and Development*, 69, 299–304.
Dusay, J. M. and Dusay, K. M. (1989) 'Transactional analysis', in R. J. Corsini and D. Wedding (eds) *Current Psychotherapies* (4th edn, pp. 405–53). Itasca, IL: Peacock.
Fagan, J. (1974) 'Three sessions with Iris'. *The Counseling Psychologist*, 4(4): 42–60.
Fagan, J. and Shepherd, I. L. (eds) (1970) *Gestalt Therapy Now: Theory, Techniques, Applications*. Palo Alto, CA: Science & Behavior Books.
Greenberg, L. S., Rice, L. N. and Elliott, R. (1993) *Facilitating Emotional Change: The Moment by Moment Process*. New York: Guilford Press.
James, M. and Jongeward, D. (1971) *Born to Win: Transactional Analysis with Gestalt Experiments*. Reading, MA: Addison-Wesley.
Levitsky, A. and Perls, F. S. (1970) 'The rules and games of gestalt therapy', in Fagan, J. and Shepherd, I. L. (eds) *Gestalt Therapy Now: Theory, Techniques, Applications* (pp. 140–9). Palo Alto, CA: Science & Behavior Books.
Mackewn, J. (1994) 'Modern Gestalt – an integrative and ethical approach to counselling and psychotherapy'. *Counselling*, 5(2): 105–8.

Parlett, M. and Hemming, J. (1996) 'Developments in Gestalt Therapy', in W. Dryden (ed.) *Developments in Psychotherapy: Historical Perspectives*. London: Sage, pp. 91–110.

Pavio, S. C. and Greenberg, L. S. (1995) 'Resolving "unfinished business": efficacy of experimental therapy using empty-chair dialogue'. *Journal of Consulting and Clinical Psychology*, 63, 419–25.

Perls, F. S. (1947) *Ego, Hunger and Aggression: A Revision of Freud's Theory and Method*. London: Allen & Unwin.

Perls, F. S. (1969a) *Gestalt Therapy Verbatim*. New York: Bantam Books.

Perls, F. S. (1969b) *In and Out of the Garbage Pail*. New York: Bantam Books.

Perls, F. S. (1970a) 'Four lectures', in J. Fagan and I. L. Shepherd (eds) *Gestalt Therapy Now: Theory, Techniques, Applications* (pp. 14–38). Palo Alto, CA: Science & Behavior Books.

Perls, F. S. (1970b) 'Dream seminars', in J. Fagan and I. L. Shepherd (eds) *Gestalt Therapy Now: Theory, Techniques, Applications* (pp. 204–33). Palo Alto, CA: Science & Behavior Books.

Perls, F. S. (1973) *The Gestalt Approach & Eyewitness to Therapy*. New York: Bantam Books.

Perls, F. S., Hefferline, R. F. and Goodman, P. (1951) *Gestalt Therapy: Excitement and Growth in the Human Personality*. London: Souvenir Press.

Perls, L. P. (1968) 'Two instances of Gestalt therapy', in P. D. Pursglove (ed.) *Recognition in Gestalt Therapy* (pp. 42–68). New York: Funk & Wagnalls.

Perls, L. P. (1970c) 'One gestalt therapist's approach', in J. Fagan and I. L. Shepherd (eds) *Gestalt Therapy Now: Theory, Techniques, Applications* (pp. 125–9). Palo Alto, CA: Science & Behavior Books.

Perls, S. (1993) 'Frederick Perls: a son's reflections'. Talk given by Stephen Perls on 23 April at the Fifteenth Annual Conference on the Theory and Practice of Gestalt Therapy, Hotel du Parc, Montreal, Canada (the text of this talk is available on www.gestalt.org).

Shepherd, I. L. (1970) 'Limitations and cautions in the Gestalt approach', in J. Fagan and I. L. Shepherd (eds) *Gestalt Therapy Now: Theory, Techniques, Applications* (pp. 234–8). Palo Alto, CA: Science & Behavior Books.

Smuts, J. (1987; original edn 1926) *Holism and Evolution*. Cape Town, SA: N & S Press.

Yontef, G. (1988) 'Assimilating diagnostic and psychoanalytic perspectives into Gestalt therapy'. *Gestalt Journal*, 11(1): 5–32.

Yontef, G. and Jacobs, L. (2000) 'Gestalt therapy', in R. J. Corsini and D. Wedding (eds) *Current Psychotherapies* (6th edn, pp. 303–39). Itasca, IL: Peacock.

Yontef, G. and Simkin, J. S. (1989) 'Gestalt therapy', in R. J. Corsini and D. Wedding (eds) *Current Psychotherapies* (4th edn, pp. 323–61). Itasca, IL: Peacock.

Perls on film, videotape and cassette

Perls, F. (1965) 'Gestalt therapy', in E. Shostrom (ed.) *Three Approaches to Psychotherapy*. Santa Ana, CA: Psychological Films.

The Gestalt Journal Press lists a comprehensive bibliography of gestalt books, articles, videotapes and cassettes.
The Gestalt Journal Press
PO Box 990
Highland
NY 12528-0990
USA
Website: www.gestalt.org

Rational Emotive Behaviour Therapy

The basic tenet of REBT is that emotional upsets, as distinguished from feelings of sorrow, regret, annoyance, and frustration, largely stem from irrational beliefs.

Albert Ellis

INTRODUCTION

When first developed in 1955, Ellis termed his approach 'rational therapy' (RT). In 1961, he changed its name to 'rational emotive therapy' (RET). In 1993, Ellis (1993a) further changed its name to 'rational emotive behaviour therapy' (REBT). What Ellis means by 'rational' is cognition that is effective in self-helping rather than cognition that is merely empirically and logically valid. He wishes that he had used the word 'cognitive' from the start since many people narrowly restrict the word 'rational' to mean intellectual or logico-empirical. People's rationality rests on judging soundly which of their desires or preferences to follow, and is therefore based on thoughts, emotions and feelings (Ellis, 1990).

Ellis introduced 'behaviour' into his approach's name for the sake of accuracy. From its start, the approach has strongly emphasized behaviour along with cognition and emotion. Ellis writes: 'So, to correct my previous errors and to set the record straight, I shall from now on call it what it has really always been – rational emotive behavior therapy (REBT)' (Ellis, 1993a, p. 258).

Ellis (2000) distinguishes between general REBT and pre-ferential REBT. General REBT is virtually the same as cognitive-behaviour therapy and aims to teach clients rational or appropriate behaviours. Preferential REBT emphasizes a profound philosophic change. At the same time as including general REBT, it also teaches clients how to dispute irrational ideas and self-defeating behaviours and how to use powerful cognitive-emotive-behavioural methods as self-helping skills. This chapter focuses on preferential REBT, which from now on will be referred to as rational emotive behaviour therapy (REBT).

ALBERT ELLIS (1913–   )

Albert Ellis was born in Pittsburgh, Pennsylvania in 1913 and grew up in New York City. He had a brother and sister who were nineteen months and four years younger than him, respectively. His father was physically absent much of the time. His Jewish mother was benignly neglectful and 'was much more immersed in her own pleasures and ego-aggrandising activities than she was in understanding and taking care of her children' (Ellis, 1991a, p. 3). At age 12 he discovered that his parents had divorced.

Another childhood misfortune was that, at age $4\frac{1}{2}$, Ellis almost died of tonsillitis and nephritis and for the next few years was frequently hospitalized. When young, Ellis had psychological as well as physical problems. He writes: 'It took me almost two decades to talk myself out of that crap of being ingratiating. I was born and reared to be shy and scared. Throughout my childhood and teens I had a real social phobia. I viewed public speaking as a fate worse than public masturbation' (Ellis, 1997a, p. 69). However, Ellis did very well at school and developed problem-solving skills to make the most of his difficult childhood. For instance, when aged 19, he overcame his terror of public speaking by persisting in giving political talks over a period of three months. Furthermore, to overcome his shyness with women, he forced himself to talk to a hundred girls in a row in the Bronx Botanical Gardens (Ellis, 1997a). As with public speaking he was able to make a 180-degree change in how he performed. These experiences were important precursors to REBT because Ellis discovered the great value of reasoning and self-persuasion in changing his dysfunctional feelings and actions.

Beginning his writing career at the age of 12, Ellis turned out scores of stories, essays and comic poems and received scores of rejection slips in return. In 1934, despite his early ambition to become the Great American Novelist, Ellis received a Bachelor's degree in business administration from the City University of New York. Early occupations included a business matching trousers to still suitable jackets and being personnel manager of a gift and novelty firm. Ellis devoted much of his spare time to writing fiction. Partly because of difficulties in getting his fiction published, Ellis turned exclusively to writing non-fiction, especially focusing on the 'sex-family revolution'.

Discovering that he liked therapy as well as writing, Ellis entered the clinical psychology programme at Columbia University in 1942, receiving a Master's degree in 1943. Soon after obtaining his Master's, Ellis began a small private practice in psychotherapy and marital and sex therapy. In 1947, he received his doctorate from Columbia University with a thesis on personality questionnaires, an earlier thesis on love having been censored before it got off the ground. After his doctorate, Ellis' ambition was to become an outstanding psychoanalyst, and so he completed a training analysis with an analyst from the Karen Horney group and began to practise psychoanalysis under his teacher's direction. From 1948 to 1952, Ellis worked for the New Jersey Department of Institutions and Agencies, mainly as chief psychologist of the New Jersey State Diagnostic Center and then as chief psychologist of the entire state of New Jersey. He also continued his private practice in New York.

For some time, Ellis had employed active-directive methods in his psychotherapy, marital and sex therapy. In addition, before undergoing analysis, Ellis had worked through many of his own problems by reading and practising the philosophies of Epictetus, Marcus Aurelius, Spinoza and Bertrand Russell, and so he started teaching clients the philosophic principles that had helped him. Between 1953 and 1955, Ellis increasingly rebelled against psychoanalysis and began calling himself a 'psychotherapist' rather than a 'psychoanalyst'. He writes: 'I finally wound up, at the beginning of 1955, with RET' (Ellis, 1991a, p. 15). He gave his first paper on RET at the American Psychological Association's annual meeting in Chicago on 31 August 1956.

In 1959, Ellis founded The Institute for Rational Living, Inc, now called the Albert Ellis Institute for Rational Emotive Behaviour Therapy, as a non-profit-making scientific and educational organization to teach the principles of rational living. Since then, Ellis has donated all his royalties and income from clients and workshops to the Institute. In 1964, the Institute bought a large New York townhouse, where it is still headquartered.

Ellis is a man of boundless energy, probably a genetic inheritance from his 'two highly energetic parents who both lived reasonably long lives and were active until the last day of their lives' (Dryden, 1989, p. 545). He spends most of his time working. Aged over 83, in a week where he was mainly in New York, 'I usually see individual and group clients from 9.30am to 11pm – with a couple of half hour breaks for meals, and mostly for half hour sessions with individual clients. So during each week I may see over 80 individual clients and over 40 more group clients' (Ellis, 1997b, p. 17). In addition, Ellis holds his 8.30 to 10.00 Friday night workshop where he interviews people in public. On Saturday night and Sunday, he works on books, writing, research, letters and various other things (Palmer, 1993). He also gives numerous workshops and seminars in America and overseas and uses the travel time to write and read.

Ellis' work is his main priority. However, he has been married and divorced twice as well as having relationships with a number of other women. Since 1964, when she was 42, he has been in a stable relationship with Janet Wolfe and comments that his life 'would be greatly bereft of laughter, warmth, and intimacy without her' (Dryden, 1989, p. 541). Ellis and Janet have no children, since they regard it as unfair that, due to his work, he would not have much time to spend with them.

Ellis has had to work around physical disabilities to attain and maintain his phenomenal productivity level (Ellis, 1997b). From age 19 he has been hampered by chronically fatiguable eyes. The upshot of this is that he rarely reads for more than twenty minutes and often keeps his eyes shut during therapy sessions. At age 40 Ellis was diagnosed as having full-blown diabetes and has had to find ways of minimizing the inconvenience attached to this condition. In his late sixties Ellis' hearing began to deteriorate and by his mid-seventies he had two hearing aids which, even when in good working order, had their limitations. More recently, Ellis has also had to suffer from a bladder that is easily filled but slow to empty, so that peeing has become a lengthy process. However, efficient as ever, Ellis has found ways of combining peeing with other activities.

Ellis' work has been controversial. His REBT ideas challenged psychoanalytic and Rogerian orthodoxies. His ideas on sex challenged conventional morality. In addition, Ellis has not been afraid to speak his mind. However, over the past thirty years or so, cognitive-behavioural ideas have become increasingly fashionable, and Ellis now regards himself as the father of REBT and the grandfather of cognitive-behaviour therapy. He has received numerous honours and awards, including the American Psychological Association's major award for Distinguished Professional Contributions to Knowledge, the American Counselling Association's major Professional Development Award, and the American Humanist Association's Humanist of the Year Award.

Ellis has always been a prolific writer, even before publishing in the area of psychology. He has published over seven hundred papers in psychological, psychiatric and sociological journals and anthologies. In addition, Ellis has authored or edited over sixty-five books and monographs including *Sex Without Guilt, Reason and Emotion in Psychotherapy, A Guide to Rational Living* (with Robert Harper), *Overcoming Resistance: Rational-Emotive Therapy with Difficult Clients, Better, Deeper and More Enduring Brief Therapy: The Rational Emotive Behaviour Approach, The Practice of Rational Emotive Behaviour Therapy* (with Windy Dryden), *Rational Emotive Behaviour Therapy: A Therapist's Guide* (with Catherine MacLaren), *How to Stubbornly Refuse to Make Yourself Miserable About Anything – Yes, Anything!, The Albert Ellis Reader* and *How to Make Yourself Happy and Remarkably Less Disturbable*. Ellis is also well known for his rational-humorous songs: for example, 'Beautiful Hangup' to the tune of Stephen Foster's 'Beautiful Dreamer', the first two lines of which are:

Beautiful hangup, why should we part
When we have shared our whole lives from the start?

Apart from humour, the guiding principles of Ellis' work have been 'Science, efficiency, honesty, revolutionism, and passionate skepticism' (Ellis, 1991a, p. 30).

THEORY

People are born, as well as reared, with greater or lesser degrees of demandingness, and therefore they can change from demanding to desiring only with great difficulty.

Albert Ellis

BASIC CONCEPTS

Fundamental and primary goals

Virtually all humans have three fundamental goals (FG): to survive, be relatively free from pain, and to be reasonably satisfied or content. As subgoals or primary goals (PG), humans want to be happy: when by themselves; gregariously with other humans; intimately, with a few selected others; informationally and educationally; vocationally and economically; and recreationally (Ellis, 1991b). Furthermore, people live in a social world, and self-interest requires putting others a close second (Ellis and Dryden, 1997).

REBT sees human beings' basic goals as preferences or desires rather than needs or necessities. Rational living consists of thinking, feeling and behaving in ways which contribute to the attainment of the chosen goals, whereas irrationality consists of thinking, feeling and behaving in ways which block or interfere with their attainment. Living rationally consists of striking a sensible balance between short-range and long-range hedonism, or between the pleasures of the here and now and the longer-range pleasures gained through present discipline. Thus rationality may be defined as the use of reason in pursuit of chosen short-range and long-range hedonism.

Emotion, cognition and behaviour

In an early paper on 'Rational psychotherapy' Ellis (1958b) proposed three fundamental hypotheses. First, thinking and emoting are closely related. Second, thinking and emoting are so closely related that they usually accompany each other, act in a circular cause-and-effect relationship, and in certain (though hardly all) respects are essentially the same thing, so that one's thinking becomes one's emotion and emoting becomes one's thought. Third, both thinking and emoting tend to take the form of self-talk or internalized sentences and, for all practical purposes, the sentences that people keep saying to themselves are or become their thoughts and emotions. Thus people's internal self-statements are capable of both generating and modifying their emotions. In addition, Ellis (1991b) stresses that thinking and emotion interact with behaviour. For instance, people usually act on the basis of thoughts and emotions, and their actions influence how they think and feel.

Healthy and unhealthy emotions

REBT is not an approach of no emotions; rather it emphasizes healthy or appropriate emotions. Negative emotions may be either healthy, unhealthy or mixed (Ellis and MacLaren, 1998). Unhealthy emotions are those which interfere with achieving a sensible balance between short-range and long-range hedonism. For instance, it may be appropriate for people in an alien and difficult world to be fearful, cautious or vigilant so that they may take any necessary steps for realistic protection. However, anxiety and over-concern are unhealthy emotions, since they are based on irrational thinking or insane beliefs and, in fact, may interfere with or block attaining goals. Similarly, hostility may have a healthy and an unhealthy part. The healthy part of hostility involves acknowledging discomfort or annoyance as a basis for action designed to overcome or minimize the irritation. The unhealthy part of hostility may involve blaming others and the world in such a way as to block effective action and possibly generate even more unhappiness for oneself and further hostility from others.

Pleasurable and enjoyable emotions can also be healthy or unhealthy. For example, people may feel excessive pride when praised by others because they possess an irrational belief in the necessity of others' approval. A sensible balance between achieving short-range and long-range hedonistic goals involves a balance between achieving short-range and long-range appropriate pleasurable emotions.

Two biological tendencies

A tension exists in all people between two opposing biological creative tendencies (Ellis, 1993b, 2000). On the one hand, people have innate tendencies to create, develop and actualize themselves as healthy, goal-attaining human beings. They have a great potential to be rational and pleasure-producing. On the other hand, they have innate tendencies to create, develop and implement irrational cognitions, unhealthy emotions and dysfunctional behaviours. REBT theorizes that often people are 'biologically predisposed to strongly, passionately, and rigidly construct and hold on to their disturbance-creating musts and other irrational beliefs' (Ellis, 1993b, p. 199). Thus, they possess a huge potential to be destructive of themselves and of others, to be illogical and to continually repeat the same mistakes.

Ellis believes that all the major human irrationalities exist in virtually all human beings regardless of culture and educational level. Human fallibility has an inherent source. The facts that people seem so easily conditioned into dysfunctional thinking and behaviour and that it is so hard to modify are both viewed as evidence for an innate tendency to irrationality (Ellis, 1980). People's failure to accept reality almost always causes them to manifest the characteristics of emotional disturbance. However, differences exist in genetic predisposition to irrationality.

People are not only born and raised to be irrational, they also have some degree of free choice in how much they make themselves emotionally disturbed. For example, when growing up, Ellis' younger sister chose to make the worst of her childhood conditions (Ellis, 1991a). However, people can use their biological tendency to have some degree of free choice to help as well as to damage themselves. First, they can choose to think differently and more effectively about what is going on. Second, because they possess the capacity to think about how they think, they can choose to acquire and maintain the cognitive skills for containing and counteracting their tendencies to irrationality.

ABC theory of personality

Ellis has an ABC theory of personality to which he has added D and E to cover change and the desirable result of change. In addition, the letter G can be placed first to provide a context for people's ABCs.

G   Goals, both fundamental and primary
A   Adversities or activating events in a person's life
B   Beliefs, both rational and irrational
C   Consequences, both emotional and behavioural
D   Disputing irrational beliefs
E   Effective new philosophy of life.

Just as cognitions, emotions and behaviours interact with each other and are virtually never entirely pure, so do the ABCs of REBT. Goals (G), activating events (A), beliefs (B) and consequences (C) 'all seem to be part of a collaboration with one another' (Ellis, 1991b, p. 145).

Rational and irrational beliefs

Ellis (Ellis, 2000; Ellis and MacLaren, 1998) divides belief systems into two basic categories: rational beliefs and irrational beliefs.

- *Rational beliefs (rBs)* are healthy, productive, adaptive, consistent with social reality, and generally consist of preferences, desires and wants. When thinking rationally about adversities (As) that either block or sabotage their goals (G), people engage in preferential thinking. Preferential as contrasted with demanding thinking involves either explicitly and/or tacitly reacting with their belief systems (Bs) in realistic ways and experiencing appropriate emotional and enacting goal-oriented behavioural consequences (Cs).
- *Irrational beliefs (iBs)* are rigid, dogmatic, unhealthy, maladaptive, largely get in the way of people's efforts to achieve their goals, and are comprised of demands, musts and shoulds. When thinking irrationally about adversities (As) that either block or sabotage their goals (Gs), people engage in demanding thinking.

In reality, people's responses to adversities (As) mainly result from a combination of rational and irrational beliefs, though often one becomes in the 'winning' mode. Ellis (2000) observes that a person's self-defeating behaviour usually follows from the interaction of A (Adversity) and B (Belief about A) and that C (disturbed Consequences) generally follow the formula A × B = C. Box 6.1 contrasts ABCs for preferential and demanding thinking.

Box 6.1   ABCs for preferential and demanding thinking

Preferential thinking

A   Adversity or activating event perceived as blocking or sabotaging goals

B   Belief system involving preferential thinking: 'I prefer to have my important goals unblocked and fulfilled!'

C   Consequences: emotional – frustration and unhappiness; behavioural – avoiding or trying to eliminate the adversity.

Demanding thinking

A   Adversity or activating event perceived as blocking or sabotaging goals

B   Belief system involving demanding thinking: 'I absolutely must have my important goals unblocked and fulfilled!'

C   Consequences: emotional – anxiety and/or excessive hostility; behavioural – self-defeating over-reaction or under-reaction to the adversity.

Demanding beliefs and their derivatives

Irrational belief systems often operate on at least four levels: primary demanding belief(s), derivatives of the primary demanding belief(s), secondary demanding belief(s), and derivatives of the secondary demanding belief(s).

- *Primary demanding belief(s)*   The primary demanding belief or beliefs involves people's main demands and commands in relation to the adversity. Ellis has coined the term 'musturbation' to indicate that these beliefs are usually expressed as musts, shoulds, ought-tos, have-tos and got-tos. He has identified three major clusters of irrational beliefs that create inappropriate emotional and behavioural consequences (1980):

(1) I *must* do well and win approval for all my performances.
(2) Others *must* treat me considerately and kindly.
(3) Conditions under which I live *must* be arranged so that I get practically everything I want comfortably, quickly and easily.

• *Derivatives of the primary demanding belief(s)* People usually create highly unrealistic and over-generalized inferences and attributions as derivatives of their musturbatory and absolutistic demands. Three common irrational derivatives often accompany their musturbatory beliefs (Ellis, 1991b; Ellis and MacLaren, 1998).

(1) *Awfulizing* 'If I don't have my important goals unblocked and fulfilled as I must, it's awful!' In this context, 'awful' means totally bad or more than bad.
(2) *I-can't-stand-it-itis* 'If I don't have my important goals unblocked and fulfilled as I must, I can't stand it!'
(3) *Damning oneself and others* 'If I don't have my important goals unblocked and fulfilled as I must, I'm a stupid, worthless person.' 'Others are bad people for blocking my important goals.'

• *Secondary demanding belief(s)* Once people make themselves miserable at C, they tend to exacerbate their misery by making themselves miserable about being miserable. In other words, they transform the negative consequence (C) of the primary demanding belief ABC into an adversity or activating event (A) for a secondary level demanding belief ABC. Box 6.2 provides an example of such chaining. Frequently, people make themselves anxious about being anxious, depressed about being depressed, guilty about feeling guilty and so on.
• *Derivatives of secondary demanding belief(s)* People can now choose to create and derive awfulizing, I-can't-stand-it-itis, and damning oneself and others from their secondary as well as their primary musturbatory beliefs. They now have two negative consequences and their derivatives for the price of one; also, in an ever-spiralling cycle, they can intensify the unhappiness they create with their beautiful hangups.

> ### Box 6.2   *ABCs for primary and secondary demanding beliefs*
>
> **Primary ABC**
>
> **A1** 'I did poorly on my job today.'
> **B1** 'Since I must do well, isn't that horrible!'
> **C1** 'I feel anxious, depressed and worthless.'
>
> **Secondary ABC**
>
> **A2(C1)** 'I feel anxious, depressed and worthless.'
> **B2**   'Since I must not feel anxious, depressed and worthless, isn't that horrible!'
> **C2**   'I feel even more anxious, depressed and worthless.'

Ego disturbance and low frustration tolerance

Ellis (1988) proposes that neurotic problems can be grouped under two main headings according to the three main musturbatory beliefs and their derivatives: (1) ego disturbance (self-damning) and (2) low frustration tolerance (LFT) or discomfort disturbance. *Ego disturbance* arises from the belief 'I *must* do well and win approval for all my performances' because it leads to people thinking and feeling that they are inadequate and undeserving persons when they do not do as well as they must. He regards this as godlike grandiosity since people demand that they be special, perfect, outstanding, superhuman.

Low frustration tolerance arises from the grandiose belief that people think they are so special that conditions must be easy and satisfying for them. They then progress to holding either or both the irrational beliefs 'Others must treat me considerately and kindly' and 'Conditions under which I live *must* be arranged so that I get practically everything I want comfortably, quickly and easily'. Awfulizing and I-can't-stand-it-itis are derivatives of such beliefs. Basically in ego disturbance and low frustration tolerance, what people are insisting is that 'I must have an easy life, I must be perfect, and people and conditions should always cater to *me, me, me, me!*' (Ellis, 1988, p. 119).

ACQUISITION

How do people acquire rational and irrational beliefs? Ellis' emphasis is much more on how people sustain their irrationality than on how they initially acquire it. The past cannot be undone and it is counter-productive to excessively focus on how people feel about the past. Ellis advises people to 'Forget your "Godawful" past' (Ellis, 1988, p. 69). He considers that psychology has focused on how people originally become illogical and that this by no means indicates how people maintain or perpetuate their illogical behaviour, or what they should do to change it. Consequently, Ellis' treatment of the development of irrational cognitions and musturbatory beliefs is cursory. However, three main strands may be identified: biology, social learning and choosing irrational cognitions. Since biological or innate tendencies to irrationality have been previously discussed, the main focus here is on social learning and choosing.

Social learning

Given that human beings are born with a distinct proneness to irrationality, this tendency is frequently exacerbated by their environment, especially early in life when people are most vulnerable to outside influences. Ellis sees humans as basically highly suggestible, but acknowledges innate differences (Ellis, 1977b). Irrational ideas, which once might have been appropriate in view of the helpless state of the child, are acquired for a number of reasons (Ellis, 1991b, 2000; Ellis and Harper, 1997). First, young children are unable to think clearly, in particular insisting on immediate rather than future gratification and being unable accurately to distinguish real from imagined fears. However, as they grow older, normal children become less insistent on having their desires and demands immediately gratified. Second, childish demands can frequently be assuaged by magic, for instance, parents saying that a fairy godmother will satisfy those demands. Third, children are dependent on the planning and thinking of others and their suggestibility or conditionability is greatest when they are very young. Fourth, parents and members of the family group themselves have irrational tendencies, prejudices and superstitions which they inculcate into their children.

Fifth, this process is exacerbated by the indoctrinations of the mass media. Finally, cultures and religions can impart irrational, self-defeating and society-defeating views.

Choosing irrational cognitions

The process of acquiring irrationality is not simply a matter of reacting to how others behave. Human beings largely create their own emotional disturbances through not developing and exercising their capacity for rational choice. Negative social learning experiences do not in themselves lead to people acquiring irrational cognitions. Many people who have had negative upbringings choose not to disturb themselves unduly. Still others, with or without support, work through their problems. The reverse is also true. Favourable social learning experiences do not in themselves lead to rational cognitions. Many people who have had favourable upbringings develop significant irrational beliefs. While social learning experiences influence people for good or ill, they still have the capacity to choose how they react to them. Ellis and Dryden (1997) conclude: 'Thus, the REBT theory of acquisition can be summed up by the view that as humans we are not disturbed simply by our experiences; rather we bring our ability to disturb ourselves to our experiences' (p. 21).

MAINTENANCE

Why do people persist in holding their irrational beliefs and their derivatives? People not only become irrational, they stay irrational. In fact, they often become even more irrational. Staying rational in an irrational world is a struggle. Once acquired, people tend to repeat their irrational beliefs again and again. Ellis continually stresses that people have strong tendencies to reindoctrinate themselves with their self-defeating ideas. People's irrrational beliefs do not continue because they were once 'conditioned' and so now hold them 'automatically'. Instead, people still, here and now, actively reinforce them, and their present active self-propagandizations and constructions keep these beliefs alive (Ellis, 2000).

Reasons contributing to human beings staying irrational

The following are some reasons that contribute to human beings staying irrational, often at great personal cost to themselves, others and society.

Biological tendencies

Human beings' biological tendencies to irrationality do not go away with maturation, but are part of their lifelong genetic inheritance. Ellis stresses that human beings 'are powerfully predisposed to unconsciously and habitually prolong their mental dysfunctioning and to fight like hell to give it up' (Ellis, 1987, p. 365). Rather than strike a realistic balance between short-range and long-range hedonism, human beings largely embrace short-range hedonism. This preference for the pleasures of the moment is the main source of resistance to change.

Emotional contributions

Absolutistic musts are often 'hot' cognitions that have a strong evaluative-feeling component in them. Such cognitions are held strongly and powerfully and, as such, can be difficult to change. In addition, people then not only develop derivatives of their primary irrational beliefs, but also secondary irrational beliefs and their derivatives. As a result they raise the level of their emotionality and then may think even more irrationally. They may fail to see how upset they are. Furthermore, they are now so upset that they fail to reality-test and dispute their irrational beliefs in ways that they might otherwise do. Instead of the consequences of irrational beliefs making people better, they make them worse.

Insufficient scientific thinking

People continue to disturb themselves because they fail to think scientifically about what is going on in the world (WIGO). To think scientifically, people need constantly to observe and check the 'facts' to see the extent to which they are 'true' and whether or not they have changed. Scientific thinking is flexible and requires evidence to uphold or negate viewpoints. In addition, the scientific method is sceptical that the universe has any absolute standards of 'good' and 'bad'. Science does not have absolute rules in regard to human behaviour.

Reinforcing consequences

People can emotionally, cognitively and behaviourally reinforce their irrational beliefs. Emotionally, absolutistic musturbatory beliefs lead to strong negative feelings – such as severe anger and depression – that make them seem true. Cognitively and behaviourally, people reinforce their beliefs in different ways according to the belief. For instance, people who must be socially approved avoid taking social risks, and by doing so convince themselves that it is too difficult and dangerous to do otherwise. Furthermore, when avoiding social situations, they may feel a sense of emotional relief. The combination of their emotional, cognitive and behavioural reactions makes them more rather than less socially anxious.

Emphasizing one's 'Godawful' past

Ellis states as an REBT insight: '*Your early childhood experiences and your past conditioning did not originally make you disturbed. You did*' (Ellis, 1988, p. 70). People maintain their emotional disturbance by looking for causes in their pasts. Focusing on the past interferes with people focusing on the present in which they may still be upsetting themselves with the same irrational beliefs with which they upset themselves in their pasts. People cannot undo their pasts, but they can change their presents and futures. Furthermore, often focusing on the past leads not only to an over-emphasis on the past relative to the present, but also to an over-emphasis on other people's behaviour relative to one's own.

Unrealistic beliefs about change

People's low frustration tolerance can be both cause and consequence of unrealistic beliefs about working to change, with or without professional assistance, their thoughts, feelings and actions. Irrational beliefs about change include the following:

- 'I must be able to change with little discomfort, work and practice on my part.'
- 'Changing how I think, feel and behave shouldn't be so hard.'
- 'I must change quickly and profoundly.'
- 'When changing, I must not have any setbacks.'
- 'Since I tried to change and failed to do so, therefore I will settle for how I function now.'

(Ellis, 1987, 1993b)

Other cognitive factors

The following are some other factors and processes whereby people maintain and worsen their irrational beliefs and emotional disturbances (Ellis, 1987; Ellis and Dryden, 1997).

- *Naivety* People can have and hang on to hugely naive personal theories about the nature of their psychological problems and how they are maintained.
- *Ignorance* People, including therapists, can consider that it is statistically normal and healthy for them to be unnecessarily upset. They fail to distinguish between healthy and unhealthy thoughts, feelings and behaviours.
- *Stupidity* Many people are too unintelligent to work effectively on their emotional problems. They fail to gain sufficient insight into the fact that that they create their own disturbances.
- *Unperceptiveness* Without therapy, many disturbed people rarely look at their irrational beliefs and ideas and how these create and drive their upsetness. Even when pointed out to them in therapy, many disturbed people are still incapable of grasping how they upset themselves.
- *Rigidity* Even when they acknowledge their self-defeating irrational beliefs, many people rigidly stick to their musturbatory beliefs and their derivatives, for instance, awfulizing and I-can't-stand-it-itis. Some such people may be psychotic or have borderline personality disorders, whereas others are plain rigid thinkers.
- *Defensiveness* Human beings are prone to avoid facing and dealing directly with their problems. They use various methods of distorting and denying problems, for instance, rationalization and avoidance.

- *Pollyannaism and indifference*   Some people who are prone to extreme anxiety and suffer from a serious illness, such as heart disease or cancer, may deal with it by denying its seriousness. Sometimes, such defensive manoeuvres may help people to cope. However, on many occasions, such thinking may block efforts to attain physical health and psychological change.
- *Changing the situation*   For many, the easy way out is to change the situation, for instance, obtain a divorce, rather than try to change themselves and then consider whether or not to change the situation. For every neurotic who really tries to have a fundamental shift in the way they think, there are probably ten times as many trying to *feel* better by changing the situations in which they behave self-defeatingly rather than *get* better. This ratio holds true whether or not people come for therapy.
- *Other palliative means*   People and their would-be helpers resort to many palliative means of dealing with emotional disturbances rather than get to the root of them. Many clients and potential clients use distraction techniques such as progressive relaxation, biofeedback, meditation and yoga. Some try superficial positive thinking. Many people lose themselves in political, religious and mystical cults. Short-term feel-good remedies like alcohol and drugs are very common. In brief, many disturbed people seek low-level and palliative remedies rather than more rigorous and long-lasting solutions.

Insufficiently challenging beliefs through action

People may reinforce their beliefs through unwillingness to change their actions. Their 'tried-and-true' self-defeating ways may bring short-term relief at the expense of long-term gain. An Ellis insight is: '*You can change irrational beliefs (iBs) by acting against them: by performing behaviours that contradict them*' (Ellis, 1988, p. 109). Why then don't people change their actions to challenge their beliefs? One reason is that they may not have insight into their irrational beliefs, their derivatives, and their emotional and behavioural consequences. Another reason is that people resist the risk and effort involved in taking action. Some people may not be clear what to do. Still others may know what to do, but lack the skills, confidence and support to do it. Another category is people who change their actions but lack the staying power to maintain them, especially when faced with difficulties and setbacks. Such people suffer from low frustration tolerance.

THERAPY

The most elegant solution to the problems resulting from irrational demandingness is to help individuals to become less demanding.

Albert Ellis

THERAPEUTIC GOALS

Earlier in this chapter, I presented Ellis' GABCDE outline. There are two meanings to E depending on whether the change goals of REBT are inelegant or elegant.

Inelegant change goals

Ellis (1980) writes: 'Inelegant change largely consists of some kind of symptom removal' (p. 13). Here, at D, REBT targets the cognitions, emotions and behaviours that accompany self-defeating feelings, like anxiety and depression, and dysfunctional behaviours, like avoiding social and public speaking situations. The goal of focused or inelegant REBT is that of focused or inelegant change. Here the letter E stands for an effective new philosophy focused on one or more specific symptoms or problems. Effectiveness in relation to these symptoms can be cognitive (similar to rational beliefs), emotional (healthy feelings), and behavioural (desirable behaviours).

Elegant change goals

In contrast to inelegant change, Ellis states: 'Elegant change in RET goes much beyond this kind of symptom removal, and aims at a significant lessening (rather than a complete removal) of clients' *disturbability*' (Ellis, 1980, p. 13). In elegant change, E goes further than an effective new philosophy that supports removal of specific symptoms in assisting clients to develop and implement an effective philosophy of life. Ellis (1997c) writes: 'To do this, clients need to acknowledge how often and how strongly they escalate their healthy goals, desires, and preferences into arrogant and grandiose *must*urbation – and apply themselves to anti-*must*urbatory thinking' (p. 337). Thus E stands for the goal of effective new philosophies for specific symptoms in inelegant REBT and for the goal of an effective philosophy of life (which includes effective new philosophies for specific symptoms) in elegant REBT.

As part of teaching anti-*must*urbatory thinking, Ellis (1999a) actively encourages practically all his clients to achieve three highly important cognitive-emotional-behavioural states or goals.

- *Unconditional self-acceptance (USA)*   Clients can always choose to accept themselves just because they are alive and human, whether or not they perform well or are approved of by others.
- *Unconditional other acceptance (UOA)*   Whatever other people do and however abominably they act, clients can choose to accept the sinner, though not their sins, to try to help them behave better, and to refuse to damn them as persons.
- *High frustration tolerance (HFT)*   Clients can choose to acknowledge that their desires are not needs, adversities are not awful but can be highly inconvenient, they can stand what they do not like, and that 'long-range hedonism, or striving for today's pleasures, without neglecting tomorrow's, will often get them more of what they want and less of what they dislike' (Ellis, 1999a, p. 39).

PROCESS OF THERAPY

Right from the start, therapists show clients that REBT is an active-directive structured therapy focusing on helping clients not only to feel better, but, by changing their thinking and behaviour, to get better. Orientation or induction can be by way of pre-therapy demonstrations, brief explanatory lectures at the start of therapy, and using client problem material to illustrate the application of REBT (Ellis and Dryden, 1997).

Before commencing therapy some REBT therapists like clients to fill out a basic biographical information form that also elicits information about clients presenting problems (see Ellis and Dryden, 1997, pp. 88–95). In addition, therapists may ask clients to fill out a personality data form which asks clients questions about their feelings in the following areas: acceptance, frustration, injustice, achievement, worth, control, certainty and catastrophizing (Ellis and Dryden, 1997, pp. 36–9).

Clients are encouraged to focus on specific problems right from the start. Early in therapy Ellis frequently reads out the client's answer to item 23 in the biographical information questionnaire which asks: 'Briefly list (PRINT) your present main complaints, symptoms and problems.' Clients are then asked to discuss what problem is most bothersome. Probably the main form of assessment in REBT is that which comes from having a number of sessions with clients and working with the material they share. Towards the end of the initial phase of REBT, both therapist and client should have an understanding of the client's main emotional and behavioural problems and start to prioritize these to provide a structure for their future work together.

The middle phase of REBT is focused on therapists adopting an educational approach to teaching clients how to strengthen their rational beliefs and weaken their irrational beliefs. This phase of REBT has two main agendas: helping clients solve their particular emotional and behavioural problems, and teaching them the skills of identifying and solving problems. In general, in addition to focusing on what clients have been most bothered about during the previous week, therapists encourage them to work through a consistent problem before moving on to the next. Homework tasks are assigned and particular attention is paid to what the client has learned or failed to learn between sessions so that blocks to the learning process can be addressed. Frequently, clients are asked to fill out REBT self-help forms as part of homework assignments. Hard and persistent challenging of irrational beliefs tends to be a prominent feature of the middle phase.

The main purpose of the end phase of REBT is to help clients become their own therapists. Termination may take place not when clients have worked through all their problems using REBT skills, but when they feel confident they can use these skills to address the remaining problems on their own. Therapists work towards termination either by decreasing the frequency of sessions or by negotiating a specific termination date. During the end phase, therapists can work with clients to anticipate problems and difficulties and articulate how they might use their REBT skills to deal with these problems. Most REBT therapists schedule follow-up sessions to monitor client progress.

REBT is committed to assisting clients to maintain their changes. However, Ellis (1988) acknowledges the likelihood of backsliding. Right from the start, clients are taught that they can only change and maintain change with work and practice. Throughout therapy, homework assignments are used to help clients build skills for both outside and after therapy. When clients find themselves backsliding, they are told to go back to the ABCs and see what they did which caused them to fall back into their old patterns. They are then encouraged to forcefully dispute (D) these irrational beliefs. They are advised to try and try again until they genuinely replace their irrational beliefs with their effective new philosophies (E).

Most clients are seen by therapists for weekly individual sessions. Ellis' own therapy sessions often last for thirty minutes. Clients normally have between five and fifty sessions. Brief therapy of one to ten sessions is used for clients who have specific problems or for those only prepared to stay in therapy for a short time (Ellis, 1996). Individuals who are not too generally disturbed can usually attain the inelegant change of symptom removal in brief therapy. Preferably, individuals with severe problems come for individual and/or group therapy for at least six months so that they can practise what they learn.

REBT can be used with most kinds of clients, ranging from those who are mildly disturbed to juvenile delinquents, borderline personality disorders, psychotics when they have some contact with reality and individuals with higher grade mental deficiency. Normally, Ellis does not consider REBT suitable for clients who are out of contact with reality, in a highly manic state, seriously autistic or brain injured, and in the lower ranges of mental deficiency. Seriously disturbed clients are often referred for medication in addition to REBT.

REBT is significantly more effective with mildly disturbed clients and with those who have a single major symptom, say sexual inadequacy, than with strongly disturbed clients. Therapists find it much more difficult to assist the latter to change, since REBT theory hypothesizes that the causes of musturbatory thinking and emotional disturbance are largely innate.

THE THERAPEUTIC RELATIONSHIP

In REBT, the main role of the therapist is that of an authoritative, but not authoritarian, teacher who strives to impart to clients self-helping skills conducive to thinking rationally, feeling appropriately and behaving effectively so that they can attain their goals. REBT practitioners often employ a fairly rapid-fire active-directive-persuasive-philosophic methodology. In most instances, they quickly pin down clients to a few basic dysfunctional beliefs (Ellis, 2000).

What kind of a therapeutic relationship best supports this active-directive teaching role? Therapists try to build rapport with clients by using empathic listening, including reflecting feelings. Ellis and Dryden (1997) distinguish between *affective* empathy – understanding how clients feel; and *philosophic* empathy – understanding the philosophies or thinking underlying these feelings. Therapists attempt to offer both kinds of empathy. In addition, therapists offer clients unconditional other acceptance (UOA), accepting them as fallible human beings and not judging the goodness or badness of their personhood against predetermined moral standards. However, frequently, and if appropriate, therapists will share their reactions to clients' negative behaviours.

REBT therapists do not show undue warmth to most of their clients. They are wary of colluding in clients' dire needs for approval. They also try to encourage clients to confront their own problems and assume responsibility for finding their own warmth and happiness rather than seeking it from therapists. Often clients perceive REBT therapists as warm and caring because of their commitment to their welfare and tolerance for all individuals.

Particularly during early sessions, therapists do most of the talking. They do not hesitate to confront clients with how they contribute to their own distress. They forcefully dispute and debate their clients' illogical thinking as well as helping clients to do this for themselves. They freely share their opinions and self-disclose, so long as this is not detrimental to clients. Furthermore they use humour, but never at their clients' expense, since they consider that many of them take themselves and their problems far too seriously. Therapists also use humour to attack disturbance-producing ideas.

A distinction exists between REBT content and the therapist's style of working with clients. Ellis' therapeutic style, like that of many of his followers, is hard-hitting and forceful. However, Ellis may well go more slowly and gently before doing any vigorous disputing when working with clients who have suffered from extreme traumas, such as rape or child abuse. Other REBT practitioners, either with specific clients or with all of their clients, choose varying degrees of passive and gentle styles.

THERAPEUTIC INTERVENTIONS

Detecting irrational beliefs and their derivatives

Therapists as teachers detect clients' irrational beliefs, their musturbations, and their derivatives – for instance, awfulizing. Furthermore, they teach clients how to do this for themselves. In order to relinquish their demandingness, it helps if clients can acknowledge that they may possess this characteristic. Ellis teaches them his ABC system. Within the ABC system, irrational beliefs can be traced cognitively, emotionally and behaviourally. Cognitively, irrational beliefs can be detected through overt or implicit signs of demandingness. In particular, Ellis looks for 'musts', 'shoulds', 'oughts', 'have tos' and 'got tos' that signal clients' musturbatory absolutistic beliefs. In addition, he looks for explicit and implicit phrases such as 'That is horrible!' and 'I can't stand it' that indicate derivatives of possessing primary and secondary irrational beliefs.

Emotionally, irrational beliefs are signalled by unhealthy feelings, such as panic and depression. Behaviourally, self-defeating actions offer clues to irrational beliefs. Sometimes the cognitive, emotional and behavioural clues are obvious to both therapists and clients. On other occasions, though obvious to therapists, clients may resist acknowledging the evidence. In still other instances, clients may hold irrational beliefs in subtle and tricky ways that make them seem natural

(Ellis, 1987). Such beliefs can challenge therapists' powers of detection.

Disputing irrational beliefs and their derivatives

It is insufficient for musts and their derivatives to disappear just to acknowledge them. Instead, therapists and clients combine to fight them by disputing them. The technique of disputing is the most typical and perhaps the most often used method of REBT. Disputing involves challenging and questioning unsubstantiated hypotheses that clients hold about themselves, others and the world. In most instances, REBT therapists quickly pin down clients to a few central irrational ideas and their derivatives that they then challenge and dispute. In addition, they teach clients how to dispute their own beliefs. Cognitions, feelings and behaviours interact in how people create and maintain irrational beliefs. Therefore, when disputing irrational beliefs and their derivatives, therapists are likely to be more effective if they work in all three of the cognitive, emotional/experiential and behavioural modalities rather than in one or two. However, no modality is entirely pure or free from the others.

Cognitive interventions

Scientific questioning

Disputing may be approached using either a didactic or a Socratic style. In a didactic or lecturing style, therapists can provide explanations and illustrations. In a Socratic or scientific questioning appproach, through a series of leading questions therapists attempt to pinpoint where clients' thinking, feeling and behaving is becoming problematic. Such questions are not only for therapists to ask clients, but for clients to learn to ask themselves. When practising disputing, it is very important that clients do so outside of stressful situations to give them the chance to build up and fine tune their skills for the actual situations.

Box 6.3 illustrates four areas of cognitive disputing (Ellis and MacLaren, 1998).

The desired cognitive outcome of disputing specific irrational beliefs and their derivatives is a sound set of preferential beliefs or effective new philosophies (E) related to each belief.

Box 6.3   Four areas of cognitive disputing

Functional disputes

Functional disputing aims to point out to clients that their beliefs may be interfering with their attainment of their goals. Typical questions are:

- 'Is it helping you?'
- 'How is continuing to think this way (or behave, or feel this way) affecting your life?'

Empirical disputes

Empirical disputing aims to help clients evaluate the factual components of their beliefs. Typical questions are:

- 'Where is the evidence that you must succed at all important tasks you prefer?'
- 'Where is the proof that it is accurate?'
- 'Where is it written?'

Logical disputes

Logical disputing aims to highlight illogical leaps that clients make from desires and preferences to demands when thinking irrationally. Typical questions are:

- 'How does it follow that just because you'd like this thing to be true and it would be very convenient, it *should* be?'
- 'Where is the logic that because you sometimes *act* badly that makes you a *bad person*?'

Philosophical disputes

Philosophical disputing aims to address the meaning of and satisfaction in life issues. Clients often get so focused on identified problems that they lose perspective on other areas of life. A typical question might be:

- 'Despite the fact that things will probably not go the way you want some/most of the time in this area, can you still derive some satisfaction from your life?'

Desirable emotional and behavioural effects should stem from and interact with the effective new philosophies. For clients seeking elegant change, the desirable effect of learning how to dispute irrational beliefs is an effective new philosophy that can be applied both now and in the future. Box 6.4 provides an ABCDE example, which includes disputing and its effects (Ellis, 1988).

Box 6.4   An ABCDE example of cognitive disputing

A   I go for an interview and fail to get the job.

iB   'I must never get rejected.'
'How awful to get rejected!'
'I can't stand the rejection!
'This rejection makes me a rotten person.'
'I'll always do poorly in job interviews.'

C   Undesirable emotional consequences: depression, worthlessness, anxiety, anger.
Undesirable behavioural consequences: Refusing to go for other job interviews. Functioning poorly on job interviews through anxiety.

D   'Why must I never get rejected?'
'Why is it awful to get rejected for a job?'
'Why can't I stand this rejection?'
'How does this rejection make me a rotten person?'
'Why must I always do poorly on job interviews?'

E   'I'd prefer to have got this job, but there is no evidence that I absolutely must have it.'
'Nothing makes it awful to get rejected, though I find it highly inconvenient.'
'I can stand rejection, though I'll never like it.'
'Rejection never makes me a rotten person, but a person with some unfortunate traits.'
'I don't always have to do poorly on job interviews, especially if I try to learn from my errors.'
Illustrative emotional effect: feeling sorrowful, but not depressed.
Illustrative behavioural effect: I went for some more job interviews.

Rational coping statements

Therapist and client can formulate rational coping statements. This step is usually taken after forceful disputing of irrational beliefs, but it can sometimes accompany such disputing. Some coping statements can be simple encouragements: for instance, 'I can accomplish this task' or 'I don't have to get upset in these situations'. Rational coping statements can also address areas of irrational thinking: for example, statements such as 'I'd prefer to have got this job, but there is no evidence that I absolutely must have it' and 'Nothing makes it awful to get rejected, though I find it highly inconvenient' as illustrated in area E of Box 6.4.

Discussion

Therapists can discuss with clients various aspects of their irrational thinking. For instance, with Roger, a 24-year-old computer programmer afraid of public speaking, Ellis discussed the harm of self-rating and how he could choose to unconditionally accept himself whether or not he failed at speaking and whether or not he was anxious about failing and showed his anxiety to others (Ellis, 1991e).

Cognitive homework

Clients repeatedly need to challenge their irrational beliefs and to practise their disputing skills both to learn them and also to reinforce their new rational philosophies. REBT uses various homework techniques to develop disputing skills.

- *Cassettes of sessions* Therapists encourage clients to record sessions and listen to each one several times.
- *Self-help forms* Clients are encouraged to fill out self-help forms. Therapists check the forms to see how accurately clients dispute their irrational beliefs. For instance, in Sichel and Ellis' (1984) form, clients identify an activating event (A) and the consequences or conditions (C) they would like to change. The form consists of three columns. In the first column, clients circle which of thirteen irrational beliefs (B), for instance, 'I MUST do well or very well!' and 'People MUST live up to my expectations or it is TERRIBLE!', lead to their consequences (C). In addition, they can add other relevant

irrational beliefs. In the second column, there is space for them to dispute (D) each circled irrational belief. In the third column, they write in effective rational beliefs (E) to replace their irrational beliefs. After the columns there is a space (F) where they can write in feelings and behaviours experienced after arriving at their effective rational beliefs. The form ends with the following self-statement about the necessity of work and practice: 'I WILL WORK HARD TO REPEAT MY EFFECTIVE RATIONAL BELIEFS FORCEFULLY TO MYSELF ON MANY OCCASIONS SO THAT I CAN MAKE MYSELF LESS DISTURBED NOW AND ACT LESS SELF-DEFEATINGLY IN THE FUTURE' (Sichel and Ellis, 1984, p. 2).

Another self-help form is known as DIBS (Disputing Irrational Beliefs). DIBS consists of six questions about the belief I want to dispute, whether the belief can be rationally supported, existing evidence for the belief, existing evidence against the belief, the worst that could happen to me if I never achieved what I wanted with regard to the belief, and good things that might happen if I never achieved what I wanted (Dryden and Ellis, 1986). A further self-help form is Dryden and Walker's written self-help form which takes clients through the ABCDE sequence (Dryden and Walker, 1992; Ellis and Dryden, 1997).

- *Reminder cards*   Clients can write out rational coping statements on 3 × 5 cards and repeat them at various times between sessions.
- *Referenting*   Referenting is a term for asking clients to do a cost benefit analysis in which they list the real advantages and disadvantages of changing their irrational thoughts and behaviours.
- *Practising REBT on others*   Encouraging clients to practise talking their friends and relatives out of their disturbances.
- *Visualizing*   Clients can be shown how to visualize themselves competently performing situations they currently fear.
- *Bibliotherapy*   Assigning clients self-help books to read, for instance, Ellis (1977a, 1988, 1999b), Ellis and Becker (1982), and Ellis and Harper (1997). Ellis (1993d) is keenly aware of the advantages and disadvantages of self-help materials.
- *Self-help cassettes*   Ellis has made innumerable audio-cassettes, including *Solving Emotional Problems* (Ellis,

1982b), *How to be Happy Though Human* (1984) and *How to Stop Worrying and Start Living* (1987b). In addition, clients can watch videotapes of therapists working with clients in areas such as coping with anger and overcoming low frustration tolerance. Many clients find listening to cassettes and observing videotapes helpful.

Problem-solving

Clients bring their goals (G) to the activating events and adversities (A) in their lives. These goals present many practical or reality problems for them to try to solve: for instance, obtaining a good education, finding a mate, getting a job, succeeding at work. Clients have a choice about whether they solve these reality problems or choose to upset themselves about them. If clients upset themselves, they have an emotional problem about their reality problem. In such cases, therapists can assist them to detect and actively dispute the relevant irrational beliefs. Sometimes it is better that clients do not address practical difficulties until they have worked through related emotional difficulties. For instance, an individual or couple might defer a decision to divorce until they have given themselves a sufficient chance to see whether or not, with a lessening of their irrational beliefs, they might happily continue to live together.

Therapists willingly assist clients to solve reality problems. However, where necessary, they also insist on vigorously detecting and disputing accompanying irrational beliefs. In assisting problem-solving, therapists help clients to state problems and goals clearly, generate and evaluate alternative strategies, outline the steps to attain goals, identify resources and supports, and develop the requisite practical skills for success.

Emotive/experiential interventions

REBT therapists use emotional/experiential interventions to supplement and reinforce cognitive interventions (Ellis and MacLaren, 1998). Such interventions include the following.

Rational emotive imagery

In rational emotive imagery (REI), clients are encouraged to imagine one of the worst activating events or adversities (A) that could happen to them, for instance, rejection by someone whose approval they really want (Ellis, 1993f; Ellis and MacLaren, 1998). They vividly imagine this adversity occurring and bringing a host of problems into their life.

They are then encouraged to get in touch with the undesirable negative emotional consequences triggered by this adversity (A) – for instance, anxiety, depression, rage, self-hatred or self-pity – and really, really feel it (C1). They should spontaneously feel what they feel and not what they are supposed to feel. Once they feel unhealthily upset at C1, they should hold on to this feeling for a minute or two. Then, keeping the same adversity (A) in their imagination, they should work on changing their disturbed negative feeling to a prescribed healthy negative feeling consequence (C2), such as sorrow, disappointment, regret, frustration, irritation or displeasure. The way to do this is by telling themselves strongly and repetitively sensible rational beliefs or coping statements: for example, 'Yes, they really did treat me shabbily and unfairly, which I wish they wouldn't have done. But there is no reason why they must treat me fairly, however preferable that would be' (Ellis, 1993f, pp. 11–19). Clients should persist with their imagery and rational statements until they change their unhealthy feeling (C1) to a healthy negative feeling (C2) – it usually takes only a few minutes. They should be set the homework assignment of carrying out this imagery procedure daily for about thirty days for each disturbed feeling they are trying to change.

Forceful disputing

Forceful disputing may be performed both by therapists on clients and clients on themselves (Ellis, 1993e). Since many irrational beliefs involve hot cognitions that possess a large emotional component, they require forceful and vigorous disputing. Therapists often need to strongly argue, persuade and point out the shaky logic of their clients' beliefs. Weak or moderately strong disputing may be insufficient. Ellis showed Roger, a computer programmer, how to create strong anti-worrying statements about public speaking and say them to himself forcefully: for example, 'I NEVER, NEVER, NEVER have to speak well or unnervously in public, though it would be nice if I did!' (Ellis, 1991e, p. 454). In addition, Ellis worked out with Roger a dialogue with himself in which he cassette-recorded some of his potent irrational beliefs, for example, 'I'm a nervous slob who deserves to be mute rather than risk making a fool of myself in public!' and in which he vigorously, forcefully and heatedly disputed them. Clients can make, and remake more powerfully, such cassettes for themselves as homework. They can then play them back to themselves, their therapists and, if in therapy groups, to the other group members.

Role-playing

Ellis uses role-playing as a way of showing clients what their false ideas are and how they affect relating to others. In role-playing, therapists place clients in simulated situations and offer assistance in thinking more effectively in them. For instance, Roger role-played giving a difficult talk in front of Ellis and the therapy group he had joined as an adjunct to individual sessions. When Roger appeared anxious during the role-play, Ellis stopped the performance to let Roger ask himself 'What am I telling myself right now to *make* myself anxious? And what can I do right now to think and feel away this anxiety?' (Ellis, 1991e, p. 454).

Reverse role-playing

Reverse role-playing is another REBT forceful disputing technique. Client and therapist switch roles, so that clients are now in a position to actively dispute their own irrational beliefs, which the therapist holds on to as strongly as the client did in earlier sessions. For example, Ellis role-played Roger tenaciously holding on to some of his irrational beliefs so that Roger could practise forcefully attacking them (Ellis, 1993e).

Unconditional acceptance

The therapist's basic acceptance of them as individuals helps clients feel and think that they are acceptable, despite any negative characteristics.

Humour

The judicious use of humour can help reduce clients' irrational beliefs and self-defeating behaviours to absurdity. Therapists frequently exaggerate clients' nutty ideas and use 'various kinds of puns, witticisms, irony, whimsy, evocative language, slang, and deliberate use of sprightly obscenity' (Ellis, 1980, p. 26). For example, Ellis said to Roger, his public speaking phobia client: 'You really should feel ashamed of avoiding making speeches. Every other person your age speaks fluently and has no anxiety. What a unique jerk you are!' (Ellis, 1991e, p. 454). Encouraging clients to sing to themselves rational humorous songs (Ellis, 1977d) and telling amusing anecdotes are further methods to counteract clients' tendencies to not take themselves, others and the world too seriously.

Behavioural interventions

As with emotional/experiential interventions, REBT therapists use behavioural interventions to supplement and reinforce cognitive interventions. Ellis doubts whether people ever truly change their irrational beliefs until they act many times against them. When young, Ellis suffered from severe fears of public speaking and meeting new women. He forced himself to repetitively engage in activities that challenged his fears, giving political talks and talking to women on a park bench in the Bronx Botanical Garden. In both instances his actions helped rid him of his irrational fears (Ellis, 1997a). The following are some REBT behavioural interventions.

Assignments that challenge demandingness

Clients who have musturbatory beliefs about approval and derivatives of these beliefs about the awfulness of rejection may be encouraged to ask someone for a date or force themselves to socialize. Simultaneously they convince themselves that it is not awful but only inconvenient to get rejected. Clients who have perfectionist beliefs may have the assignment of deliberately making a real attempt to speak badly in public.

Clients are encouraged to do their assignments *repetitively*. For instance, Roger, the speech-anxious client, was asked to speak in public as often as he could, once or twice a week (Ellis, 1991e). Often clients are asked to do their assignments *floodingly*, staying in situations they perceive as highly dangerous until they see that their 'danger' is largely imagined. For instance, clients who are afraid of riding on buses or underground trains are urged to do this immediately, many times a day in rush-hour, if that is what they most fear. Concurrently, in all instances where clients dispute their musturbatory beliefs behaviourally, they can dispute them cognitively too.

Shame attacking exercises

Ellis hypothesizes that ego anxiety is highly related to feelings of shame, guilt, embarrassment and humiliation. Consequently, the more people confront the irrational beliefs behind these feelings, the less they are likely to disturb themselves. Clients are encouraged to do things in public that they regard as particularly shameful or embarrassing. Examples are yelling out the stops on elevators, buses or underground trains or asking for sex-related items in loud voices in chemist shops.

After explaining the principle of shame attacking exercises, REBT therapists can negotiate exercises with clients. The purpose of these exercises is to prove that these behaviours in themselves are really not shameful and that they can be done with relative comfort and self-acceptance. In addition, clients are urged to disclose more about what they perceive, or what they perceive others perceive, as shameful. Box 6.5 provides an example of a shame attacking exercise (Ellis, 1996, pp. 91–4).

Skills training

The distinction between behavioural skills and cognitive skills is imprecise. Always, when therapists assist clients with behavioural skills, for instance, assertion and communication skills, they train clients cognitively in disputing the accompanying irrational beliefs and derivative self-statements. Clients are sometimes asked to seek additional training experiences to acquire relevant skills. For instance, Ellis thought that speech-anxious Roger showed insufficient assertion skills at work, for

---

Box 6.5 Example of a shame attacking exercise

The therapist

Albert Ellis

The client

Chana, who was anxious about test-taking, kept procrastinating in her studies, and refused to take some important subjects at school because she knew that this would entail sitting several tests during the term. Chana was afraid of people finding out how poorly she did in tests.

The shame attacking exercise

Chana chose the exercise of asking strangers for a dollar bill. Ellis instructed Chana, when asking strangers for dollar bills, to work on possible feelings of humiliation and embarrassment and then choose not to make herself feel unashamed and unembarrassed.

During the exercise

At first Chana felt very nervous and tongue-tied about going up to a stranger. However, she reminded herself that she did not need the stranger's approval and, by the third time she tried it, she really began to feel shameless and, by the fifth time, started enjoying the exercise.

After the exercise

As a result of the exercise Chana saw that she could do shame attacking exercises with people who knew her in which she talked about her test-taking problems. As part of this process, Chana developed the effective new philosophy: 'I don't need their goddamned approval. Let them think what they think!'

---

instance, not refusing to give presentations when genuinely unprepared. Ellis encouraged Roger to attend a six-week assertion course at his institute as well as a five-month public speaking course at a local college (Ellis, 1991e).

Use of rewards and penalties

REBT therapists use rewards and penalties to encourage clients to do homework and implement self-change pro- grammes (Ellis, 1980; Ellis and Dryden, 1997). For instance, every time Roger filled out an RET self-help report or gave a public speech, he would reward himself by listening to one of his favourite CDs. Whenever he failed to carry out an assign- ment, he would talk to his boring aunt for thirty minutes. Two doses of this excruciating penalty cured Roger of not doing assignments! (Ellis, 1991e).

OVERCOMING RESISTANCE

When clients resist following therapy procedures and doing homework assignments, they mainly do so because of the following irrational beliefs (Ellis, 1986a): (1) 'I *must* do well at changing myself'; (2) 'You (the therapist and others) *must* help me change'; and (3) 'Changing myself *must* occur quickly and easily'. Stemming from such beliefs (B), resisters have negative feelings consequences, for instance, depression and self-pity, and behavioural consequences, for instance, procrastination and withdrawal. In addition, they employ derivatives of irrational beliefs, such as awfulizing. The main REBT approach to resistant clients is to teach them to find and forcefully dispute the main irrational beliefs contributing to their resistance.

Therapists can encourage resistant clients to use rational coping statements, for instance, 'Therapy doesn't have to be easy. I can, in fact, enjoy its difficulty and its challenge' (Ellis, 1986a, p. 262). In addition, therapists can ask clients to list the disadvantages of resisting and the advantages of working at therapy and then regularly reviewing and think- ing about these lists. Furthermore, some resistant clients can be helped by proselytizing REBT and using it on friends and relatives.

CASE MATERIAL

Ellis has been conscientious about providing case demonstra- tions of REBT in action, only some of which are mentioned here. Ellis presents a case example containing verbatim transcripts of the first, second and fourth sessions with a woman who comes to therapy because she is self-punishing, impulsive and compulsive, afraid of males, has no goals in life, and is guilty about her relationship with her parents (Ellis, 1971; Wedding and Corsini, in press).

Ellis provides verbatim transcript, plus commentary, of his conducting a first session of REBT brief therapy with Ted, a 38-year-old African-American, married for twenty years with two children, who became panicked whenever he took the train to work or back to his office and whenever he thought about having intercourse with his wife (Ellis, 1996). Another verbatim transcript case example is that of the first fifteen minutes of an initial interview Ellis conducted with a 25-year-old single woman, Sara, who worked as the head of a computer programming section, and who, without any traumatic or violent history, was very insecure and self-denigrating (Ellis, 2000). Ellis also discusses Sara's overall treatment of a further six sessions of individual work, followed by twenty-four weeks of REBT group therapy and one weekend of a rational encounter marathon group.

A further verbatim transcript case example is that of Ellis working with a woman therapist who volunteers to bring up problems of feeling inadequate as a therapist and as a person. Ellis and Dryden then review the transcript and analyse its REBT aspects (Ellis and Dryden, 1997). In yet another case example of REBT, though this time without transcripts, Ellis illustrates the cognitive, emotive and behavioural methods he used during therapy with Jane, a 27-year-old woman afflicted with severe social and work anxiety (Ellis and Dryden, 1997).

Ellis may also be seen conducting therapy. An early example is his work with Gloria in the *Three Approaches to Psychotherapy* film series (Ellis, 1965). In addition, videos of Ellis and other prominent REBT therapists conducting sessions are available from the Albert Ellis Institute (address and website at the end of this chapter). For example, Ellis has made a videotape in which he conducts therapy with a woman dealing with guilt over her husband's suicide. In another videotape entitled *Dealing with Addictions*, Ellis interviews a 32-year-old man with low frustration tolerance, short-term hedonism and polyabuse.

FURTHER DEVELOPMENTS

Other applications of REBT include group therapy and marathons either along with individual counselling or instead of it (Ellis, 1992; Ellis and Dryden, 1997). In group REBT, members are taught to apply detecting and disputing irrational beliefs on one another (Ellis, 2000). They also practise attacking their ego disturbance irrational beliefs through disclosing material they perceive as risky. In addition, clients in groups, while working on assertion and other communication skills, can partake in role-plays.

Ellis has a major interest in the application of REBT to marital, couples and family relationship problems (Ellis, 1986b, 1991c, 1991d, 1993c, 2000; Ellis and Dryden, 1997). Therapists usually see marital or love partners together, listen to their complaints, and then teach them that even though their complaints may accurately describe behaviour at A, their upsetness at C is not justified. In particular, work focuses on musturbatory beliefs generating hostility. In addition, therapists frequently teach partners compromising and relationship skills. In family REBT, tolerance for oneself and others, independent of how obnoxious specific behaviours may be, is repeatedly taught to both parents and children.

Ellis is possibly the most influential English-speaking psychological educator of the twentieth century in terms of helping ordinary people learn how to overcome their emotional disturbances and become more self-actualizing. Through his books and cassettes he has made a major contribution to educating the public in America and elsewhere on how to live more effectively. He has also influenced numerous other writers of self-help books. A recent public education application of REBT has been the development of nine-hour intensive workshops (Ellis and Dryden, 1997).

REBT is practised widely throughout the world, with institutes or centres established in Britain, Australia, the United States, France, Germany, Holland, Italy, India, Israel and Mexico. Ellis concludes that REBT is what its name implies: rational and emotive, realistic and visionary, empirical and humanistic. Such an approach befits human beings in all their complexity (Ellis, 2000).

SUMMARY

- *Rational emotive behaviour therapy (REBT) is not a purely intellectual approach, but strongly emphasizes the interplay of feeling, behaviour and cognition.*
- *Human beings' fundamental goals are survival, freedom from pain and happiness. Their feelings can be healthy and appropriate or unhealthy and inappropriate.*
- *People have biological tendencies both to actualizing themselves as healthy goal-attaining human beings and to being irrational and disturbing themselves.*
- *Ellis has expanded his ABC theory of personality to a GABCDE theory: G, goals; A, adversities or activating events; B, beliefs, both rational and irrational; C, consequences, both emotional and behavioural; D, disputing irrational beliefs; and E, effective new philosophy.*
- *In pursuit of their goals (G), people create unhealthy emotions and self-defeating behaviours at C because they have demanding, as contrasted with preferential, beliefs at B in relation to adversities and activating events at A. In addition, they have derivatives of their demanding beliefs, for instance, awfulizing, I-can't-stand-it-itis, and damning themselves and others. These beliefs and their derivatives can be grouped into two main headings: ego disturbance and low frustration tolerance.*
- *As well as their innate tendencies to irrationality, human beings acquire irrational beliefs partly by social learning, but also because they do not develop and exercise their capacity for rational choice.*
- *Reasons why people persist in maintaining irrational beliefs include biological tendencies to irrationality, the emotional strength of their beliefs, insufficient scientific thinking, reinforcing consequences, emphasizing their 'Godawful' pasts, unrealistic beliefs about change, and insufficiently challenging their beliefs through action.*
- *REBT has inelegant goals, symptom removal, and elegant goals, helping clients become less disturbable through possessing an effective new philosophy. It aims to help clients not only feel better but get better, by changing from rigid and demanding to preferential thinking. As part of this process clients are helped to develop unconditional self-*

acceptance (USA), unconditional other acceptance (UOA) and high frustration tolerance (HFT).

- REBT is an active-directive structured therapy in which clients are encouraged to focus on specific problems right from the start.
- The REBT therapist is a teacher who uses a variety of cognitive, emotive/experiential and behavioural interventions to assist clients to dispute (D) their irrational beliefs and their derivatives so that they can develop an effective new philosophy (E).
- Disputing by means of scientific questioning is the main cognitive intervention. Four areas of cognitive disputing are functional, empirical, logical and philosophical. In addition, therapists help clients to solve genuine problems in their lives.
- Emotive/experiential interventions include rational-emotive imagery, forceful disputing, role-playing and reverse role-playing, unconditional acceptance and humour.
- Behavioural interventions include assignments that challenge demandingness, shame attacking exercises, skills training and use of rewards and penalties.
- REBT aims to assist clients to maintain their changes through stressing work and practice, assigning homework, and teaching clients, if they backslide, to go back to their ABCs and then dispute irrational beliefs that cause them to revert to previous behaviours.
- Other applications of REBT include group therapy, marital and family therapy, and psychological education. REBT institutes and centres exist in North and South America, Europe, the Middle East and Australia.

REVIEW AND PERSONAL QUESTIONS

Review questions

1. Why does Ellis now call his approach rational emotive behaviour therapy?
2. Describe the differences between healthy or appropriate and unhealthy or inappropriate emotions?
3. What does Ellis consider to be the biological basis of personality?

4. Give an example of Ellis' ABC theory where B represents:

   - demanding musturbatory thinking
   - preferential thinking?

5. Critically discuss Ellis' ideas about the derivatives of irrational beliefs.

6. Discuss the roles of social learning and free choice in acquiring irrational beliefs.

7. Describe the contribution of each of the following factors to maintaining, and possibly strengthening, irrational beliefs:

   - biological tendencies
   - emotional contributions
   - insufficient scientific thinking
   - reinforcing consequences
   - emphasizing one's 'Godawful' past
   - unrealistic beliefs about change
   - insufficiently challenging beliefs through action.

8. What are the differences between inelegant and elegant therapy goals?

9. Outline the process of REBT individual therapy.

10. What is the nature of the therapist–client relationship in REBT?

11. Give at least one example of each of the following ways of disputing irrational beliefs: functional, empirical, logical and philosophical. Apart from scientific questioning, what other cognitive interventions do REBT therapists use?

12. Describe emotional/experiential interventions used in REBT.

13. Describe behavioural interventions used in REBT.

14. Critically discuss the issue of overcoming resistance in REBT.

Personal questions

1. Identify at least two of your irrational beliefs based on absolutistic demanding thinking in relation to each of the following:

   - yourself
   - others
   - the conditions under which you live.

2. For one of the irrational beliefs you identified above, state

   - how you acquired it
   - how you maintain it.

3. From your own life, give an example of each of the following:

   - the ABCs of rational thinking
   - the ABCs of irrational thinking.

4. Choose one of your irrational beliefs (B) that you wish to change. How could you dispute (D) it by:

   - cognitive methods?
   - emotive/experiential methods?
   - behavioural methods?

   What new effective new philosophy (E) would you arrive at?

5. What relevance, if any, has the theory and practice of rational emotive behaviour therapy for how you conduct therapy?

6. What relevance, if any, has the theory and practice of rational emotive behaviour therapy for how you live?

ANNOTATED BIBLIOGRAPHY

Ellis, A. and Dryden, W. (1997) *The Practice of Rational Emotive Behaviour Therapy*. London: Free Association Books, and New York: Springer.

This book presents the general theory and basic practice of rational emotive behaviour therapy (REBT), with special chapters on how it is used in individual, couples, family, group, marathon, and sex therapy. It brings the original seminal book on REBT, *Reason and Emotion in Psychotherapy* (Ellis, 1962), up to date, and gives details of many REBT procedures.

Ellis, A. and MacLaren, C. (1998) *Rational Emotive Behavior Therapy: A Therapist's Guide*. San Luis Obispo, CA: Impact Publishers.

Practical and accessible, this REBT therapist guide includes chapters on the philosophical and personality theory foundations of REBT, its theory of personality disturbance and change, assessment, cognitive techniques, emotive/experiential techniques, behavioural techniques and the integration of REBT with other systems of therapy.

Ellis, A. (2000) 'Rational emotive behavior therapy', in R. J. Corsini and D. Wedding (eds) *Current Psychotherapies* (6th edn, pp. 168–204). Itasca, IL: Peacock.

An authoritative overview of the theory and practice of rational emotive behaviour therapy written by its originator.

Ellis, A. (1991b) 'The revised ABC's of Rational-emotive therapy (RET)'. *Journal of Rational-Emotive & Cognitive Behavior Therapy*, 9, 139–72.

An important paper in which Ellis discusses basic human goals and values; the ABCs of emotional disturbance; interactions of As, Bs and Cs; the ABCs of interpersonal relationships; and using the ABCs in therapy.

Ellis, A. and Harper, R. A. (1997) *A Guide to Rational Living*. North Hollywood, CA: Wilshire Books.

This is a completely revised and rewritten version of the REBT self-help classic which is often recommended to clients by cognitive-behaviour therapists. The book is a succinct, straightforward approach to REBT based on self-questioning and homework and shows how readers can help themselves with various emotional problems.

Ellis, A. (1999b) *How to Make Yourself Happy and Remarkably Less Disturbable*. Atascadero, CA: Impact Publishers.

Every therapist is at risk of crooked thinking. An excellent way to learn about REBT is to apply it to yourself. This entertaining self-help book presents Ellis' views on emotional disturbance and on the importance of scientific thinking. Readers are then presented with a series of chapters showing them in simple language 'how to' take and maintain more control of their thoughts, feelings and actions.

Dryden, W. (1999) *Rational Emotive Behaviour Counselling in Action* (2nd edn). London: Sage.

This introductory book succinctly and systematically presents the theory and practice of REBT. The book's three parts comprise: (1) the basic principles of rational emotive behavioural counselling; (2) the rational emotive behavioural counselling sequence; and (3) the rational emotive behavioural counselling process.

REFERENCES

Dryden, W. (1989) 'Albert Ellis: an efficient and passionate life'. *Journal of Counseling and Development*, 67, 539–46 (interview with Albert Ellis).

Dryden, W. (1999) *Rational Emotive Behaviour Counselling in Action* (2nd edn). London: Sage.

Dryden, W. and Ellis, A. (1986) 'Rational-emotive therapy (RET)', in W. Dryden and W. Golden (eds) *Cognitive-Behavioural Approaches to Psychotherapy* (pp. 129–68). London: Harper & Row.

Dryden, W. and Walker, J. (1992) *ABC of Emotional and Behavioural Problems* (self-help form). New York: Albert Ellis Institute for Rational Emotive Behaviour Therapy.

Ellis, A. (1958a) *Sex Without Guilt*. New York: Lyle Stuart.

Ellis, A. (1958b) 'Rational psychotherapy'. *Journal of General Psychology*, 59, 35–49.

Ellis, A. (1962) *Reason and Emotion in Psychotherapy*. Secaucus, NJ: Citadel.

Ellis, A. (1971) 'A twenty-three-year-old woman, guilty about not following her parents' rules', in A. Ellis, *Growth Through Reason: Verbatim Cases in Rational-Emotive Therapy*. Hollywood: Wilshire Books, pp. 223–86. Reprinted in D. Wedding and R. J. Corsini (eds) (2000) *Case Studies in Psychotherapy*. Itasca, IL: Peacock.

Ellis, A. (1977a) *Anger: How to Live With and Without It*. Sydney: Macmillan Sun Books.

Ellis, A. (1977b) 'The basic clinical theory of rational-emotive therapy', in A. Ellis and R. F. Grieger (eds) *Handbook of Rational-emotive Therapy* (pp. 3–34). New York: Springer Publishing.

Ellis, A. (1980) 'Overview of the clinical theory of rational-emotive therapy', in R. Grieger and J. Boyd (eds) *Rational-emotive Therapy: A Skills-based Approach* (pp. 1–31). New York: Van Nostrand Reinhold.

Ellis, A. (1985) *Overcoming Resistance: Rational-Emotive Therapy with Difficult Clients*. New York: Springer.

Ellis, A. (1986a) 'Rational-emotive therapy approaches to overcoming resistance', in A. Ellis and R. M. Grieger (eds) *Handbook of Rational-emotive Therapy* (Vol. 2, pp. 246–74). New York: Springer.

Ellis, A. (1986b) 'Application of rational-emotive therapy to love problems', in A. Ellis and R. M. Grieger (eds) *Handbook of Rational-emotive Therapy* (Vol. 2, pp. 162–82). New York: Springer.

Ellis, A. (1987) 'The impossibility of achieving consistently good mental health'. *American Psychologist*, 42, 364–75.

Ellis, A. (1988) *How to Stubbornly Refuse to Make Yourself Miserable about Anything, Yes Anything!* Sydney: Pan Macmillan.

Ellis, A. (1990) 'Is Rational-Emotive Therapy (RET) "rationalist" or "constructivist"?', in A. Ellis and W. Dryden, *The Essential Albert Ellis* (pp. 114–41). New York: Springer.

Ellis, A. (1991a) 'My life in clinical psychology', in C. E. Walker (ed.) *The History of Clinical Psychology in Autobiography* (Vol. 1, pp. 1–37). Pacific Grove, CA: Brooks/Cole.

Ellis, A. (1991b) 'The revised ABC's of Rational-emotive therapy (RET)'. *Journal of Rational-Emotive and Cognitive Behavior Therapy*, 9, 139–72.

Ellis, A. (1991c) 'Using RET effectively: reflections and interview', in M. E. Bernard (ed.) *Using Rational-emotive Therapy Effectively* (pp. 1–33). New York: Plenum.

Ellis, A. (1991d) 'Rational-emotive behavior marriage and family therapy', in A. M. Horne (ed.) *Family Counseling and Therapy* (3rd edn, pp. 489–513). Itasca, IL: Peacock.

Ellis, A. (1991e) 'Rational-emotive treatment of simple phobias'. *Psychotherapy*, 28, 452–6.

Ellis, A. (1991f) 'Achieving self-actualization: the rational-emotive approach', in A. Jones and R. Crandall (eds) *Handbook of Self-actualization* (Special Issue). *Journal of Social Behavior and Personality*, 6(5): 1–18.

Ellis, A. (1992) 'Group rational-emotive and cognitive-behavioral therapy'. *International Journal of Group Psychotherapy*, 42, 63–80.

Ellis, A. (1993a) 'Changing Rational-Emotive Therapy (RET) to Rational Emotive Behavior Therapy (REBT)'. *The Behavior Therapist*, 16, 257–8.

Ellis, A. (1993b) 'Reflections on rational-emotive therapy'. *Journal of Consulting and Clinical Psychology*, 61, 199–201.

Ellis, A. (1993c) 'The rational-emotive therapy (RET) approach to marital and family therapy'. *The Family Journal: Counselling and Therapy for Couples and Families*, 1, 292–307.

Ellis, A. (1993d) 'The advantages and disadvantages of self-help therapy materials'. *Professional Psychology: Research and Practice*, 24, 335–9.

Ellis, A. (1993e) 'Vigorous RET disputing', in M. E. Bernard and J. L. Wolfe (eds) *The RET Resource Book for Practitioners* (p. 117). New York: Institute for Rational-Emotive Therapy.

Ellis, A. (1993f) 'Rational-emotive imagery: RET version', in M. E. Bernard and J. L. Wolfe (eds) *The RET Resource Book for Practitioners* (pp. 11, 8–11, 10). New York: Institute for Rational-Emotive Therapy.

Ellis, A. (1994) *Reason and Emotion in Psychotherapy* (rev. edn). Secaucus, NJ: Citadel.

Ellis, A. (1996) *Better, Deeper and More Enduring Brief Therapy:*

The Rational Emotive Behavior Approach. New York: Brunner/ Mazel.
Ellis, A. (1997a) 'The evolution of Albert Ellis and rational emotive behavior therapy', in J. K. Zeig (ed.) *The Evolution of Psychotherapy: The Third Conference* (pp. 69–82). New York: Brunner/Mazel.
Ellis, A. (1997b) 'Using rational emotive behavior therapy techniques to cope with disability'. *Professional Psychology Research and Practice*, **28**, 17–22.
Ellis, A. (1997c) 'Extending the goals of behavior therapy and of cognitive behavior therapy'. *Behavior Therapy*, **28**, 333–9.
Ellis, A. (1999a) 'Three methods of rational emotive behavior therapy that make my psychotherapy effective'. *Psychotherapy Bulletin*, **34**, 38–9.
Ellis, A. (1999b) *How to Make Yourself Happy and Remarkably Less Disturbable*. Atascadero, CA: Impact Publishers.
Ellis, A. (2000) 'Rational emotive behavior therapy', in R. J. Corsini and D. Wedding (eds) *Current Psychotherapies* (6th edn, pp. 168–204). Itasca, IL: Peacock.
Ellis, A. and Becker, I. M. (1982) *A Guide to Personal Happiness*. Hollywood, CA: Wilshire Books.
Ellis, A. and Blau, S. (eds) (1998) *The Albert Ellis Reader*. Secaucus, NJ: Carol Publishing.
Ellis, A. and Dryden, W. (1997) *The Practice of Rational Emotive Behaviour Therapy*. London: Free Association Books, and New York: Springer.
Ellis, A. and Harper, R. A. (1997) *A Guide to Rational Living*. North Hollywood, CA: Wilshire Books.
Ellis, A. and MacLaren, C. (1998) *Rational Emotive Behavior Therapy: A Therapist's Guide*. San Luis Obispo, CA: Impact Publishers.
Palmer, S. (1993) 'In the counsellor's chair: Stephen Palmer interviews Dr. Albert Ellis'. *Counselling*, **4**, 171–4.
Sichel, J. and Ellis, A. (1984) 'RET self-help form'. New York: Institute for Rational-Emotive Therapy.
Wedding, D. and Corsini, R. J. (eds) (in press) *Case Studies in Psychotherapy* (3rd edn). Itasca, IL: Peacock.

Ellis on cassette (illustrative)

Ellis, A. (1977d) *A Garland of Rational Songs* (with songbook). New York: Institute for Rational Emotive Behavior Therapy.
Ellis, A. (1982b) *Solving Emotional Problems*. New York: Institute for Rational Emotive Behavior Therapy.

Ellis, A. (1984) *How to Be Happy Though Human*. New York: Institute for Rational Emotive Behavior Therapy.
Ellis, A. (1987b) *How to Stop Worrying and Start Living*. Washington, DC: Psychology Today Tapes.

Ellis on videotape (illustrative)

Coping with the Suicide of a Loved One (49 mins).
Dealing with Addictions (55 mins).

For further details of REBT publications, cassettes and videotapes, contact:
Albert Ellis Institute for Rational Emotive Behavior Therapy
45 East 65th Street
New York, NY 10021-6593
USA
Telephone: (212) 535-0822
Fax: (212) 249-3582
website: www.rebt.org
e-mail: info@rebt.org

Ellis on film

Ellis, A. (1965) 'Rational-emotive therapy', in E. Shostrom (ed.) *Three Approaches to Psychotherapy*. Santa Ana, CA: Psychological Films.

Cognitive Therapy

*Cognitive therapy aims to adjust information-pro-
cessing and initiate positive change in all systems by
acting through the cognitive system.*

Aaron Beck

INTRODUCTION

Cognitive therapy was initially developed in the early 1960s by
Dr Aaron Beck of the University of Pennsylvania. The theory
postulates that during clients' cognitive development they
learn incorrect habits of processing and interpreting information. Cognitive therapists attempt to unravel clients' distortions and help them to learn different and more realistic ways
of processing and reality-testing information.

Cognitive therapy's theoretical underpinnings come from
three main sources (Beck and Weishaar, 2000). First, the
phenomenological approach to psychology, which posits that
the individual's view of self and personal world are central to
how they behave. Second, structural theory and depth psychology; in particular Freud's theory contributed to Beck's
structuring cognition into primary and secondary processes.
Third, the work of more modern cognitive psychologists like
George Kelly influenced Beck; for example, Kelly's concept of
personal constructs is similar to Beck's idea of schemas (Beck
et al., 1990).

Influences on the practice of cognitive therapy include
Rogers, Ellis and the behaviour therapists. The gentle style of
questioning and emphasis on unconditional acceptance owes
much to person-centred therapy. The emphasis on finding
solutions to conscious problems resembles rational emotive
behaviour therapy. Setting goals and session agendas, testing
hypotheses, using specific behaviour change procedures and
assigning homework are among the contributions from behaviour therapy.

AARON BECK (1921–   )

Aaron Temkin 'Tim' Beck was born on 18 July 1921, in Providence, Rhode Island, the fourth but third surviving son of Russian Jewish immigrant parents. In 1919, Beck's parents lost their only daughter in an influenza epidemic, an event that precipitated a deep depression in his mother which lasted off and on for the rest of her life. At age 7, Beck had a near fatal illness which reinforced his mother's over-protectiveness. While his father was calm, Beck did not like his mother's moody, inconsistent and excitable behaviour. Beck's father, who ran a printing business, encouraged his interest in science and nature. At high school, Beck edited the school paper and graduated first in his class. While growing up, Beck developed many anxieties and phobias, including fears of abandonment, surgery, suffocation, public speaking and heights (Weishaar, 1993).

In 1942 Beck graduated from Brown University, having majored in English and political science. He took pre-medical courses both before and after graduating and, in 1946, received his MD from Yale University School of Medicine. From 1946 to 1948 he served a rotating internship and a residency in pathology at the Rhode Island Hospital. In 1950 he started a neurology residency at the Cushing Veterans Administration Hospital in Framingham, Massachusetts. Due to a shortage of psychiatry residents, against his wishes Beck was forced to complete a six-month rotation in psychiatry. Deciding to remain in psychiatry, from 1950 to 1952, he was a Fellow in psychiatry at the Austen Riggs Center in Stockbridge, Massachusetts. In 1953 the American Board of Psychiatry and Neurology certified Beck in psychiatry and, in 1958, Beck graduated from the Philadelphia Psychoanalytic Institute. Since 1954 Beck has been a faculty member in the University of Pennsylvania's Department of Psychiatry. He is currently University Professor Emeritus of Psychiatry and President of the independent Beck Institute for Cognitive Therapy and Research, where staff are affiliated with the University Psychiatry Department.

The period from 1960 to 1963 saw the development of cognitive therapy (Beck, 1963, 1964). Beck was researching and re-examining psychoanalytic theory and ended by discarding it. Beck observes: 'There's nothing that I've been associated with since 1963 the seeds of which were not in the 1962 to 1964 articles. That was the critical period: changing from psychoanalysis to developing a new theory of therapy' (Weishaar, 1993, p. 21). Beck's process of developing theory is that he first observes patients, then develops ways of measuring these observations, then formulates a theory if the observations are validated by a number of cases, then designs interventions congruent with the theory, then over time and through further experimentation continues to assess whether the theory is confirmed or negated. When developing theory Beck also uses self-observation.

Beck has authored or co-authored over 375 articles in professional and scientific journals. His fourteen books include *Cognitive Therapy and the Emotional Disorders*; *Cognitive Therapy of Depression*, co-authored with Rush, Shaw and Emery; *Anxiety Disorders and Phobias*, co-authored with Emery and assisted by Greenberg; *Love is Never Enough*; *Cognitive Therapy of Personality Disorders*, co-authored with Freeman and associates; *The Integrative Power of Cognitive Therapy*, co-authored with Alford; *Scientific Foundations of Cognitive Theory and Therapy of Depression*, co-authored with Clark and Alford; and *Prisoners of Hate: The Cognitive Basis of Anger, Hostility and Violence*. Tests and measures that Beck has developed with colleagues include the *Beck Depression Inventory*, the *Beck Hopelessness Scale*, the *Suicide Intent Scale*, the *Scale for Suicide Ideation*, and the *Beck Self-Concept Test*.

Beck's awards and honours include being awarded, in 1979, the American Psychiatric Association's Foundation Fund Prize for Research in Psychiatry for his research in depression and the development of cognitive therapy; in 1989, the American Psychological Association's Distinguished Scientific Award for Applications of Psychology; in 1997, the Cummings PSYCHE Award for Lifetime Achievement; and, in 1998, the Lifetime Achievement Award of the Association for the Advancement of Behavior Therapy. In addition, in 1987, Beck was elected a Fellow of Britain's Royal College of Psychiatrists.

Beck continues to be highly active in writing, research and training. In 1950, he married Phyllis, a continuing source of strength and support, who developed her own career by becoming a Pennsylvania Superior Court Judge. The Becks have four adult children and many grandchildren.

THEORY

In the theory of cognitive therapy, the nature and function of information processing (i.e., the assignment of meaning) constitute the key to understanding maladaptive behavior and positive therapeutic processes.

Aaron Beck

BASIC CONCEPTS

Cognition is the key to understanding and treating psychological disorders. Alford and Beck write: ' "Cognition" is defined as that function that involves inferences about one's experiences and about the occurrence and control of future events' (1997, p. 14). Human beings need to adapt to changing environmental circumstances. Cognition includes the processes involved in identifying and predicting complex relations among events for the purposes of adaptation. Human beings have the capacity both for primal/primitive and for higher level cognitive processing.

Schemas

Schemas are structures that consist of people's fundamental beliefs and assumptions. Schemas are meaning-making cognitive structures. There are two categories of meaning: first, the objective or public meaning of an event, which may have few significant implications for the individual; and second, its personal or private meaning. Meaning assignment controls the psychological systems, such as behavioural, emotional, attentional and memory, so that the individual can activate strategies for adaptation.

Schemas are relatively stable cognitive patterns that influence, through their beliefs, how people select and synthesize incoming information. They are developed early in life from personal experiences and identifications with significant others and reinforced by further learning experiences. Schemas are not pathological by definition – they may be adaptive or maladaptive. They are analogous to George Kelly's (1955) formulation of personal constructs. People categorize and evaluate their experiences through a matrix of schemas.

Schemas possess structural qualities such as degree of breadth, flexibility, and their relative prominence in a person's cognitive organization. In addition, according to the degree of energy invested in them at any time, schemas can range from latent to predominant. When schemas are hypervalent, they are prepotent and easily triggered. Psychopathology is characterized not only by the activation of inappropriate schemas but, in all probability, by their crowding out or inhibiting more adaptive schemas.

Modes

Contemporary cognitive theory stresses the concept of modes. Modes are networks of cognitive, affective, motivational and behavioural schemas. Modes are fundamental to personality since they interpret and adapt to emerging and ongoing situations (Beck and Weishaar, 2000). In earlier writings, cognitions were viewed as the mediating variable that triggered people's affective, motivational and behavioural systems. Instead of a linear relationship, all aspects of human functioning are viewed as acting together as a mode. Alford and Beck observe: 'The operation of a mode (e.g, anger, attack) across diverse psychological systems (emotion, motivation) is determined by the idiosyncratic schematic processing derived from an individual's genetic programming and internalised cultural/social beliefs' (1997, p. 10).

Modes can be primal, which means they are universal and linked to survival. Anxiety is an example of a primal mode. Examples of modes under conscious control include conversing and studying. Primal modes include primary process thinking that is primitive and that conceptualizes situations in global, rigid, biased and relatively crude ways. Primal modes of thinking may have originally been adaptive in an evolutionary sense, yet they can become maladaptive in everyday life when triggered by systematically biased thinking and misinterpretations.

In addition, humans are capable of higher levels of cognitive processing that tests reality and corrects primal, global conceptualizations. However, in psychopathology, these corrective functions become impaired and primary responses can escalate into full-blown psychiatric disorders. Nevertheless, conscious or higher level thinking can override primal thinking and make it more flexible and realistic. Cognitive therapy approaches dysfunctional modes by deactivating them, modifying their content and structure, and by constructing adaptive modes to neutralize them.

Cognitive vulnerability

The term *cognitive vulnerability* refers to human beings' cognitive frailty. Because of their schemas, each person has a set of unique vulnerabilities and sensitivities that predispose them to psychological distress. People's schemas and beliefs influence the way they process data about themselves. When they exhibit psychological problems, their dysfunctional schemas and beliefs lead them to systematically bias information in unhelpful ways.

Beck (Beck *et al.*, 1990) gives the example of Sue, who heard noises coming from the next room where her boyfriend Tom was working on some chores. Sue's first thought was that 'Tom is making a lot of noise'. However, Sue's information processing continued and she made the following interpretation of her experience: 'Tom is making a lot of noise *because he's angry at me.*' Her attribution of causality was produced by a conditional schema or belief that 'If an intimate of mine is noisy, it means he is angry at me'. Further down her hierarchy were the beliefs that 'If people reject me, I will be all alone' and 'Being alone will be devastating'. At the most basic level Sue had the belief or schema that 'I am unlovable'. When activated, Sue's basic belief (or schema) 'I am unlovable' acted as a 'feed-forward' mechanism moulding the information about Tom's behaviour in a way to fit the schema. Beck provides an alternative explanation that might have better fitted the information available to Sue, namely that 'Loud hammering is a sound of exuberance'.

Automatic thoughts

Automatic thoughts are less accessible to awareness than voluntary thoughts, but not so deeply buried as beliefs and schemas. These thoughts are similar to what Freud termed 'preconscious' thinking and what Ellis terms 'self-statements'.

People's self-evaluations and self-instructions appear to be derived from deeper structures – their self-schemas. Automatic thoughts reflect schema content – deeper beliefs and assumptions. In normal functioning self-appraisals and self-evaluations operate more or less automatically to help people stay on course. However, in psychopathology certain automatic thoughts operate to help people stay off course. Most psychological disorders are characterized by specific systematic biases in processing information. For example, depressive disorders are characterized by a negative view of self, experience and the future, and anxiety disorders by fear of physical or psychological danger.

The following are some salient characteristics of automatic thoughts. Automatic thoughts:

- are part of people's internal monologue – what and how they talk to themselves;
- can take the form of words, images, or both;
- occur very rapidly and usually at the fringe of awareness;
- can precede and accompany emotions, including feelings and inhibitions – for instance, people's emotional responses to each other's actions follow from their interpretations rather than from the actions themselves;
- are generally plausible to people who assume that they are accurate;
- have a recurring quality, despite people trying to block them out;
- affect tone of voice, facial expression and gestures, even though they may not be expressed verbally;
- can be linked together with more subtle thoughts underlying more obvious thoughts – for instance, when a husband boasts about his wife's cooking, his wife's secondary obvious automatic thought is 'He's fishing for a compliment', while her primary subtle automatic thought is 'They'll think that's all I'm good for' (Beck, 1988); and
- though often hard to identify, therapists can train clients to pinpoint these thoughts with great accuracy.

Cognitive distortions

Dysfunctional beliefs embedded in cognitive schemas contribute to systematic cognitive distortions, more accessible in automatic thoughts, that both characterize and maintain psychological distress. Box 7.1 includes some of the main cognitive distortions (Beck and Weishaar, 2000).

Box 7.1 Cognitive distortions

Arbitrary inference

The process of drawing specific conclusions without supporting evidence and sometimes in the face of contradictory evidence. An example of arbitrary inference is that of the working mother who after a busy day concludes, 'I am a terrible mother.'

Selective abstraction

Selectively attending to a detail taken out of context at the same time as ignoring other more salient information. An example of selective abstraction is that of the boyfriend who becomes jealous at seeing his girlfriend tilt her head towards a man at a noisy party in order to hear him better.

Over-generalization

Drawing a general rule or conclusion from one or a few isolated incidents and then applying the rule too broadly to unrelated situations. An example of over-generalization is the woman who concludes after a disappointing date, 'All men are alike. I'll always be rejected.'

Magnification and minimization

Evaluating particular events as far more or far less important than they really are. An example of magnification is the student who catastrophizes 'If I appear the least bit nervous in class it will mean disaster.' An example of minimization is that of a man describing his terminally ill mother as having a 'cold'.

Personalization

Having a tendency without adequate evidence to relate external events to oneself. For instance, concluding, when

---

an acquaintance walking down the opposite side of a busy street does not acknowledge a wave of greeting, 'I must have done something to offend him/her.'

Dichotomous thinking

Black-and-white, either/or, and polarized thinking are other terms for dichotomous thinking. Thinking in extreme terms, for instance, 'Unless I do extremely well on this exam, I am a total failure.'

Evolutionary and genetic factors

The cognitive structures and schemas relevant to depression, anxiety disorders and personality disorders reflect our evolutionary history (Beck, 1991; Beck *et al.*, 1990). Beck writes: 'It is reasonable to consider that the notion of long-standing cognitive-affective motivational processes influence our automatic processes: the way we construe events, what we feel, and how we are disposed to act' (Beck *et al.*, 1990, p. 24). Much animal behaviour is regarded as programmed, with underlying processes reflected in overt behaviour. Though there are risks in extrapolating from animal to human ethology, similar developmental processes may be operative in human beings. Animal analogies may clarify many aspects of normal and abnormal human behaviour. For instance, observations of primate behaviour seem highly relevant to depressed behaviour in human beings.

'Strategies' are forms of programmed behaviour designed to serve biological goals. Regarding anxiety and anger, Beck (in Beck and Emery, 1985) suggests four 'primal' survival strategies – fight, flight, freeze and faint – to perceptions of threat. He also proposes that strategies associated with traditional personality disorders may have possible antecedents in our evolutionary past (Beck *et al.*, 1990). The dramatic strategy of the histrionic personality may have roots in the display rituals of non-human animals. The attack strategy of the antisocial personality may have roots in predatory behaviour.

Human strategies may be adaptive or maladaptive depending on their circumstances. The strategies adopted by people with personality disorders are maladaptive exaggerations of normal strategies. For instance, with the dependent personality disorder the cognitive substrate or basic belief is 'I am helpless' which leads to a strategy of attachment based on fear of abandonment. With the avoidant personality disorder, the basic belief is 'I may get hurt' which leads to a strategy of avoidance.

Genetic factors

Mention was made above of the role of evolution in laying the foundation for cognitive schemas and behavioural strategies. In addition, biological factors, such as variation in the gene pool, differentiate individuals in terms of their vulnerability to different kinds of distress. For instance, predisposing factors in depression are hereditary susceptibility and diseases that cause persistent neurochemical abnormalities.

Beck (in Beck *et al.*, 1990) regards the evidence as strong for relatively stable temperamental and behavioural differences being present at birth. These innate 'tendencies' can be strengthened or weakened by experience. For instance, because of the quality of their interpersonal interactions and learning experiences, not all shy children become shy adults. Furthermore, mutually reinforcing cycles can be established between people's innate tendencies and others' reactions to them. For instance, individuals with innate care-eliciting tendencies can elicit care-producing behaviour in others, even beyond the age when such behaviour is adaptive.

ACQUISITION

This section on acquisition seeks to answer two main, yet interrelated, questions. First, how are cognitive schemas, automatic thoughts and cognitive distortions initially acquired? Second, how are symptoms of psychiatric and other disorders activated? Here my focus is on dysfunctional cognitions and behaviour, though much that follows is relevant to acquiring adaptive cognitions and behaviour.

Acquisition of vulnerability

Cognitive therapy views the acquisition of the potential for psychological distress as the result of many interacting factors:

evolutionary, biological, developmental and environmental. Though many of the factors are common across individuals, each individual has their unique variations and way of attaching personal meaning to events. Below are some ways in which people acquire vulnerabilities.

Childhood traumas

Specific affect-laden incidents in childhood may create the potential for later distress by generating dysfunctional underlying beliefs (Beck and Emery, 1985). One example is the client who suffered a sense of doom and dread every Christmas season. His earliest memory of this feeling was when, aged 7, he witnessed his mother being taken away to a tuberculosis sanatorium. His underlying belief became 'Something bad is going to happen over the Christmas holidays'. Another example is the 5-year-old, who went away on a trip and returned to find the family dog dead, developing the belief 'When I'm not physically close to others, something bad will happen to them'. A further example is that of the 7-year-old whose father left the family permanently after a marital fight developing the underlying belief 'If I make others angry they will leave me'.

Negative treatment in childhood

Children can be subject to ongoing negative treatment which affects their self-esteem and later makes them vulnerable to psychological distress. Furthermore, parents and significant others can model abusive behaviour which their children later use against others. Box 7.2 provides examples of acquiring cognitive vulnerability in childhood (Beck, 1988; Beck *et al.*, 1990).

Social learning

Beck endorses social learning theory. However, he also stresses that individuals have unique learning histories and idiosyncratic ways of attaching meanings to earlier events. Many reasons exist for personality disorders – for example, obsessive-compulsive and paranoid behaviour may develop either as a compensation or from fear. However, the reinforcement

---

Box 7.2   Childhood abuse and later cognitive vulnerability

Example 1.   Dysfunctional belief: 'I am a wimp'

Gary had periodic violent outbursts against Beverley, whom he perceived as needling him all the time for not doing chores. Gary had suffered from being brought up in a household where people controlled each other through power and might. His father and older brother intimidated him and Gary developed a core schema, 'I am a wimp'. To compensate for this belief, Gary adopted an interpersonal strategy of intimidation to control other people's inclination to dominate him, as his family had done earlier.

Example 2.   Dysfunctional belief: 'I am a bad kid'

In her childhood, a 28-year-old single woman who now suffered from panic disorder had come home from school early one day and her mother screamed at her for waking her up, saying 'How dare you interrupt my sleep!' Despite the fact that her mother drank a lot and was irritable and unpredictable, the woman developed the beliefs 'I am a bad kid' and 'I am wrong because I upset my mother'.

Example 3.   Dysfunctional tendency to self-criticism

A female client kept criticizing herself unnecessarily. She lessened her self-criticism when she re-experienced childhood scenes of criticism and obtained the insight 'I criticize myself now not because it's right to do so, but because my mother always criticized me and I took this over from her'.

---

of relevant strategies by parents and significant others is among the reasons for specific personality disorders. For instance, the dependent personality's help-seeking and clinging strategies may have been rewarded and attempts at self-sufficiency and mobility discouraged. Identification with other family members can be important in what personality disorder strategies are developed. In addition, negative life experiences may worsen an initial predisposition so that, for instance, the shy child turns into an avoidant personality.

Modelling is a key process in social learning theory. For example, marital partners have memories about how their parents behaved. Parental modelling provides a basis for rules, shoulds and should nots that they bring into their own marriages. Beck (1988) provides the example of Wendy and Hal who married very young and had trouble freeing themselves from parental modelling and reinforcement. Wendy had absorbed her mother's traditional rule that 'The role of a wife is to take care of her husband'. When Wendy failed to live up to the rule, she disparaged herself. Hal's father had stressed and rewarded perfectionism so much so that Hal had developed the belief 'I can never do anything right'. His mother reinforced his self-doubts because she had a negative attitude towards men: 'Men can't do anything – they're weak and helpless.' Hal's rules and beliefs made him vulnerable both to creating and dealing with difficulties in his marriage.

Inadequate experiences for learning coping skills

People may have been inadequately provided with personal experiences to learn coping skills. For example, an element in the anxious person's assessment of a threat is their ability to cope with the threat. A boy who has developed the coping skills of dealing with a bully is likely to feel less anxious about the bully because of this. People who fail to develop adequate assertion skills may be more prone to depression, first, they may lose self-esteem through others' actions and, second, they may then disparage themselves for lack of assertion. Most couples have learned insufficient skills in marital communication 'and so unwittingly produce continual abrasions, misunderstandings, and frustrations' (Beck, 1988, p. 275).

Activation of vulnerability

The term *cognitive shift* describes the shift of energy away from normal or higher level cognitive processing to a predominance of processing by pathological primal schemas. According to the disorder, energy is used to activate and inhibit unconscious patterns. For instance, in depression, generalized anxiety disorders and panic attacks, the depressive, danger and panic modes are energized, respectively. The concept of mode reflects the manner in which a schema is expressed. For example, a schema such as 'I'm inadequate' may lead to a predominance of catastrophizing cognitions when the anxiety mode is activated and to a predominance of self-blame and hopelessness cognitions when the depressed mode is activated.

Thinking and behaving in ways that indicate vulnerability is a matter of degree. The *continuity hypothesis* suggests that anxiety depression and personality disorders are exaggerated mechanisms of normal functioning. People can acquire dysfunctional schemas, rules, automatic thoughts and behaviours and not have them activated so that they become full-blown disorders or highly damaging factors in marital relationships.

The *cognitive shift* is triggered when people perceive their vital interests are at stake or have been affected. Initially, the shift into psychopathology is often activated in response to major life stressors. Later the shift may be activated by less severe stressors (A. Butler, personal communication, 8 April 1994). With repeated activations over the life span, people become increasingly sensitive to triggers so that it takes objectively less severe or salient stressors to precipitate a shift.

In non-endogenous unipolar depression, people have a cognitive vulnerability that is triggered by stressful life events or a series of traumatic experiences. An example of the development of vulnerability to activation of the cognitive shift is that of a person with recurrent depression whose first episode may have been precipitated by a severe life stressor (for example, losing a job). Later episodes may be precipitated by relatively minor and less directly relevant stressors (for example, hearing of a friend in another field being fired) that take on inordinate meaning due to prior experiences.

Three activating or precipitating factors are proposed for generalized anxiety disorders (Beck and Emery, 1985). First, people may face increased demands, for instance, after the birth of a child or a job promotion. Second, there may be increased threat in an area of a person's life, for example, a new mother having a baby susceptible to infection, or an employee getting a hostile new boss. Third, stressful events and reversals may undermine confidence. An example is that of a young lawyer who failed his bar examination and, about the same time, was told by his girlfriend that she did not love him. Fearing for his future as a lawyer and family man, he became chronically anxious.

MAINTENANCE

When people's cognitive vulnerabilities get activated and their cognitive processes go awry, why do they stay that way? Many people cope with the activation of their cognitive vulnerabilities by instigating adaptive cognitive and behavioural strategies. However, those with psychopathological disorders and those with deeply distressed marriages may remain stuck in faulty patterns of information processing and behaviour, to their own and other people's great disadvantage. There is no single cause why people continue to process information inefficiently. The evolutionary history of the species and genetic influences play a part. In addition, the extent and depth of people's experiences of childhood traumas, negative treatment in childhood, faulty social learning and inadequate experiences of learning coping skills play their parts too.

Failure to turn off predominant modes

The type of schema that is evoked may be determined by the mode that is active at any given time. Normally there is a balance between modes so that when one predominates or is hypervalent for a long time, an opposing mode is activated. For instance, during a period of elation a person may become aware of negative feedback, or hostility may be counter-balanced by anxiety. In psychopathological disorders there seems to be an interference in the turn-off of the dominant mode. This results in systematically biased interpretations of negative events in depression, of positive events in mania and of dangerous events in anxiety disorders. Beck considers the reasons are obscure as to why the opponent mode remains relatively inactive, thus failing to contribute to a more balanced view of reality. One possibility is that neurochemical disturbances either stimulate a prolonged overactivity of the dominant mode or fail to stimulate sufficient activity in the opposing mode.

Inability to reality-test dysfunctional interpretations

Since clients accept their dysfunctional beliefs so readily during anxiety and depression, Beck believes they have temporarily lost their ability to reality-test their interpretations.

Their information processing, based on dysfunctional schemas and beliefs, is permeated with automatic thoughts containing cognitive distortions. Cognitive distortions are not only manifestations of psychopathology, they also serve to maintain it by interfering with clients' ability to test the reality of their thinking. Clients think in rigid, stereotypical terms. They fail to distinguish adequately between fact and inference. Instead of viewing the content of their thoughts as testable hypotheses, they jump to conclusions on inadequate evidence and then view their conclusions as facts. They insufficiently take into account any feedback that might modify or negate their thoughts and perceptions. Thus information-processing systems become closed, instead of remaining open to assessing new data as they become available.

Resistances to change

Many reasons exist for why clients resist change. For instance, clients may be fearful of the negative effects on others of their changing. Marta was a 42-year-old woman living with her mother and diagnosed as having a dependent personality disorder. Whenever she thought of moving house she feared that this would kill her mother – and her mother reinforced this thinking (Beck *et al.*, 1990). Many highly anxious, depressed and suicidal clients fear change as an unknown. Clients sometimes fear the positive as well as the negative consequences of change, for instance, having to deal with the added responsibility of a promotion or marriage.

Beck (1988) considers that partners in distressed relationships may need to confront many beliefs, possibly expressed in the form of automatic thoughts, that weaken their motivation for change. Such thoughts include: 'My partner is incapable of change' and 'He/she hurt me. He/she deserves to be hurt'.

COGNITIVE MODELS

A systematic bias in information process characterizes most psychological disorders. Overviews of Beck's cognitive models of depression, anxiety disorders, distressed couple relationships and personality disorders are presented below.

Cognitive model of depression

Beck views depression as not just a mood state, but a cognitive state as well (Beck, 1991; Beck *et al.*, 1979). Depression entails clients activating three major cognitive patterns known as *the cognitive triad*, involving negative views of:

- *themselves* as unlovable, worthless, helpless and lacking in ability to attain happiness;
- *their past and present experiencing of the world* – their personal world is extremely demanding and presents huge obstacles to achieving goals;
- *their future* which is viewed as hopeless and unlikely to improve – this hopelessness may bring about thoughts of suicide.

These cognitive patterns lead to the motivational, behavioural and physical symptoms of depression. An illustrative motivational symptom is *paralysis of will* created by the belief that one lacks the ability to cope or control an event's outcome. Inertia and fatigue are illustrative behavioural and physical symptoms, respectively.

Depressive schemas are formed early in life. Situations of loss similar to those originally embedding the schema may trigger a depression. Series of traumatic events may also activate depressions. As the depression worsens, depressive schemas become hypervalent to the point where clients may become unable to view their negative thoughts objectively and find themselves completely preoccupied with repetitive negative thoughts. As dysfunctional schemas become more activated, so does the incidence of systematic cognitive distortions.

Cognitive model of anxiety disorders

The main cognitive theme in anxiety disorders is danger. Anxiety is a strategy in response to threat. In anxiety disorders the normal evolutionary survival mechanism of anxiety becomes exaggerated and malfunctioning. Beck (in Beck and Emery, 1985) adopts Lazarus' (1966) distinction between primary and secondary appraisal. Primary appraisal is the first impression of a situation that suggests the situation is noxious. Subsequent successive reappraisals are made concerning the nature and relevance of the threat to a person's vital interests, including physical and psychological injury. Secondary appraisal involves the person assessing his or her resources for dealing with the threat. This process takes place at the same time as evaluating the nature of the threat. As with depression, a person's underlying dysfunctional schemas and beliefs may predispose them to anxiety. Their dysfunctional beliefs may be activated by increased demands, threats and stresses which may interact with previous problems. Cognitive distortions reflecting dysfunctional schema include overestimating the probability and severity of the threat, magnification of the negative consequences (catastrophizing), underestimating one's resources for dealing with the threat, and insufficiently taking into account support factors, for instance, the presence of others who might help. In brief, anxious individuals maximize the likelihood of harm and minimize their ability to cope.

Cognitive model of distressed couples relationships

Beck observes 'what attracts partners to each other is rarely enough to sustain a relationship' (Beck, 1988, p. 46). Poor communication skills are one reason for marital difficulties. In addition, partners bring much personal baggage into the relationship in terms of hidden expectations of each other and the relationship. The expectations in marriage are less flexible than in uncommitted relationships. Furthermore, much behaviour in marriage has idiosyncratic symbolic meanings attached to it revolving around symbols of love or rejection, security or insecurity.

When disappointment in a relationship sets in and emotions run high, partners lose some or virtually all of their ability to reality-test their interpretations of their own and each other's thoughts, feelings and actions. Instead they react to their 'invisible reality' which is likely to be based more on their internal states, fears and expectations than on what actually happens. Dysfunctional schemas and beliefs can be triggered leading to a negative cognitive set about the other person. A distressed couple's voluntary and automatic thinking contains numerous cognitive distortions. Partners tend to fixate on what is wrong in their relationship rather than on what is right. They misperceive and misinterpret what the other says or does, engage in mind-reading and attribute undesirable and malicious motives to each other, and fail to check out the accuracy of their negative explanations and illogical conclusions.

In addition, partners send each other barbed messages that trigger hurt and anger. They perceive they have been wronged, get angry, feel impelled to attack, and attack. Hostility is part of a primitive fight-flight survival mechanism. However, acting on the primitive urge to attack is often destructive to the relationship. It increases the level of threat in the relationship and hence partners' tendencies to think in rigid and erroneous ways. Furthermore, hostility can increase partners' resistances to working on their relationship.

Cognitive model of personality disorders

Personality disorders, along with other kinds of psychopathology, partly represent evolutionary strategies that have been insufficiently adapted to today's individualized and technological society (Beck *et al.*, 1990). In addition, genetic predisposition and differing learning experiences influence which disorders different individuals develop. Each personality disorder is characterized by a basic belief and a corresponding overt behavioural strategy. Different overt responses represent important structural differences in basic beliefs (or schemas). The dependent personality disorder has the basic belief, 'I am helpless' and the overt strategy of attachment. The corresponding beliefs and strategies in the other personality disorders are: avoidant disorder, 'I may get hurt', avoidance; passive aggressive disorder, 'I could be stepped on', resistance; paranoid disorder, 'People are potential adversaries', wariness; narcissistic disorder, 'I am special', self-aggrandizement; the histrionic disorder, 'I need to impress', dramatics; obsessive-compulsive disorder, 'Errors are bad. I must not err', perfectionism; antisocial disorder, 'People are there to be taken', attack; and schizoid disorder, 'I need plenty of space', isolation. Another way of looking at strategies is that each personality disorder reflects both overdeveloped and underdeveloped strategies: for example, in the paranoid disorder 'mistrust' is overdeveloped and 'trust' is underdeveloped. A fuller cognitive profile may be drawn for each personality disorder.

When particular schemas are hypervalent, their constituent schemas are readily triggered. In personality disorders a cognitive shift occurs in which there is a redirection of energy away from normal cognitive processing into the different schemas that constitute the disorders. As part of this process more adaptive schemas may get inhibited. Because of the tenacity of their dysfunctional schemas, cognitive therapy with clients with personality disorders is generally longer term and involves a fuller exploration of the origin of schemas than for clients with depression or anxiety disorders.

THERAPY

Cognitive therapy initially addresses symptom relief, but its ultimate goals are to remove systematic biases in thinking and modify the core beliefs that predispose the person to future distress.

Aaron Beck

THERAPEUTIC GOALS

Cognitive therapy 'aims explicitly to "reenergize" the reality-testing system' (Beck *et al.*, 1990, p. 37). In varying degrees, clients with psychopathological disorders and couples in distressed relationships have lost the ability to reality-test dysfunctional interpretations. Cognitive therapy teaches clients adaptive metacognition – how to think about their thinking – so that they can correct faulty cognitive processing and develop assumptions that allow them to cope. While cognitive therapy may initially address symptom relief, its ultimate goal is to remove systematic biases in how clients think. In addition, cognitive therapy aims to impart behavioural skills relevant to clients' problems, for instance, listening and communication skills for distressed couples or assertion skills for shy people.

Clients are told that a goal of cognitive therapy is for them to learn to become their own therapists (Beck and Weishaar, 2000). When working with clients' cognitions, goals include teaching them to: (1) monitor their negative automatic thoughts; (2) recognize the connections between cognition, affect and behaviour; (3) examine and reality-test the evidence for and against distorted automatic thoughts; (4) substitute more realistic interpretations for biased cognitions; and (5) learn to identify and alter the beliefs that predispose them to distort their experiences (Beck *et al.*, 1979). Clients need not be highly intelligent to gain from cognitive therapy – in fact Beck's researches show no relationship between intelligence and cognitive therapy outcomes.

Cognitive therapy works best with clients who can focus on their automatic thoughts and take some responsibility for self-help. It is not recommended for clients with impaired reality testing, such as hallucinations and delusions, or for clients with impaired memory and reasoning abilities, such as with organic brain syndromes. For some disorders, such as recurrent major depressive episodes, a combination of cognitive therapy and medication is recommended.

PROCESS OF THERAPY

At the Beck Institute for Cognitive Therapy and Research in suburban Philadelphia, clients undergo a three-hour intake protocol consisting of a clinical interview and psychological tests. The clinical interview provides a thorough history of the background factors contributing to the client's distress. The interview also assesses current level of functioning, prominent symptoms and expectations for therapy. The *Beck Depression Inventory* (Beck *et al.*, 1961), the *Anxiety Checklist* (Beck, 1978), and the *Dysfunctional Attitudes Scale* (Weissman, 1979) are prominent among psychological tests used during the intake protocol.

The initial interview has many purposes: initiating a relationship, providing a rationale for cognitive therapy, producing symptom relief and eliciting important information. Right from the start therapists impart to clients the expectation that cognitive therapy will be time-limited. During the initial interview, therapists start to define problems. Definitions of problems entail both functional and cognitive analyses.

- The *functional* analysis seeks to answer questions such as: 'What are the component parts of the problem?', 'How is it manifested?', 'In what situations does it occur?', 'What is its frequency, intensity and duration?', and 'What are its consequences?'

- The *cognitive* analysis identifies the client's thoughts and images when emotion is triggered, the extent to which the client feels in control of thoughts and images, and predictions about the likelihood of the problem occurring and what will happen. From the beginning, therapists train clients to monitor their feelings, thoughts and behaviour and to recognize the connections between them. *Homework* is a feature throughout cognitive therapy. An example of an early homework assignment might be asking clients to record their automatic thoughts when distressed.

During initial sessions, therapists and clients draw up *problem lists*. Problem lists can consist of specific symptoms, behaviours or pervasive problems. Their function is to assign treatment priorities. Considerations in prioritizing treatment include magnitude of distress, symptom severity, and pervasiveness of theme. Therapists approach each problem by choosing the appropriate cognitive and behavioural techniques to apply. Therapists always offer a rationale for each technique. In addition, both when suggesting and implementing techniques, therapists elicit feedback from clients.

While the early stages of therapy may focus on symptom removal, middle and later stages are more likely to emphasize changing clients' patterns of thinking. Clients are helped to understand the interrelationships between their thoughts, feelings and behaviours. Once they can challenge automatic thoughts that interfere with effective functioning, they can identify and examine the underlying assumptions or beliefs generating such thoughts. Assumptions may be revealed as themes in automatic thoughts across time and across situations. Once assumptions and core beliefs have been identified and their disruptive power understood, cognitive therapy aims to assist clients to examine their validity and current usefulness and then discard or amend them, as appropriate.

As cognitive therapy progresses, clients develop their skills of being their own therapists. Clients assume more responsibility for identifying problems, analysing their thinking and creating suitable homework assignments. The role of the therapist shifts from being fairly didactic to facilitating clients as they develop their cognitive self-helping skills. The frequency of sessions decreases as clients become more proficient.

Being mainly a short-term structured approach, cognitive therapy tends to have its ending built into its beginning. Therapy ends when goals are reached and clients feel confident about implementing their new skills. From the outset, therapists discuss with clients criteria and expectations for termination. There are a number of ways of assessing progress including relief from symptoms, changes in reported and observed behaviour, and changes in thinking both inside and outside therapy. Performance in homework assignments, such as filling in the daily record of automatic thoughts and carrying out specific tasks and experiments, also assists in assessing progress. In particular, therapists look out for clients' ability to reality-test and, if necessary, modify or discard distorted interpretations. Termination is often gradual, say from weekly to bi-weekly sessions, followed by booster sessions one and two months after termination. The purpose of such sessions is to consolidate gains and assist clients to keep employing their new skills (Beck and Weishaar, 2000).

Cognitive therapy sessions generally last for forty-five minutes. The standard treatment length for unipolar depression is eight to sixteen sessions at weekly intervals. Moderately to severely depressed clients may be seen twice a week for the first two or three weeks. Clients with anxiety disorders generally receive between five and fifteen sessions (Clark and Beck, 1988). The treatment of personality disorders generally takes longer and may last for a year or more.

THE THERAPEUTIC RELATIONSHIP

Cognitive therapy is an educational process in which therapists are active in developing relationships with clients and using their expertise in helping clients examine and modify beliefs and behaviour. The quality of the therapist–client relationship is an important medium for improvement. Cognitive therapy is not an impersonal approach, but one in which therapists seek to understand their clients as individuals. Beck regards his therapeutic style as somewhat Rogerian. Therapists strive to create an emotional climate of genuine warmth and non-judgemental acceptance. Furthermore, cognitive therapists give clients their phone numbers in case of emergency.

Cognitive therapists attempt to demystify counselling by using language that clients can understand. They treat clients with respect by offering rationales both for their overall approach and for each technique they propose. In addition, they share responsibility for what happens in therapy by discussing case conceptualizations and involving clients in setting goals and session agendas. Cognitive therapists also elicit feedback from clients about both their suggestions and their behaviour. Therapists are sensitive to signs of transference and allow clients' reactions to them to be aired. Therapists can use these transference reactions to identify and work with clients' automatic thoughts and interpersonal distortions.

With most personality-disordered clients, cognitive therapists offer a closer and warmer relationship than in acute disorders, such as anxiety and depression. Therapists can face problems of non-collaboration from clients, especially those with personality disorders (Beck *et al.*, 1990).

Serving as co-investigator – collaborative empiricism

In addition to offering accepting and warm relationships, cognitive therapists play an active role in the therapy process. Therapists encourage clients to play an active role too. All the client's cognitions are viewed as testable hypotheses. Therapist and client collaborate in the scientific endeavour of examining the evidence to confirm or negate the client's cognitions. Based on what clients say and how they say it, therapists develop hypotheses that can identify cognitive errors as well as underlying assumptions and beliefs. Therapists then ask clients to comment on whether their hypotheses fit the facts. By this means, clients are encouraged both to view their thoughts as personal views of reality and to build their skills of evaluating their validity. Throughout the process of identifying and exploring the evidence for biased thinking, either the therapist or the client takes the more active role as appropriate.

Serving as a guide – guided discovery

There are a number of different facets to guided discovery. Therapists can operate as guides to assist clients to discover the themes that run through their present automatic thoughts and beliefs. This can be taken one stage further where therapists and clients link the beliefs to analogous experiences in the past and collaboratively piece together the developmental history of the beliefs. Another use of guided discovery is that therapists act as guides in assisting clients to reality-test their possible errors in logic by designing new experiences that involve the client experimenting with different behaviour. Therapists do not use cajoling, disputation and indoctrination to assist clients to reality-test their thinking and adopt new beliefs. Rather, they encourage clients to develop their own skills of using and assessing information, facts and probabilities in order to obtain more realistic perspectives than sometimes offered by their initial thoughts.

THERAPEUTIC INTERVENTIONS

Both cognitive and behavioural interventions are used in cognitive therapy. The interventions selected depend on such factors as the nature of the client's problems, the therapeutic goals, and how well they are functioning.

Cognitive interventions

The following are some of the main cognitive interventions used by cognitive therapists to assist clients to replace their distorted automatic thoughts and beliefs with more realistic ways of processing information.

Eliciting and identifying automatic thoughts

In order to change their thinking, clients need first become aware of their thought processes. Included below are some specific interventions for eliciting and identifying automatic thoughts.

- **Providing reasons** Therapists can provide reasons for the importance of examining the connections between how clients think, feel and act. Furthermore, they can introduce the concept of automatic thoughts and provide an example of how underlying perceptions influence feelings. In addition, therapists can communicate that a major assumption of cognitive therapy is that clients are experiencing difficulties in reality-testing the validity of their interpretations. Box 7.3 provides an example of a cognitive therapist showing the relationship between cognition, affect and behaviour (Beck and Rush, 1979, pp. 147–8).

Box 7.3 Example of showing the influence of cognitions on affect and behaviour

The client

A 43-year-old depressed male patient.

The scene

The therapist instructed the client to imagine that a person was home alone one night and heard a crash in another room.

Interpretation 1

This person thinks, 'There's a burglar in the room.'

Possible consequences of Interpretation 1

The therapist then asked the client:

- 'How do you think this person would feel?', to which the client answered, 'Very anxious, terrified.'
- 'And how might he behave?', to which the client replied he might hide or phone the police.

Interpretation 2

The therapist then instructed the client to imagine that the person heard the same noise and thought: 'The windows have been left open and the wind has caused something to fall over.'

Possible consequences of Interpretation 2

The therapist then asked the client:

- 'How would he feel?', to which the client replied the person wouldn't be afraid, though he might be sad if he thought something valuable had been broken.
- 'And would his behaviour be different following this thought?', to which the client replied it would be different in that he would probably go and see what the problem was and certainly wouldn't phone the police.

Main teaching points

The therapist emphasized that this example showed:

- that usually there were a number of ways the client could interpret a situation
- the way he interpreted a situation would affect how he felt and behaved.

- **Questioning**   Clients may be questioned about automatic thoughts that occur during upsetting situations. Where clients experience difficulty in recalling thoughts, imagery or role-playing may be used. When questioning, therapists observe clients carefully for signs of affect that may offer leads for further questioning.
- **Using a whiteboard**   When clients see their initial thoughts written up on the board, this may trigger them to reveal less obvious and more frightening thoughts.
- **Encouraging clients to engage in feared activities**   Frequently, during sessions, clients are encouraged to engage in anxiety-evoking activities: for instance, making phone calls or writing letters they had been putting off. As they perform the activity, therapists can ask the question 'What is going through your mind right now?' Therapists can also go with clients into real-life situations where they experience difficulty, for instance, crowded places, and get them to verbalize what they think.
- **Focusing on imagery**   Gathering information about imagery can be an important way of accessing automatic thoughts. Though individual differences exist, clinical observations suggest that many people visualizing scenes react to them as though they were real.
- **Self-monitoring of thoughts**   Clients may be set homework in which they record their thoughts. They may complete a

daily record of automatic thoughts log in which they record in their respective columns:

- *date*
- *situation* leading to negative emotion(s)
- *emotion(s)* felt and their degree on a 0–100 per cent scale
- *automatic thought(s)* and a rating of how strongly they believed the automatic thought(s) on a 0–100 per cent scale.

Therapists may encourage some clients to use wrist counters to help them learn to recognize automatic thoughts as they occur.

Reality-testing and correcting automatic thoughts

Interventions for assisting clients to treat their thoughts as hypotheses that require testing against reality and, if necessary, discarding, modifying or replacing, include the following.

- **Conducting Socratic dialogues** Questions comprise the largest category of verbal statements in cognitive therapy. Questions reflect the basic empirical orientation of the approach and have the immediate goal of converting clients' closed belief systems into open systems. More specifically questions seek to help clients become aware of what their thoughts are; examine them for cognitive distortions; substitute more balanced thoughts; and make plans to develop new thought patterns. A basic awareness raising question is to ask clients 'What is going through your mind right now?'
  Therapists use questioning rather than indoctrination and disputation. Conducted in an emotional climate of warmth and acceptance, the Socratic style of questioning assists clients to expand and evaluate how they think. Typical questions are:

  - 'Where is the evidence?'
  - 'Where is the logic?'
  - 'Are there other ways of perceiving the situation?'
  - 'What do I have to lose?'
  - 'What do I have to gain?'
  - 'What would be the worst thing that could happen?'
  - 'What can I learn from this experience?'
                                                    (Beck and Emery, 1985)

Clients learn to ask themselves the same questions that their therapists have asked. For instance, however plausible their automatic thoughts may 'feel', clients in distressed relationships can question their validity by asking themselves the following series of questions:

– 'What is the evidence in *favour* of my interpretation?'
– 'What evidence is *contrary* to my interpretation?'
– 'Does it *logically follow* from my spouse's actions that my spouse has the motive that I assign to him or her?'
– 'Is there an *alternative* explanation for his or her behaviour?'   (Beck, 1988)

Box 7.4 provides an example of some of Beck's questions to challenge a client's thinking (Beck, 1976, pp. 249–52).

Box 7.4   *Case example: Challenging the thought that 'failure is a catastrophe'*

The client

A medical student inhibited in numerous situations where assertion was essential. Here the therapist focuses on the client's fears of giving a talk in front of his class the following day.

The therapist's questions

- 'What are you afraid of?'
- 'Suppose you *do* make a fool of yourself, why is that so bad?'
- 'Now look here, suppose they ridicule you, can you die from it?'
- 'Suppose they decide that you are the worst public speaker who ever lived, will this ruin your career?'
- 'But if you flubbed it would your wife or parents disown you?'
- 'Well what would be so awful about it?'

When the client answers that he would feel pretty bad, the therapist asks:

- 'For how long?' and the client replies 'For about a day or two' and the therapist then says:
- 'And then what?', to which the client replies 'Then I'd be OK.'

The therapist's summary

The therapist pointed out to the client that, somewhere along the line, his thinking got fouled up, and he tended to regard failure as a catastrophe. The client needed to start challenging his wrong premises and to label failures accurately as failures to attain goals and not as disasters.

Subsequent therapy sessions

As therapy proceeded, the therapist coached the client in changing his notion that failure was a catastrophe and also challenged maladaptive attitudes producing psychological distress in other social situations.

- **Identifying cognitive distortions** Therapists can teach clients what the common cognitive distortions are, for instance, arbitrary inference and magnification. Both during therapy and as homework, clients can be challenged to identify the distortions in how they think. Clients may use the three-column technique for this:

  - Column 1 – describe a situation that elicits negative emotions;
  - Column 2 – identify their automatic thoughts in the situation;
  - Column 3 – list the types of distortions in these thoughts.

- **Decatastrophizing** In decatastrophizing, the basic question is 'So what if it happens?' Areas covered in this technique include: the event's probability and severity, the client's coping capacity and support factors, and the client's ability to accept and deal with the worst possible outcomes.
- **Reattribution** Reattribution techniques test automatic thoughts and underlying beliefs by considering alternative ways of assigning responsibility and cause. Clients can be

encouraged to rate on a 0–100 scale the degree of responsibility they feel for negative events and feared outcomes. By means of questioning, the therapist attempts to loosen them up by generating and evaluating alternative explanations.

- **Redefining**   Redefining problems entails making them more concrete and stating them in terms of what the client might do. For example, a lonely person who feels uncared for may redefine his or her problem as 'I need to reach out to other people and be caring'.

- **Decentring**   Decentring involves assisting clients to challenge their belief that everyone is focusing on them. Clients can be encouraged to evaluate more closely what others are doing: for instance, other students may be day-dreaming, looking at their lecturer, or taking notes. In addition, clients can be asked to closely observe how frequently they attend to others. This may help them realize how limited their observations are, and thus infer that other people's observations are the same.

- **Forming rational responses**   Cognitive therapists train clients in how to form more rational responses to their automatic thoughts. Again, questioning is an important way to assist clients in learning to use their inner monologue for rather than against themselves. Box 7.5 provides an example of a client providing a counteracting rational response to herself (Beck, 1988, p. 264). Finding a rational response can help clients see their automatic thoughts as an interpretation rather than as 'the truth'.

Box 7.5   *Example of forming a rational response*

The situation

Wendy was phoned by her husband Hal to say he was tied up at the office.

- *Emotional reaction*   Anger.
- *Automatic thought*   'It's not fair – I have to work too. If he wanted to, he could be home on time.'
- *Rational response*   'His job is different. Many of his customers come in after work.'

- **Daily recording of rational responses**   When ready, clients can be encouraged to fill out rational response and outcome columns on their daily record of automatic thoughts. In the outcome column, clients:

  – re-rate their beliefs in their automatic thought(s) on a 0–100 per cent scale
  – specify what their subsequent emotions are and rate them on a 0–100 per cent scale.

- **Imagery techniques**   Numerous imagery techniques are discussed by Beck and Emery (1985). Among these techniques are assisting clients to gain more realistic perspectives through repeated visualizations of fantasies, through projecting themselves into the future and looking back on their present situations, and by getting them to exaggerate images, for instance, of harming others.

Identifying and modifying underlying beliefs

Underlying beliefs may be harder for therapists and clients to access than automatic thoughts. They often fall into one of three main belief clusters centring on issues of

- *acceptance* – for instance, 'I'm flawed and therefore unacceptable.'
- *competence* – for instance, 'I'm inferior.'
- *control* – for instance, 'I have no control.'

Underlying beliefs are signposted by the themes in clients' automatic thoughts. Clients' behaviour, coping strategies and personal histories are additional sources for therapists to form belief hypotheses. Most clients find it difficult to articulate their beliefs without assistance. Generally, therapists present hypotheses to clients for verification. Where clients disagree, therapists can work with them to form more accurate statements of their beliefs.

The following are some cognitive interventions for modifying beliefs.

- **Socratic questioning**   Therapists can use questions that encourage clients to examine their beliefs: for instance, 'Does the belief seem reasonable?', 'Can you review the

evidence for it?', and 'What are the advantages and disadvantages of maintaining the belief?'
- **Hypothesis testing**   Together, therapists and clients can set
  up experiments that encourage clients to test the reality of
  their beliefs. Box 7.6 provides an example of such an
  experiment (Beck, 1988, p. 224).
- **Using imagery**   Imagery can be used to assist clients to
  'relive' past traumatic events and so restructure their
  experiences and the beliefs derived from them.

Box 7.6   Example of hypothesis testing concerning a belief

The client

Marjorie, who was afraid to make a mental commitment to her
spouse, Ken, because she feared she might find out that she
could not trust him.

Marjorie's underlying belief

'I must never allow myself to be vulnerable.'

Consequence of Marjorie's distorted thinking

Her aloof behaviour and fault-finding created distance in their
relationship.

The experiment

Beck and Marjorie set up a three-month experiment for her to
test the hypothesis: 'If I totally commit myself to the relationship, look for the positive instead of the negative, I will feel
more secure.' During the experiment, Marjorie was to change
how she thought and acted.

Result of the experiment

Marjorie discovered that she was more secure and had fewer
thoughts about leaving Ken.

- **Reliving childhood memories** Beck (Beck *et al.*, 1990) considers that with chronic personality disorders it is crucial to use childhood material to assist clients in reviewing and loosening their underlying beliefs. By re-creating 'pathogenic' developmental situations through role-playing and role reversal, clients have an opportunity to restructure or modify beliefs formed during this period.
- **Refashioning beliefs** Therapists can assist clients to refashion their beliefs. Beck gives the example of MK, a director of a research institute at a major university who suffered from a major depressive disorder and generalized anxiety disorder. The client had strong beliefs of inadequacy and rejection which he crystallized as 'I must be *the best* at everything I do'. One of MK's beliefs was refashioned thus: 'It is rewarding to succeed highly, but lesser success is rewarding also and has no bearing on my adequacy or inadequacy. I am adequate no matter what' (Beck and Rush, in press, p. 48).

Behavioural interventions

Behavioural interventions serve many purposes in cognitive therapy. First, behavioural interventions can lay the foundation for later cognitive work. An issue arises whether to focus on behaviour first, cognition first, or both concurrently. Behavioural interventions may sometimes be used before cognitive interventions to promote symptom relief and enhance motivation. For instance, severely depressed clients may be encouraged to perform small tasks to counteract their withdrawal, get them involved in constructive activities, and open their minds to the possibility of gaining satisfaction from previously pleasurable activities. However, in contrast to normal people, depressed clients can change their behaviour markedly, but do not necessarily change their negative hypervalent cognitions (Beck *et al.*, 1979). In working with couples, Beck (1988) concentrates on changing behaviour first, since he regards it as easier to change actions than thinking patterns; also, spouses may immediately reward each other's changes in behaviour.

Second, behavioural interventions can be used to assist clients in reality-testing their automatic thoughts and beliefs. A third use of behavioural interventions is, along with cognitive interventions, to assist clients to engage in feared activities. A fourth use is to train clients in specific behavioural skills. Since the uses of behavioural interventions overlap, they are not categorized according to purpose. The following are some of the main behavioural interventions used by cognitive therapists.

Activity scheduling

Activity scheduling is a form of timetabling. Planning specific activities with clients can be important in helping clients to realize that they can control their time. A principle of activity scheduling is to state what activity the clients agree to engage in rather than how much they will accomplish. Clients can set aside time each evening to plan their activities for the following day.

Rating mastery and pleasure

Using 0–10 scales, clients can rate the degree of mastery and the degree of pleasure they experienced in each activity during the day. Mastery and pleasure ratings can give depressed clients an insight into the activities that reduce their dysphoria.

Hypothesis testing

Hypothesis testing has both behavioural and cognitive components (Beck and Weishaar, 2000). Especially later in therapy, behavioural experiments may be designed to provide information that may contradict existing automatic thoughts, faulty predictions and underlying beliefs. A young man about to cancel a date because of the fear 'I won't know what to say' was encouraged to go on the date and treat not knowing what to say as an experimental hypothesis. The findings of this particular experiment disproved his hypothesis (Beck and Emery, 1985). In the earlier example (Box 7.6) Marjorie was engaging in a behavioural as well as a cognitive experiment to test her underlying belief 'I must never allow myself to be vulnerable'.

Rehearsing behaviour and role-playing

Behaviour rehearsal can be used to develop clients' skills for specific social and stressful situations. Demonstration and video feedback can be used as part of skills training. Behaviour rehearsals should have a number of trials and rehearse clients in a variety of responses. Clients also can rehearse situations by using their imaginations.

Assigning graded tasks

Clients often fail at tasks because they try to do too much too soon. Therapists and clients can develop hierarchies of feared or difficult situations. Clients can then perform less threatening before moving on to more threatening activities.

Using diversion techniques

Clients may be encouraged to engage in activities that divert them from their strong negative emotions and thinking. Such activities include work, play, socializing and doing something physical.

Assigning homework

Homework forms an important part of cognitive therapy. Its purpose is both to shorten the time spent in therapy and facilitate the development of cognitive and behavioural skills for use after counselling. Homework assignments include self-monitoring, activities designed to reality-test automatic thoughts and underlying beliefs, implementing procedures for dealing with specific situations, and activities for developing cognitive skills such as identifying cognitive distortions, rational responding and refashioning beliefs.

CASE MATERIAL

Beck, collaborating with Rush and other colleagues (1979, pp. 225–43), presents an initial interview with a depressed 40-year-old female clinical psychologist client who had recently been left by her boyfriend. The interview transcript is broken down into five parts: questioning to elicit vital information, broadening the client's perspective, 'alternative therapy', obtaining more accurate data, and closure. Beck and Young (1985, pp. 206–44) illustrate in the case example of a depressed young female client how cognitive therapists elicit and challenge maladaptive thoughts and assumptions throughout treatment. Beck and Weishaar (2000) illustrate in the case example of a 21-year-old highly anxious male college student both behavioural and cognitive interventions for attaining therapeutic goals. Throughout his book *Love is Never Enough*, Beck (1988) provides numerous vignettes of the use of cognitive interventions in relationship therapy.

Other sources of case material include Scott *et al.*'s edited *Cognitive Therapy in Clinical Practice: An Illustrative Casebook* (1989); Freeman and Dattilio's edited *Comprehensive Casebook of Cognitive Therapy* (1992); and Judith Beck's *Cognitive Therapy: Basics and Beyond* (1995), which uses cases throughout to illustrate how to employ various cognitive therapy interventions.

FURTHER DEVELOPMENTS

Cognitive therapy has been used with all ages, from children to the elderly. Beck reports that several controlled studies have shown it to be at least as effective as antidepressant medication in treating elderly depressed clients. Cognitive therapy has been used for group work with families. Some newer applications of cognitive therapy include working with clients with schizophrenia, post-traumatic stress disorders, substance abuse problems, hypertension and dissociative disorders as well as with clients who have committed sexual offences, such as exhibitionism and incest. Schema-focused approaches to personality disorders have been an important development in cognitive therapy.

There are over ten training centres for cognitive therapy in the United States, including the Beck Institute for Cognitive Therapy and Research, directed by Beck's daughter, Dr Judith Beck. In addition, training in cognitive therapy is widely available elsewhere, including Britain and Australia. With the current emphasis on containing costs through managed care, cognitive therapy's short-term approach will be increasingly popular with both third-party payers and clients (Beck and Weishaar, 2000).

SUMMARY

- *Beck's cognitive therapy views clients as faulty processors of information. Human beings have the capacity for primal and higher level cognitive processes. As well as voluntary thoughts, thinking consists of schemas and automatic thoughts.*
- *Schemas are relatively stable cognitive patterns that influence through people's beliefs how they select and synthesize incoming information. When activated, dysfunctional schemas and beliefs can lead people to systematically bias information. Modes are networks of cognitive, affective, motivational and behavioural schemas.*
- *Automatic thoughts, which occur very rapidly and at the fringe of awareness, are not so deeply buried as schemas and reflect schema content. Dysfunctional beliefs can lead to systematic cognitive distortions.*
- *Evolutionary and genetic causes contribute to how people think and behave. Human beings acquire cognitive vulnerability through childhood traumas, negative treatment in childhood, social learning, and inadequate experiences for learning coping skills. Cognitive vulnerability can be activated by perceived losses, increased demands and stress.*
- *Factors maintaining psychological distress include failure to turn off hypervalent modes, inability to reality-test dysfunctional interpretations, and resistances to change. Beck's cognitive models of depression, anxiety disorders, distressed couple relationships and personality disorders are overviewed.*
- *The main goal of cognitive therapy is to re-energize the client's reality-testing system. Cognitive therapy teaches clients how to evaluate and modify their thinking. In addition, therapy focuses on symptom relief and helping clients to develop adaptive behaviours.*
- *Cognitive therapy tends to be highly structured and short-term. The process of therapy starts with defining problems and case conceptualization. While the early stages of therapy may focus on symptom relief, middle and later stages of therapy focus on using cognitive and behavioural interventions to change clients' patterns of thinking.*
- *Therapists provide clients with good human relationships. In addition, they collaborate with clients to investigate*

*problems and act as guides in helping them to reality-test
possible errors in logic.*

- *Cognitive interventions focus on eliciting and identifying
  automatic thoughts, reality-testing and correcting automatic thoughts, identifying underlying beliefs and modifying underlying beliefs. Socratic questioning is a central
  activity of the cognitive therapist.*
- *Behavioural interventions may be used to support both
  cognitive and behavioural change. Behavioural interventions include activity scheduling, conducting experiments
  to test thinking, and rehearsing behaviour and role-playing.*
- *Training in cognitive therapy is available in many countries.
  Especially in an era emphasizing short-term managed care,
  cognitive therapy has wide applicability.*

REVIEW AND PERSONAL QUESTIONS
Review questions

1. What are schemas and modes and why are they important?
2. What are automatic thoughts and why are they important?
3. What are cognitive distortions and why are they important?
4. What are Beck's views on the following causes of cognitions and behaviour:

   - evolutionary causes?
   - genetic causes?

5. What is the nature and role of each of the following
   factors in helping people acquire cognitive vulnerability:
   childhood traumas, negative treatment in childhood,
   social learning, and inadequate experiences for learning
   coping skills?
6. What are some factors relevant to activating cognitive
   vulnerability?
7. What is the nature and role of each of the following
   factors in helping people maintain cognitive vulnerability:
   failure to turn off hypervalent modes, inability to reality-
   test dysfunctional interpretations, and resistances to
   change?

8. Critically discuss the goals of cognitive therapy.
9. Describe the nature of the therapist–client relationship in cognitive therapy.
10. Describe the process of cognitive therapy.
11. What are some of the main cognitive interventions used in cognitive therapy for:

   - eliciting and identifying automatic thoughts?
   - reality-testing and correcting automatic thoughts?
   - identifying and modifying underlying beliefs?

12. What are some of the main behavioural interventions used in cognitive therapy?

Personal questions

1. List any significant factors when you were growing up that may have contributed to your acquiring faulty ways of processing information.
2. Think of a specific problem in your life. Elicit and identify some of your automatic thoughts regarding it.
3. Identify characteristic cognitive distortions, if any, in the way you process information.
4. Identify one of your automatic thoughts in a problem area and challenge it by means of Socratic questioning.
5. In a problem area, identify a thought that lends itself to being reality-tested through changing your behaviour. Design and implement a behavioural experiment to reality-test your thought.
6. What relevance, if any, has the theory and practice of cognitive therapy for how you conduct therapy?
7. What relevance, if any, has the theory and practice of cognitive therapy for how you live?

ANNOTATED BIBLIOGRAPHY

Beck, A. T., Rush, A. J., Shaw, B. F. and Emery, G. (1979) *Cognitive Therapy of Depression*. New York: John Wiley.

This book presents Beck's cognitive model of depression. The bulk of the book is a clinical handbook devoted to practical aspects of treating depressed clients, for instance, the therapeutic relationship, the application of both cognitive and behavioural interventions, and problems related to termination and relapse.

Beck, A. T. and Emery, G. (1985) *Anxiety Disorders and Phobias: A Cognitive Perspective.* New York: Basic Books.

Part 1 of the book, written by Beck, is entitled 'Theoretical and clinical aspects' and presents his cognitive model of anxiety. Part 2 of the book, written by Emery, is entitled 'Cognitive therapy: techniques and applications' and has chapters on the principles of cognitive therapy, techniques for cognitive restructuring, modifying imagery, affect and behaviour, and on restructuring assumptions.

Beck, A. T. (1988) *Love is Never Enough: How Couples Can Overcome Misunderstandings, Resolve Conflicts, and Solve Relationship Problems Through Cognitive Therapy.* New York: Harper & Row.

This book describes the power of negative and biased thinking in couple relationships. Beck shows how partners can improve their relationship by identifying and modifying their maladaptive automatic thoughts and underlying beliefs.

Beck, A. T., Freeman, A. and associates (1990) *Cognitive Therapy of Personality Disorders.* New York: Guilford Press.

Part 1 of this book, written by Beck and Freeman, presents Beck's cognitive model of personality disorders as well as the history of and research on cognitive therapy for personality disorders. Part 2, written by a series of associates, focuses on clinical applications of cognitive therapy for each of the personality disorders.

Beck, A. T. and Weishaar, M. E. (2000) 'Cognitive therapy', in R. J. Corsini and D. Wedding (eds) *Current Psychotherapies* (6th edn, pp. 241–72). Itasca, IL: Peacock.

An authoritative chapter reviewing the theory and practice of contemporary cognitive therapy.

Beck, J. S. (1995) *Cognitive Therapy: Basics and Beyond.* New York: Guilford Press.

Beck's daughter Judith wrote this manual for cognitive therapy. Starting with case conceptualization, she shows the reader how to identify and work with deeper level cognitions, prepare for termination and anticipate problems.

Padesky, C. A. and Greenberger, D. (1995) *Clinician's Guide to Mind Over Mood*; and Greenberger, D. and Padesky, C. A. (1995) *Mind Over Mood: Change How You Feel by Changing The Way You Think.* New York: Guilford Press.

These companion volumes are designed as step-by-step guides to the techniques and strategies of cognitive therapy. The manual is designed as a self-help workbook and the clinician's guide provides therapists with instructions on how to incorporate the workbook into individual and group psychotherapy.

Weishaar, M. E. (1993) *Aaron T. Beck*. London: Sage.

Weishaar has been both a student and collaborator of Beck, so she writes with authority. The five chapters in the book cover Beck's life, his theoretical contributions, his practical contributions, some criticisms and rebuttals, and Beck's overall influence.

REFERENCES

Alford, B. A. and Beck, A. T. (1997) *The Integrative Power of Cognitive Therapy*. New York: Guilford Press.

Beck, A. T. (1963) 'Thinking and depression. 1. Idiosyncratic content and cognitive distortions'. *Archives of General Psychiatry*, 9, 324–33.

Beck, A. T. (1964) 'Thinking and depression. 2. Theory and therapy'. *Archives of General Psychiatry*, 10, 561–71.

Beck, A. T. (1976) *Cognitive Therapy and the Emotional Disorders*. New York: New American Library.

Beck, A. T. (1978) *Anxiety Checklist*. Philadelphia, PA: Center for Cognitive Therapy.

Beck, A. T. (1988) *Love is Never Enough: How Couples Can Overcome Misunderstandings, Resolve Conflicts, and Solve Relationship Problems Through Cognitive Therapy*. New York: Harper & Row.

Beck, A. T. (1991) 'Cognitive therapy: a 30-year retrospective'. *American Psychologist*, 46, 368–75.

Beck. A. T. (1999) *Prisoners of Hate: The Cognitive Basis of Anger, Hostility and Violence*. New York: HarperCollins.

Beck, A. T. and Emery, G. (1985) *Anxiety Disorders and Phobias: A Cognitive Perspective*. New York: Basic Books.

Beck, A. T. and Rush, A. J. (in press) 'Cognitive therapy', in H. I. Kaplan and B. J. Sadock (eds) *Comprehensive Textbook of Psychiatry* (Vol. VI). Baltimore, MD: Williams & Williams.

Beck, A. T. and Weishaar, M. E. (2000) 'Cognitive therapy', in R. J. Corsini and D. Wedding (eds) *Current Psychotherapies* (6th edn, pp. 241–72). Itasca, IL: Peacock.

Beck, A. T. and Young, J. E. (1985) 'Cognitive therapy of depression', in D. Barlow (ed.) *Clinical Handbook of Psychological Disorders: A Step-by-Step Treatment Manual* (pp. 206–44). New York: Guilford Press.

Beck, A. T., Freeman, A. and associates (1990) *Cognitive Therapy of Personality Disorders*. New York: Guilford Press.

Beck, A. T., Kovacs, M. and Weissman, A. (1979) 'Assessment of suicide intention: the Scale for Suicide Ideation'. *Journal of Consulting and Clinical Psychology*, 47, 343–52.
Beck, A. T., Rush, A. J., Shaw, B. F. and Emery, G. (1979) *Cognitive Therapy of Depression*. New York: John Wiley.
Beck, A. T., Ward, C. H., Mendelson, M., Mock, J. E. and Erbaugh, J. K. (1961) 'An inventory for measuring depression'. *Archives of General Psychiatry*, 4, 561–71.
Beck, J. S. (1995) *Cognitive Therapy: Basics and Beyond*. New York: Guilford Press.
Clark, D. M. and Beck, A. T. (1988) 'Cognitive approaches', in C. G. Last and M. Hersen (eds) *Handbook of Anxiety Disorders* (pp. 362–85). New York: Pergamon.
Clark, D. M., Beck, A. T. and Alford, B. A. (1999) *Scientific Foundations of Cognitive Theory and Therapy of Depression*. Philadelphia, PA: John Wiley.
Freeman, A. and Dattillio, F. M. (eds) (1992) *Comprehensive Casebook of Cognitive Therapy*. New York: Plenum Press.
Greenberger, D. and Padesky, C. A. (1995) *Mind Over Mood: Change How You Feel by Changing The Way You Think*. New York: Guilford Press.
Kelly, G. (1955) *The Psychology of Personal Constructs*. New York: Norton.
Kendall, P. C., Hollon, S. T., Beck, A. T., Hammen, C. L. and Ingram, R. E. (1987) 'Issues and recommendations regarding use of the Beck Depression Inventory'. *Cognitive Therapy and Research*, 11, 289–99.
Lazarus, R. S. (1966) *Psychological Stress and the Coping Process*. New York: McGraw-Hill.
Padesky, C. A. and Greenberger, D. (1995) *Clinician's Guide to Mind Over Mood*. New York: Guilford Press.
Scott, J., Williams, J. M. G. and Beck, A. T. (eds) (1989) *Cognitive Therapy in Clinical Practice: An Illustrative Casebook*. London: Routledge.
Weishaar, M. E. (1993) *Aaron T. Beck*. London: Sage.
Weissman, A. (1979) *The Dysfunctional Attitudes Scale*. Philadelphia, PA: Center for Cognitive Therapy.

Beck on audio-cassette and videotape

Beck, A. T. (1977) *Demonstration of the Cognitive Therapy of Depression: Interview #1 (Patient with Family Problem)*. Audio and video available.
Beck, A. T. (1979) *Cognitive Therapy of Depression: Interview #1 (Patient with a Hopelessness Problem)*. Audio and video available.

Beck, A. T. (1985) *Cognitive Therapy of Anxiety and Panic Disorders: First Interview Techniques.* Audio and video available.
Beck, A. T. (1990) *Cognitive Therapy of an Avoidant Personality.* Two audio-cassettes.

All the above are available from:
The Beck Institute
GSB Building, City Line and Belmont Avenues, Suite 700
Bala Cynwyd
PA 19004-1610
USA
Phone: 610.664.3020
Fax: 610.664.4437
e-mail: beckinst@gim.net
website: www.beckinstitute.org

Evaluating Counselling and Therapy Approaches

Life is the art of drawing sufficient conclusions from insufficient premises.

Samuel Butler

You have now had a chance to read about the six key counselling and therapy approaches presented in this book. Undoubtedly, you have already started drawing your own conclusions about the usefulness of the different approaches and how comfortable you would be implementing each of them. In this final chapter I want to broaden your perspectives about evaluating counselling and therapy approaches by reviewing eight relevant issues. Some of these issues are also pertinent to the whole enterprise of originating counselling and therapy approaches.

ISSUE 1 What is the relationship between theorists' personal histories and their therapeutic approaches?

Theories of counselling and therapy are created by human beings. Without exception, all the theorists whose work is described in this book encountered periods of significant psychological suffering in their lives. Box 8.1 illustrates this point. Jung's observation 'Only the wounded physician heals' (Jung, 1961), might be amended to become 'Only the wounded healer creates a counselling and therapy approach'.

If you accept that many of the originators of therapeutic approaches experienced more than their fair share of psychological suffering, the question still remains how this affected their theorizing. All the theorists in this book seem to have been motivated to develop theoretical positions that would

---

Box 8.1 Wounded theorists

- **Sigmund Freud (Psychoanalysis)** suffered for many years from periodic depressions, mood variations and anxiety attacks. Freud also had occasional attacks of dread of dying, some psychologically induced fainting spells, and became very frightened about train travel.

- **Carl Jung (Analytical therapy)** was a solitary child who, at one stage, used fainting spells to get out of going to secondary school. In his late thirties and early forties Jung experienced schizophrenic-like symptoms.

- **Carl Rogers (Person-centred therapy)** was an extremely shy and solitary child who grew up in a home where he considered his parents as masters of subtle emotional manipulation. Rogers felt it unsafe to share much of his personal feelings at home for fear of being judged negatively.

- **Fritz Perls (Gestalt therapy)** grew up in a distressed family where his parents had many bitter verbal and physical fights. Perls' mother beat him with carpet-beating rods. He hated his father's pompous righteousness.

- **Albert Ellis (Rational emotive behaviour therapy)** was a sickly child who was unusually shy and introverted during his childhood and adolescence. Ellis' mother was self-involved and neglectful while, for much of the time, his father was physically absent. At age 12, Ellis discovered his parents had divorced.

- **Aaron Beck's (Cognitive therapy)** mother was periodically deeply depressed. She could also be moody, inconsistent and excitable. While growing up, Beck developed many anxieties, including fears related to abandonment, surgery, suffocation, public speaking and heights.

---

help not just their clients but themselves. For example, Freud's self-analysis helped him address his personal suffering at the same time as providing important insights for his main work, *The Interpretation of Dreams* (Freud, 1976; Jones, 1963). Jung's confrontation with his own unconscious archetypes and primordial images provided a rich source of ideas for helping both himself and others (Jung, 1961). Rogers' person-centred therapist has the attributes of empathy, respect and non-possessive warmth that Rogers found missing in his parents and required for his own growth. In his late teens Albert Ellis regularly went to the Bronx Botanical Gardens in New York and forced himself to sit next to women on park benches and strike up conversations with them so that he could learn to control his shyness and build his relating skills. Here, early in life, Ellis was trying to think and behave more rationally in one of his problem areas.

Being highly motivated to develop therapeutic approaches that they could use themselves has both advantages and disadvantages. In evaluating the theory and practice of the different originators, relevant questions are: 'How much of their own problems were or are the theorists projecting on to clients at large?' and 'Is the approach that worked or works for any particular theorist necessarily that which is best for all clients?' The same sorts of questions can be asked of those studying counselling and therapy approaches. For example, when evaluating the different theoretical approaches, 'How much are your own needs and problems restricting your ability to be objective?'

ISSUE 2 What is the influence of the theorists' historical and cultural contexts on their therapeutic approaches?

Therapeutic approaches do not incubate and emerge in vacuums. Theorists are influenced by the historical and cultural contexts in which they live. For example, the prevalence of sexual repression in turn-of-the-century Austria influenced Freud to develop a theoretical position in which unacknowledged sexuality plays a large part. Another example is that, during the first half of the twentieth century, parents tended to dominate their families more than they do now. Carl Rogers was brought up in the first quarter of the century. His person-centred counselling reflects the need for individuals to have nurturing and accepting relationships within which to work through the effects of judgemental family upbringings so that they can 'become persons' (Rogers, 1961, 1980).

A relevant question here is that of how much the problems

affecting clients change over time. For instance, the current breakdown of respect for authority may mean that, unlike Rogers, many young people are facing problems of too little rather than too much structure. In addition, the materialism and rampant consumerism of Western societies may be exacerbating people's tendencies to greed and consequent feelings of depression and alienation when their attempts to buy happiness fail. In the twenty-first century, the increasing pace of technological change may also create new sets of problems, which current therapeutic approaches may be insufficiently equipped to address, stemming from changes in how people work and communicate.

Culture also plays a part in influencing theory. For example, ideas of desirable behaviour can differ greatly between Western and Eastern cultures. Western therapeutic approaches reflect a value on individualism that people from Eastern cultures, with their greater emphasis on group harmony, may find uncongenial (Ho, 1985). All the theorists presented in this book were or are from the West: Freud was Austrian; Jung Swiss; Rogers, Ellis and Beck American; and Perls was born German and lived for the second half of his life in South Africa and then in the United States.

ISSUE 3   What is the influence of all the major theorists being men?

In *The Female Eunuch*, Germaine Greer observed that Freud was the father of psychoanalysis and that it had no mother (Greer, 1971). Most readers have probably noticed that all the major theorists presented in this book are men. In addition, none of the theoretical approaches presented either in my longer book *Theory and Practice of Counselling and Therapy* (Nelson-Jones, in press) or *Current Psychotherapies* (Corsini and Wedding, 2000), probably the most authoritative American therapy text, were developed by women. However, women have been prominent in psychodynamic approaches to therapy: for instance, Melanie Klein, Karen Horney and Anna Freud. In addition, Perls' wife Laura is considered by many to be the co-founder of gestalt therapy. Furthermore, women have been the driving force behind feminist therapy.

A number of interesting questions are raised by the predominance of men in developing therapeutic approaches such as 'Do some theories contain male bias?' For instance, Freud's notion of penis envy is uncongenial to many women. Furthermore, if women had been more prominent in theorizing, 'Might we have seen the emergence of different and more humane therapeutic approaches?' In addition, given equal mental ability between the sexes and women's greater interest than men in relationships, 'Why have women not made more of a contribution to originating major counselling and therapy approaches?'

ISSUE 4   What is the nature of human nature?

Allport (1964) observed that debasing theoretical assumptions degrade human beings and generous assumptions exalt them. Maslow (1971) raises the issue of whether psychology has been based too much on a 'bad animal' rather than a 'good animal' underlying view of human nature. Both Freud and Jung were mainly pessimistic about human nature and emphasized the darker individual and collective unconscious forces lying beneath the veneer of civilization. One of Freud's favourite quotes came from the Roman writer Plautus: 'Man is a wolf to man.' If anything, the psychodynamic theories stress curbing negative instincts and impulses rather than cultivating positive ones.

The traditional behaviourists view people's behaviour as the result of evolutionary drives, for instance, for sex, food and shelter, and conditioning. Their mechanistic view of human nature is scarcely flattering to humans. The cognitive-behaviourists allow for personal agency. Nevertheless, if anything, theorists like Ellis, with his focus on biological tendencies to irrationality, and Beck, with his underlying maladaptive schemas, have focused more on the darker than on the brighter aspects of human nature. Of the theorists in this book, Rogers is perhaps the only one to take predominantly a good animal view of human nature. For Rogers, the actualizing tendency in human beings is positive and it only becomes negative to the extent that it is blocked and frustrated by environmental forces.

Charles Darwin referred to humans possessing an 'instinct of sympathy' and this appears to be an important survival instinct for the species (Dalai Lama and Cutler, 1998). In addition, there is ample evidence that humans can be co-operative and caring as well as hostile and uncaring (Argyle, 1991). The make-up of human nature is a complex area. In addition to being very pessimistic or very optimistic, other possibilities include being neutral or cautiously optimistic about the positive aspects of human nature. Neither neutrality nor cautious optimism involves the need to deny human beings' huge potential for destructive and aggressive behaviours, but just balances it out by noting their huge potential to think, feel, act and communicate constructively. Thus therapy can become a matter of releasing and cultivating higher human potentials as well as of containing and over-coming destructive tendencies.

ISSUE 5 To what extent does the approach address subnormal, normal and supra-normal functioning?

When evaluating the different therapeutic approaches, con-sider the populations for which their originators intended them. You may remember that Jung thought his analytical therapy more suited to patients searching for meaning in the afternoon of their lives than those requiring help with conven-tional adaptation in the morning of their lives.

It is possible to look at human functioning in three broad categories – subnormal, normal and supra-normal – with, at any given moment, individuals being placed somewhere along this continuum. Subnormal functioning is that where indivi-duals are psychologically distressed and have problems that are more severe than the normal run of the population. Such clients might suffer from the mental disorders that are listed in the American Psychiatric Association's *Diagnostic and Statis-tical Manual of Mental Disorders* (APA, 1994). Normal functioning is that where people are capable of conventional adaptation to the societies in which they live. Such individuals may still experience problems for which counselling and therapy is appropriate: for instance, relationship problems, stress problems, and study problems.

Some clients who are functioning well may want to function even better. Supra-normal functioning refers to going above, beyond or transcending normal human functioning. Drawing on Eastern and Western traditions, qualities of supra-normal functioning include equanimity, autonomy, mental purification, human sympathy, honesty both with oneself and others, inner strength, heightened concentration and compassionate or selfless service (Dalai Lama and Cutler, 1998; Maslow, 1970; Walsh, 2000).

Psychotherapy has its origins more in dealing with the problems of the subnormal and normal than in trying to assist well-functioning people to develop their full human potential. Of the theorists presented in this book, four were or are psychiatrists – Freud, Jung, Perls and Beck – and two, clinical psychologists – Rogers and Ellis. There has yet to be a major therapeutic approach developed by professionals, such as counselling psychologists or counsellors, who predominantly deal with normal client populations, let alone superior functioning ones.

Some theorists in this book, for instance, Rogers and Ellis, have paid attention to defining full human functioning. Nevertheless, none of the approaches presented sufficiently addresses helping clients to be compassionate, engage in selfless service and synergistically foster the interests and ideals both of themselves and humankind. A possible criticism of Western psychotherapy is that it errs too much in the direction of being self-centred therapy. The Austrian psychiatrist, Alfred Adler, with his emphasis on social interest and community feeling, stands out as an advocate of the need to show more concern for others and for the human species (Adler, 1998).

ISSUE 6   To what extent does the therapeutic approach foster self-therapy for afterwards?

Sooner or later all clients are going to part from their therapists. Though a full course of psychoanalysis or of analytical therapy may last for years, that option is for the few. Nowadays there is great pressure from those paying for therapeutic services, for example, governments and insurance companies, to encourage short-term managed care. Furthermore, most private clients have limited resources, which makes paying for long-term therapy either difficult or impossible. Even though some clients genuinely require longer term contact, increasingly most counselling and therapy is short-term, say between one and ten sessions or medium-term, say between eleven and twenty-five sessions. Important questions then become: 'What are the ingredients of effective time-limited therapy?' 'How can therapeutic gains best be maintained afterwards?' and 'To what extent is the therapy a training in self-therapy?'

In Chapter 1 I mentioned that one of the functions of theories was to provide languages both for the therapeutic conversation and so that clients can converse with themselves. Of the six theories presented here, Freud's psychoanalysis, Jung's analytical therapy, Rogerian person-centred therapy and Perlsian gestalt therapy appear not to give high priority to sharing the language in which the therapy is conceptualized with clients. For instance, Rogerian therapists do not share concepts like actualizing tendency, conditions of worth, and organismic valuing process with their clients. Though clients in each of these four approaches may end therapy able to lead their lives more skilfully, the skills of so doing tend not to be clearly articulated during therapy. Clients may learn self-therapy skills, but this is more a by-product of the therapy rather than an integral part of it. For example, person-centred therapists assist clients to listen to their feelings and 'inner voices' and in so doing clients can learn to do this better on their own.

In the cognitive-behavioural school the therapist's role is more that of an educator than in either the psychodynamic or the humanistic schools. As part of the therapeutic process, the language of the approach gets shared with clients. For instance, in rational emotive behaviour therapy, clients learn to detect, analyse in ABC terms, dispute and restate irrational beliefs both during therapy sessions and when completing homework assignments. In inelegant REBT, this sharing of language may be only in relation to specific symptoms, but in elegant REBT, this sharing can lead to disputing irrational beliefs becoming a way of life.

In cognitive therapy, clients learn that they need to test the reality of their thinking and are taught how to do this. By sharing a common language with clients and educating them in cognitive and, sometimes, in behavioural skills as well, these cognitive-behavioural approaches may be more clearly helping clients to become better at self-therapy than those approaches leaving relevant skills to be indirectly acquired and maintained. Perhaps adherents of other than cognitive-behavioural approaches might further develop their theory and practice, without losing the essence, so that clients can learn more about how to conduct self-therapy for afterwards.

ISSUE 7   What is the role of research in evaluating therapeutic approaches?

Though counselling and therapy approaches may have different goals, nevertheless a pertinent question in evaluating any approach is always going to be 'Where is the research evidence for its effectiveness?' Dictionary definitions of research tend to use adjectives like 'careful' and 'systematic' and nouns like 'study', 'inquiry' and 'investigation'. In Chapter 1, I stated that a function of counselling and therapy theories was to provide research hypotheses. Good theory provides good research hypotheses, poor theory provides poor hypotheses.

Research can have a role in laying the scientific base for a therapeutic approach. However, here my emphasis is on the role of research in evaluating the practice of therapeutic approaches. A pertinent question is 'What therapy, conducted by which therapists, is appropriate for which clients, with which problems, under what circumstances?' Conducting research into therapeutic approaches can be difficult since there are so many considerations to take into account.

Research variables

Below are suggestions of variables, albeit sometimes interrelated, that can be explored when researching therapeutic approaches.

- *Therapist variables*   Therapist variables include age, sex, race, culture, professional training, relevant background and experience, and emotional well-being.
- *Client variables*   Client variables include age, sex, race, culture, nature of problem or problems, prior history of therapy, severity of disturbance, degree of family and environmental support, and whether any and what medication is involved.
- *Process variables*   Process variables consist of specific details concerning the content and management of therapy. Such variables include frequency and duration of sessions,

what interventions were used and how, and how between-session time was used.

- *Outcome variables* Outcome variables are criteria for measuring what changes occurred at the end of therapy and the degree to which they were maintained. Sources of outcome information include tests and measures, and therapist, client and third-party observations.

Research methods

Methods for evaluating counselling and therapy approaches fall into two main categories: qualitative and quantitative. Qualitative approaches to researching therapeutic methods include detailed case descriptions and open-ended interviews. Quantitative approaches emphasize the systematic collection and analysis of quantitative information. Both quantitative and qualitative research methods can be used in evaluating therapeutic approaches – they are not mutually exclusive.

In quantitative research, client change can be estimated by comparing information obtained at different times: for example, at the start of therapy, when it ends, and after one or more stipulated follow-up periods. Quantitative information is often in the form of answers to standardized questionnaires measuring variables such as anxiety or depression. Another important source of quantitative information can be recording the frequency and duration of specific thoughts and behaviours.

Quantitative research designs fall into two main categories: comparison group designs and single case designs. In a simple comparison group design, those receiving treatment would form a treatment group and those not receiving treatment would form a control group. Comparison group designs can be more elaborate: for example, as well as a control group, there could be two or three experimental groups, each being varied in some clearly defined way.

Increasingly, single case research designs are being used in counselling and therapy research. Kazdin writes: 'Single case experiments permit inferences to be drawn about intervention effects by using the patient as his or her own control. The impact of treatment is examined in relation to the patient's dysfunction over time' (Kazdin, 1986, p. 39). He states that there are four main characteristics of single case designs: clear specification of goals, use of repeated observations, the delineation of time periods in which different conditions (baseline, treatment) apply, and relatively stable data – the more variable the data, the more difficult it is to draw conclusions about intervention effects (Kazdin, 1986).

Empirically supported treatments

Especially in the United States, research into therapeutic approaches is being used to establish empirically supported treatments (ESTs). In 1993, the Society of Clinical Psychology (Division 12) of the American Psychological Association established a task force to identify treatments with scientifically proven effectiveness for particular mental disorders. This task force has identified a number of effective, or probably effective, psychological treatments for disorders including depression, eating disorders, marital discord, panic disorder with and without agoraphobia, post-traumatic stress disorder, social phobia, and smoking cessation (Barlow *et al.*, 1999).

A number of observations are relevant about empirically supported treatments. Where such treatments exist, there is a professional and ethical obligation on the part of therapists to find out about them. Furthermore, unless they have good reason for not doing so in terms of particular clients' circumstances, therapists must seriously consider either implementing the treatments themselves or referring clients to those competent to do so. Currently, there is a research–practice gap in which therapists under-utilize evidence-based treatments emanating from the findings of their research-oriented colleagues (McLeod, 2000). One reason for this gap is that some therapists require further training before they can properly implement the protocols for specific empirically supported treatments. Another reason is that the presentation of therapy research findings tends not to be user-friendly to practitioners. Relatively few empirically supported or evidence-based treatments come from outside the area of cognitive-behaviour therapy (Lazarus, 1998).

Limitations of research

Clearly, research studies have an important role to play in evaluating therapeutic approaches. Furthermore, all therapists should be reflective practitioners willing to honestly evaluate their own therapeutic processes and outcomes. However, good researchers, like good practitioners, should acknowledge the limitations as well as the strengths of their endeavours. Even in those areas where empirically supported treatments exist, there may be still better ways of treating clients. Skilled researchers not only find out what they know, they often obtain a sharper insight into what remains to be discovered.

The concerns of many clients do not fall into circumscribed problem areas and the unavoidable messiness of much of therapeutic practice does not easily lend itself to narrow research studies. In addition, currently some important issues, such as how to encourage supra-normal functioning, scarcely obtain any research attention. Research at its best consists of creating ideas as well as evaluating them. In academic institutions the evaluative component may be stifling the creative component of research, what Einstein called the 'holy curiosity of inquiry'. To some extent, scientific therapy research has turned against itself by undervaluing and undermining its creative base. It is much easier to evaluate existing approaches than to create them in the first place and then evaluate them.

ISSUE 8 How adequately is the theory of each therapeutic approach stated?

In Chapter 1, I mentioned that counselling and therapy theories may be viewed as possessing four main dimensions if they are to be stated adequately: (1) a statement of the *basic concepts* or assumptions underlying the theory; (2) an explanation of the *acquisition* of helpful and unhelpful behaviour; (3) an explanation of the *maintenance* of helpful and unhelpful behaviour; (4) an explanation of how to help clients *change* their behaviour and *consolidate* their gains when therapy ends. Box 8.2 provides the reader with a basic checklist of questions to ask when assessing how adequately a therapeutic approach's theory is stated.

Readers can use the checklist in Box 8.2 to identify gaps in how thoroughly theories are stated. For example, a theoretical statement may be more thorough in assessing how behaviour is maintained than how it was acquired in the first place, or vice versa.

Box 8.2   A checklist for assessing a therapeutic approach's theoretical statement

Model of human development

1. What are the basic concepts of the theory and how adequate are they?
2. How well does the theory say how helpful and unhelpful thoughts, feelings, physical reactions, and communications/actions are acquired?
3. How well does the theory say how helpful and unhelpful thoughts, feelings, physical reactions, and communications/actions are maintained?

Model of therapy

4. How clear and adequate are the approach's therapeutic goals?
5. How clearly articulated and adequate is the approach's process of therapy?
6. What is the nature of the therapeutic relationship and what are its strengths and weaknesses?
7. What interventions are used in the approach and what are their strengths and limitations?
8. How consistent is the approach's model of human development with its model of therapeutic practice?
9. What is the research evidence for the effectiveness of the approach with different kinds of clients?

Another way to use the checklist is to evaluate how well the theoretical statement answers each question. For example, one way to answer the question about the basic concepts of the theoretical statement is in terms of how adequately they lay the building blocks for the therapeutic approach. Freud's concepts of levels of consciousness and the tripartite structure of the mental apparatus provide a good foundation for the remainder of his theory and practice.

Another way of reviewing an approach's basic concepts involves assessing its assumptions about human nature. I find some theoretical statements contain an overly negative view of human nature. Furthermore, I would like to see a clearer statement about the concept of mind and a clearer acknowledgement of the importance of mental development and discipline throughout life in the basic concepts of all theoretical approaches, even rational emotive behaviour therapy and cognitive therapy. Above, I have provided you with a few ideas on how to answer the first question on the checklist. When answering all questions on the checklist, remember to have the courage to think for yourself and to think critically.

CONCLUDING COMMENT

You have now been introduced to six key counselling and therapy approaches. I hope that you have enjoyed studying these approaches and want to learn more about this fascinating field. All people are personality theorists, with ideas about what makes themselves and others 'tick'. The systematic study of counselling and therapy approaches should assist you in developing a good working model of human development and therapy to guide your practical work with clients. Reading an introductory counselling and therapy textbook like this is an early step along the path of what should be a very stimulating and rewarding journey. I hope that the results of this journey are of great benefit to you and those whom you help both now and in the future.

SUMMARY

- *Counselling and therapy approaches may be influenced for good or ill by the personal histories of their originators. All approaches in this book were developed by 'wounded theorists'.*
- *Approaches to therapy also reflect the historical and cultural contexts of their originators. The new century is likely to throw up fresh problems that existing therapeutic approaches may inadequately address.*
- *All the really first-rank counselling and therapy theorists are men. Though many women have also been prominent in developing therapeutic approaches, it is interesting to speculate why they have not made an even greater contribution.*
- *The make-up of human nature is a complex area. Possibly most therapeutic approaches are based on an overly negative or bad animal view of human nature that leads to*

insufficient emphasis on acknowledging and cultivating human beings' higher potentials.

- *Human functioning may be viewed on subnormal, normal and supra-normal dimensions. A possible criticism of Western psychotherapy is that it errs too much in the direction of being self-centred therapy.*
- *In particular it is the cognitive-behavioural approaches, with their educational emphasis, that share their languages with clients so that clients can perform a degree of self-therapy once formal therapy ends.*
- *Research plays an important role in evaluating therapeutic approaches. Research can focus on therapist, client, process and outcome variables. Therapy research can be qualitative, quantitative, or a mixture of both. Attempts are being made to identify empirically supported treatments (ESTs).*
- *Limitations of research include the complexity of the subject matter, insufficient attention to supra-normal functioning, and an undervaluing of the creative as contrasted with the evaluative aspects of research.*
- *A nine-item checklist for assessing the adequacy of a therapeutic approach's model of human development and model of therapy is presented.*
- *The systematic study of counselling and therapy approaches should assist readers in developing a good working model of human development and of therapy to guide their practical work with clients.*

REVIEW AND PERSONAL QUESTIONS

Review questions

1. What do you consider the influence of each of the following factors on the development of the counselling and therapy approaches presented in this book:

   - the theorists' personal histories?
   - the theorists' historical and cultural contexts?
   - the fact that all the theorists were or are men?

2. Do you consider that the six theorists are too negative or positive in their views about human nature? Provide reasons for your answer.

3. Critically discuss the role of research in evaluating therapeutic approaches.
4. Apply the checklist for assessing the adequacy of a therapeutic approaches' theoretical statement (see Box 8.2) to at least one of the counselling and therapy approaches presented in this book.

Personal questions

1. What do you consider the influence of each of the following factors on how you might develop your own approach to counselling and therapy:

   - your personal history?
   - your historical and cultural context?
   - your biological sex?

2. In light of reading this book, what are your present preferences regarding counselling and therapy approaches and why?
3. If and when you develop a theoretical statement for your own therapeutic approach, use the checklist provided in Box 8.2 to assess its adequacy and guide you in strengthening your statement.

REFERENCES

Adler, A. (1998; original edition 1933) *Social Interest: Adler's Key to the Meaning of Life*. Oxford: Oneworld.

Allport, G. W. (1964) 'The fruits of eclecticism: bitter or sweet?' *Acta Psychologica*, 23, 27–44.

American Psychiatric Association (APA) (1994) *Diagnostic and Statistical Manual of Mental Disorders* (4th edn). Washington, DC: Author.

Argyle, M. (1991) *Cooperation: The Basis of Sociability*. London: Routledge.

Barlow, D. H., Levitt, J. and Bufka, L. F. (1999) 'The dissemination of empirically supported treatments; a view to the future'. *Behaviour Research and Therapy*, 37, S147–62.

Corsini, R. J. and Wedding, D. (eds) (2000) *Current Psychotherapies* (6th edn). Itasca, IL: Peacock.

Dalai Lama, His Holiness the, and Cutler, H. C. (1998) *The Art of Happiness: A Handbook for Living*. Sydney: Hodder.

288 *Six Key Approaches to Counselling and Therapy*

Freud, S. (1976; original edition 1900) *The Interpretation of Dreams*. Harmondsworth: Penguin Books.

Greer, G. (1971) *The Female Eunuch*. London: Paladin.

Ho, D. Y. F. (1985) 'Cultural values and professional issues in clinical psychology: the Hong Kong experience'. *American Psychologist*, 40, 1212–18.

Jones, E. (1963) *The Life and Work of Sigmund Freud*. New York: Anchor Books.

Jung, C. G. (1961) *Memories, Dreams and Reflections*. London: Fontana Press.

Kazdin, A. E. (1986) 'Research designs and methodology', in S. L. Garfield and A. E. Bergin (eds) *Handbook of Psychotherapy and Behavior Change* (3rd edn, pp. 23–68). New York: John Wiley.

Lazarus, A. A. (1998) *Brief but Comprehensive Psychotherapy: The Multimodal Way*. New York: Springer.

Maslow, A. H. (1970) *Motivation and Personality* (2nd edn). New York: Harper & Row.

Maslow, A. H. (1971) *The Farther Reaches of Human Nature*. Harmondsworth: Pelican.

McLeod, J. (2000) 'Research issues in counselling and psychotherapy', in S. Palmer (ed.) *Introduction to Counselling and Psychotherapy: The Essential Guide* (pp. 331–40). London: Sage.

Nelson-Jones, R. (in press) *The Theory and Practice of Counselling and Therapy* (3rd edn). London: Continuum.

Rogers, C. R. (1961) *On Becoming a Person*. Boston, MA: Houghton Mifflin.

Rogers, C. R. (1980) *A Way of Being*. Boston, MA: Houghton Mifflin.

Walsh, R. (2000) 'Asian psychotherapies', in R. Corsini and D. Wedding (eds) *Current Psychotherapies* (6th edn, pp. 407–44). Itasca, IL: Peacock.

Glossary

ABBREVIATIONS

AT – analytical therapy; CT – cognitive therapy; GT – gestalt therapy; PA – psychoanalysis; PCT – person-centred therapy; REBT – rational emotive behaviour therapy

ABCDE theory (REBT)   A theoretical model for understanding psychological distress and change: A – Adversities or activating events in a person's life; B – Beliefs, both rational and irrational; C – Consequences, both emotional and behavioural; D – Disputing irrational beliefs; and E – Effective new philosophy of life.

active imagination (AT)   A technique devised by Jung to help people get in touch with unconscious material. Clients begin by concentrating on a starting point. They then allow their unconscious to produce a series of images, which may make up a complete story.

activity scheduling (CT)   Activity scheduling involves planning and timetabling specific activities with clients. A principle of activity scheduling is to state what activity the client agrees to engage in rather than how much they will accomplish.

actualizing tendency (PCT)   An active process representing the inherent tendency of the organism to develop its capacities in the direction of maintaining, enhancing and reproducing itself.

anima and animus (AT)   The anima is the personification of the feminine nature in a man's unconscious, whereas the animus is the personification of the masculine nature in a woman's unconscious.

archetypes (AT)   'Primordial images' and 'primordial thoughts' rather than the representations of the images or thoughts themselves. Archetypes provide instinctive patterns for mental activity.

automatic thoughts (CT)   Less accessible to awareness than voluntary thoughts, but not so deeply buried as beliefs and schemas. Automatic thoughts are part of people's internal monologue – what and how they talk to themselves; can take the form of words, images, or both; occur very rapidly and are usually at the fringe of awareness.

awareness technique (GT)   A concentration technique in which clients are asked to become aware of their body language, their breathing, their voice quality and their emotions as much as of any pressing thoughts.

collective unconscious (AT)   At its deepest levels the unconscious is a vast collective and universal historical storehouse whose contents belong to mankind in general. The contents of the collective unconscious have never been in consciousness, but owe their existence to heredity.

complexes (AT)   An important feature of the personal unconscious; accumulations of associations, sometimes of a traumatic nature, that possess strong emotional content – for example, the mother complex.

cognitive-behaviour therapy   A term describing therapies that extend behaviour therapy to have a major focus on changing covert thoughts as well as overt behaviours: examples include cognitive therapy and rational emotive behaviour therapy. These therapies are criticized by traditional behaviour therapists for insufficient adherence to scientifically established principles of behaviour.

cognitive distortions (CT)   Information-processing errors that both characterize and maintain psychological distress: for instance, arbitrary inference, selective abstraction, over-generalization and dichotomous thinking.

cognitive vulnerability (CT)   Human beings' cognitive frailty. Because of their schemas, each person has a set of unique vulnerabilities and sensitivities that predispose them to psychological distress.

collaborative empiricism (CT)   Therapists and clients collaborate in the scientific endeavour of examining the evidence to confirm or negate the client's cognitions, all of which are viewed as testable hypotheses.

conditions of worth (PCT)   The internalization or introjection of others' evaluations, which do not truly reflect the person's actualizing tendency but may serve to impede it.

congruence (PCT)   Consistency between the thoughts and

feelings the therapist experiences and her or his professional demeanour. Not putting on a professional façade.

contact boundary (GT) The boundary between organism and environment where all feelings, thoughts and actions take place. Contacting the environment represents forming a gestalt, whereas withdrawal is either closing a gestalt completely or mobilizing resources to make closure possible.

counselling A relationship in which counsellors assist clients to understand themselves and their problems better. Then, where appropriate, counsellors use various interventions to assist clients to feel, think, communicate and act more effectively. The term counselling is often used interchangeably with psychotherapy. Since there are many different theoretical orientations, it may be more accurate to speak of counselling approaches than counselling.

defence mechanisms (PA) Infantilisms which operate unconsciously to protect the ego and may impede realistic behaviour long after they have outlived their usefulness. Examples include repression, reaction formation, projection, fixation and regression.

disputing (REBT) Involves challenging and questioning unsubstantiated hypotheses that clients hold about themselves, others and the world.

dream analysis (AT) Dreams are utterances or statements from the unconscious and are comparable to texts that appear unintelligible, but the therapist has to discover how to read them. An understanding of myths and symbols is fundamental for analysing dreams.

dreamwork (GT) Dreams are existential messages, not just unfinished situations, current problems or symptoms. There are four stages to dreamwork: sharing the dream, retelling the dream in the present tense, talking to the different actors in the dream, and conducting a dialogue between different elements in the dream.

eclecticism The practice of drawing from different counselling and therapy approaches in formulating client problems and implementing treatment interventions. A distinction can be made between theoretical eclecticism and practical or technical eclecticism.

ego (PA) The ego or 'I' acts as an intermediary between the id and the external world and strives to bring the reality principle to bear upon the id in substitution for the pleasure principle.

ego disturbance (REBT) Arises from the demanding and irrational belief 'I *must* do well and win approval for all my performances' because it leads to people thinking and feeling that they are inadequate and undeserving when they do not do as well as they must.

empathy (PCT) The therapist's capacity to comprehend accurately the client's inner world or internal frame of reference and to sensitively communicate back this understanding.

excitement (GT) The energy people create, which coincides with the physiological function of excitation.

experiments (CT) Beliefs are treated as testable hypotheses. Together, therapists and clients set up cognitive and behavioural experiments that encourage clients to test the reality of their beliefs.

experiments (GT) Therapists and clients develop experiments in which clients try out different ways of thinking and acting. Clients are repeatedly encouraged to 'Try this and see what you experience'.

free association (PA) Clients must tell their analysts everything that occurs to them, even if it is disagreeable and even if it seems meaningless. The object of free association is to help lift repressions by making unconscious material conscious.

frustration (GT) Providing situations in which clients experience being stuck in frustration and then frustrating their avoidances still further until they are willing to mobilize their own resources.

gestalt (GT) Means form or shape; among the meanings of the German verb *gestalten* are to shape, to form, to fashion, to organize and to structure. Other terms for gestalt are pattern, configuration or organized whole.

homeostasis (GT) Homeostasis or organismic self-regulation is the process by which the organism satisfies its needs by restoring balance when faced with a demand or need which upsets its equilibrium.

id (PA) The id or 'it' contains everything that is inherited and fixed in the constitution. Filled with energy from the instincts, the id strives to bring about the satisfaction of instinctual needs on the basis of the pleasure principle.

incongruence (PCT) A discrepancy between the self as perceived and the actual experience of the organism.

individuation (AT) The process by which the person becomes differentiated as a separate psychological individual, a separate whole as distinct from the collective psychology.

inelegant and elegant change (REBT) Inelegant change largely consists of some kind of symptom removal. Elegant change goes further than developing an effective new philosophy that supports removal of specific symptoms to assisting clients to develop and implement an effective philosophy of life.

instincts (PA) Somatic or biological demands upon the mind, which are grouped into two basic instincts: *Eros* and the *destructive instinct*.

integration Attempting to blend together theoretical concepts and/or practical interventions drawn from different counselling and therapy approaches into coherent and integrated wholes.

interpretation (PA) Involves offering constructions or explanations. Interpreting dreams represents an important – sometimes the most important – part of the analyst's work.

introjections (GT) Experiences which are swallowed as a whole rather than being properly digested and assimilated. The outcome of introjection is that undesirable as well as desirable thoughts, feelings and behaviours get retained.

irrational beliefs (REBT) Rigid, dogmatic, unhealthy, maladaptive beliefs that mostly get in the way of people's efforts to achieve their goals, and are comprised of demands, musts and shoulds.

low frustration tolerance (REBT) Low frustration tolerance or discomfort disturbance arises from the grandiose belief that people think they are so special that conditions must be easy and satisfying for them.

modes (CT) Networks of cognitive, affective, motivational and behavioural schemas. Modes are fundamental to personality since they interpret and adapt to emerging and ongoing situations.

openness to experience (PCT) Allowing all significant sensory and visceral experiences to be perceived, the capacity for realistic perception without defensiveness.

organismic valuing process (PCT) A person's continuous weighing of experience and the placing of values on that experience in terms of its ability to satisfy the actualizing tendency.

persona (AT)   A concept derived from the mask worn by actors in antiquity. At one level, the persona is the individual's system of adaptation or way of coping with the world. At a different level, the persona is not just an individual mask but a mask of the collective psyche.

personal unconscious (AT)   The contents, which are definitely personal, fall into two main categories: material that lost its intensity because it was either forgotten or repressed; and material which never possessed sufficient intensity to reach consciousness but has somehow entered the psyche – for instance, some sense-impressions.

preconscious (PA)   The preconscious is latent and capable of becoming conscious, while the unconscious is repressed and is unlikely to become conscious without great difficulty.

psychodynamics (PA)   The concept of psychical or mental energy and its distribution among the id, ego and super-ego is central to psychoanalysis.

psychotherapy   Literally 'mind healing'. More accurate to speak of the psychotherapies since there are many different theoretical and practical approaches to psychotherapy.

rational beliefs (REBT)   Healthy, productive and adaptive beliefs that are consistent with social reality and are stated as preferences, desires and wants.

rational coping statements (REBT)   Range from articulating simple words of encouragement to generating longer statements containing preferential thinking. This step often, but not necessarily, follows vigorous disputing.

rational emotive imagery (REBT)   In rational emotive imagery (REI) clients vividly imagine an adversity, next, once feeling unhealthily upset, hold on to the image for a minute or two, and then tell themselves strongly and repetitively sensible rational beliefs or coping statements.

reattribution techniques (CT)   Test automatic thoughts and underlying beliefs by considering alternative ways of assigning responsibility and cause.

schemas (CT)   Structures that consist of people's fundamental beliefs and assumptions. They are relatively stable cognitive patterns that influence, through their beliefs, how people select and synthesize incoming information.

self (AT)   The self is the central archetype, the archetype of order. The self, which expresses the unity of personality as a whole, encompasses both conscious and unconscious components.

self-actualizing (GT) A process involving an effective balance of contact and withdrawal at the contact boundary and the ability to use energy or excitement to meet real rather than phoney needs.

self-actualizing (PCT) A process of living and of personal development, based on an individual's organismic valuing process, that genuinely reflects their unique actualizing tendency.

self-concept (PCT) The self as perceived and the values attached to these perceptions, or what a person refers to as 'I' or 'me'.

shadow (AT) The shadow archetype reflects the realm of human beings' animal ancestors and, as such, comprises the whole historical aspect of the unconscious. For the most part, the shadow consists of inferior traits of personality that individuals refuse to acknowledge.

Socratic dialogue (CT) A Socratic style of questioning assists clients to expand and evaluate how they think. Typical questions are: 'Where is the evidence?'; 'Where is the logic?'; 'Are there other ways of perceiving the situation?'; and 'What would be the worst thing that could happen?'

super-ego (PA) The super-ego is a residue formed within the ego in which parental influence is prolonged. Parental influence may be broadly defined to include cultural, racial and family influences.

transference (PA) Clients perceive their analysts as reincarnations of important figures from their childhoods and transfer on to them moderate to intense feelings and emotions appropriate to these earlier models.

unconditional positive regard (PCT) This consists of two dimensions: first, prizing and feeling positively towards clients, and second, non-judgemental acceptance of clients' experiencing and disclosures as their subjective reality.

unconditional self-acceptance (REBT) Clients can always choose to accept themselves just because they are alive and human, whether or not they perform well or are approved of by others.

unconscious (PA) The unconscious, or unconscious proper, consists of material that is inadmissible to consciousness through repression. The censorship on unconscious material coming into awareness is very strong indeed.

Appendix 1
Training information

The following is a selective listing of sources of training information in Britain and Australia.

FREUD'S PSYCHOANALYSIS

Britain
The Chair
Psychoanalytic and Psychodynamic Psychotherapy Section
United Kingdom Council for Psychotherapy
167–169 Great Portland Street
London W1N 5FB

Australia
Centres for the training of psychoanalysts exist in Adelaide, Melbourne and Sydney.
Information may be obtained from:
The Australian Psychoanalytic Society
c/o Francis Thomson-Salo, Secretary
PO Box 22261
Caulfield Junction
Melbourne
Victoria 3161

JUNG'S ANALYTICAL THERAPY

Britain
Association of Jungian Analysts
7 Eton Avenue
London N3 7EL

British Association for Psychotherapists
37 Mapesbury Road
London NW2 4HJ

Independent Group of Analytical Psychologists
PO Box 1175
London W3 6DS

Society of Analytical Psychology
1 Daleham Gardens
London NW3 5BY

Australia
Regional centres for the training of Jungian analysts exist in
  Melbourne, Perth and Sydney.
Information may be obtained from:
Australian and New Zealand Society of Jungian Analysts –
  ANZSJA
c/o Anne Brown, Secretary
11 Eckersley Court
Blackburn South
Melbourne
Victoria 3130
e-mail: anne@preston.starway.net.au

PERSON-CENTRED THERAPY

Britain
Centre for Counselling Studies
School of Education and Professional Development
University of East Anglia
Norwich NR4 7TJ

Counselling Unit
Faculty of Education
University of Strathclyde
76 Southbrae Drive
Glasgow
Scotland G13 1PP

Australia
Masters in Counselling
School of Education
La Trobe University
Bundoora
Melbourne
Victoria 3083

GESTALT THERAPY

Britain
The Gestalt Psychotherapy Training Institute in the UK
2 Bedford Street
London Road
Bath BA1 6AF

Professor Petruska Clarkson
PHYSIS
12 North Common Road
London W5 2QB
Tel/Fax: 020 8567-3531

Australia
Gestalt Institute
Suite 40, 45 Riversdale Road
Hawthorn
Melbourne
Victoria 3122
Tel: 03-9815-0050

Gestalt Institute
81 Frederick Street
Toowong
Queensland 4066
Tel: 07-3371-8163

RATIONAL EMOTIVE BEHAVIOUR THERAPY

Britain
MSc Rational Emotive Behaviour Therapy
PACE
Goldsmiths College
New Cross
London SE14 6NW
Tel: 020 7919-78720
Contact person: Professor Windy Dryden

Centre for Rational Emotive Behaviour Therapy
156 Westcombe Hill
Blackheath
London SE3 7DH
Tel: 020 8293-4114 (course details)
Website: http://www.managingstress.com

Australia
Australian Institute for REBT
118 Balcombe Road
Mentone
Victoria 3802
Tel: 03-9585-1881
Contact person: Monica O'Kelly

COGNITIVE THERAPY

Britain
Information about behavioural and cognitive therapies train-
ing is available from:
British Association for Behavioural & Cognitive Psycho-
therapies (BABCP)
PO Box 9
Accrington BB5 2DG
Executive Officer: Howard Lomas
Tel/Fax: 01254-875277
e-mail: membership@babcp.org.uk

Australia
Information about Australian behavioural and cognitive
therapies training is available from:
Dr Ray Wilks
Victorian Branch of the Australian Association for Cognitive
and Behaviour Therapy (AACBT)
PO Box 1170D
Bundoora
Melbourne
Victoria 3083
Tel: 03-9925-7722
Fax: 03-9925-7303
e-mail: wilks@rmit.edu.au

PROFESSIONAL ASSOCIATIONS

Training information may also be obtained from the following
professional associations.

Britain
British Association for Counselling
1 Regent Place
Rugby CV21 2PJ
Tel: 01788-57832
Fax: 01788-562189
email: bac@bac.co.uk
Website: http//www.counselling.co.uk

British Psychological Society
St Andrews House
48 Princess Road East
Leicester LE1 7DR
Tel: 0116-254-9568
Fax: 0116-247-1787

United Kingdom Council for Psychotherapy
167–169 Great Portland Street
London W1N 5FB

Australia
Australian Psychological Society
PO Box 126
Carlton South
Melbourne
Victoria 3053
Tel: 03-9663-6166
Fax: 03-9663-6177
e-mail: naltoff@psychsociety.com.au
Website: http//www.aps.psychsociety.com.au

Appendix 2
Journal information

The following is a selective listing of counselling and therapy journals.

PSYCHOANALYSIS

International Journal of Psycho-Analysis
British Psychoanalytic Society
Byron House
112 Shirland Road
London W9 2EQ
UK

Journal of the American Psychoanalytic Association
American Psychoanalytic Association
309 East 49th Street
New York
NY 10017
USA

Psychoanalytic Quarterly
175 Fifth Avenue, Room 810
New York
NY 10010
USA

ANALYTICAL THERAPY

The Journal of Analytical Psychology
1 Daleham Gardens
London NW3 5BY
UK

Quadrant
28 East 39th Street
New York
NY 10016
USA

The San Francisco Jung Institute Library Journal
2040 Gough Street
San Francisco
CA 94109
USA

Harvest
194 Castellain Mansions
Castellain Road
London W9 1HD
UK

PERSON-CENTRED THERAPY

The Person-Centered Journal
ADPCA
PO Box 6881
San Carlos
CA 94090
USA
Tel: (415) 493 5000 ext: 4334

Person-Centred Practice
PCCS Books
Llangarron
Ross-on-Wye HR9 6PT
UK
Fax: (01989) 770 700
e-mail: books@pccs.telme.com

GESTALT THERAPY

The Gestalt Journal
The Gestalt Journal Press
PO Box 990
Highland
NY 12528-0990
USA
Tel: (914) 691 7192
Fax: 1 209 671 3843
e-mail: tgjournal@gestalt.org
Website: www.gestalt.org

The Gestalt Review
PO Box 1807
Lawrence
KS 66044-8897
USA
Tel: 1 785 843 1236
Fax: 1 785 843 1274
e-mail: TAPJournal@analyticpress.com

British Gestalt Journal
PO Box 2994
London N5 1UG
UK
Tel/Fax: 0117 907 7539

RATIONAL EMOTIVE BEHAVIOUR THERAPY

The Journal of Rational-Emotive & Cognitive-Behavior Therapy
Human Sciences Press Inc
72 Fifth Avenue
New York
NY 10011 8004
USA

The Rational Emotive Behaviour Therapist
Centre for Rational Emotive Behaviour Therapy
156 Westcombe Hill
Blackheath
London SE3 7DH
UK

Cognitive Therapy and Research
Plenum Press
233 Spring Street
New York
NY 10013
USA
(This journal focuses on the cognitive therapies)

COGNITIVE THERAPY

Cognitive Therapy Today Newsletter
The Beck Institute
GSB Building City Line and Belmont Avenues, Suite 700
Bala Cynwyd
PA 19004-1610
USA
Tel: 610 664 3020
Fax: 610 664 4437
e-mail: beckinst@gim.net
Website: www.beckinstitute.org

*Journal of Cognitive Psychotherapy: An International Quar-
    terly*
International Association for Cognitive Psychotherapy
Department of Psychology
University of Southern Mississippi
Hattiesberg
MS 39406
USA

Cognitive Therapy and Research
Plenum Press
233 Spring Street
New York
NY 10013
USA
(This journal focuses on the cognitive therapies)

Behaviour Change (Journal of the Australian Association for
   Cognitive and Behaviour Therapy)
Australian Academic Press
32 Jeays Street
Bowen Hills
Queensland 4006
Australia

Name Index

Subject Index

gestalt therapy 150–1
person of tomorrow 121
self-concept 109–10, 112, 114–20
self-regard 119–20, 123, 132–3
self-standards
 beliefs, rational and
  irrational 189–92
 conditions of worth 109–10,
  112, 119
 super-ego 26–9
sexual development 32–5
shadow 66–7, 78
shame attacking exercises 214–15
shuttle technique 168–9
skills training
 cognitive therapy 263
 rational emotive behaviour
  therapy 214–15
Socratic questioning 255–7
stages
 of analytical therapy 80–1
 of life 74–5
 of sexual development 32–5
structure of mental apparatus 26–9
subception 116, 119
subjective frame of reference 104–5
Suicide Ideation Scale 230
Suicide Intent Scale 230

super-ego 26–9
symbols
 analytical therapy 87–91
 psychoanalysis 48–9
sympathy and frustration 166–7
systematic bias in psychological
  disorders 243–7

theories
 defining 6–7
 evaluating 272–85
 functions of 7–8
 learning about 12–15
 limitations of 10–12
therapeutic schools and
  approaches 1–4
transcendent function 70, 79
transference
 analytical therapy 84–6
 psychoanalysis 45–6

unconditional positive
  regard 128–9, 132–3
unconscious
 analytical therapy 63–7, 78
 psychoanalysis 25–6

videotapes 180, 217, 270–1
vulnerability, cognitive 233, 237–41